THE PIPER AND THE BARD

a study of William Blake

a study of William Blake

The PIPER
· & The ·
BARD

by Robert F. Gleckner

1959   WAYNE STATE UNIVERSITY PRESS   DETROIT

First printing May 1959
Second printing August 1960

Copyright © 1959 by Wayne State University Press
Library of Congress Catalog Number: 59-9651

to my wife
who worked, inspired, endured
and
to my mother and father

PREFACE

૨ৡ

F. W. Bateson begins the Preface of his recent *Selected Poems of William Blake* with: "The total intelligibility of Blake's poetry is a modern discovery." He refers particularly to the later prophetic works here (*The Four Zoas, Milton, Jerusalem*), but from his notes it is clear that he also refers to the complexity and obscurity of much of Blake's great lyric achievement, *Songs of Innocence and of Experience*. Northrop Frye, S. Foster Damon, Jacob Bronowski, David V. Erdman, Stanley Gardner and others have all grappled with the many problems to some extent, and to them I am obviously indebted; but there is still much to be done. Joseph Wicksteed's *Blake's Innocence and Experience* (1928) is still today the only book devoted exclusively to the *Songs*. Despite my frequent disagreement with Wicksteed's critical strategy and interpretation, his accomplishment must be applauded. Above all he recognized what seems to me the incontrovertible fact that Blake's songs must be examined closely, probed into, dissected (even at the risk of "murder," as Wordsworth warned us)—not merely read and enjoyed. For they are integral parts of the growth of Blake's poetic ability, his philosophical-religious-aesthetic concepts, and his own very special technique for conveying those concepts.

It is mainly with the *Songs,* then, that I shall deal in the following pages. Blake as a mystic, a lunatic, a pre-Romantic or Romantic, a sociologist, a husband and lover, a painter and engraver, a revolutionary, are all outside my scope. So too is anything like a full examination of Blake's possible sources or contemporary allusions; that I leave, gratefully, to the Erdmans, the Raines, the Harpers, and others.

My object, then, is to limit myself rather severely to the Blake canon, and to provide a close reading of most of the *Songs of Innocence* and *Songs of Experience* and of four other works written in the crucial period between the appearance of the two song series: *Tiriel, The Book of Thel, The Marriage of Heaven and Hell,* and *Visions of the Daughters of Albion.* These, I believe, are the key elements of an organic and ever-developing "system" that began with the seeds of innocence and resulted finally in the prophetic books. Although I do not think I meant to lean on him, Blake himself offers sound reasons for such an approach in his *Vision of the Last Judgment:*

> General Knowledge is Remote Knowledge; it is in Particulars that Wisdom consists. . . . Both in Art & in Life, General Masses are as Much Art as a Pasteboard Man is Human. Every Man has Eyes, Nose & Mouth; this Every Idiot knows, but he who enters into & discriminates most minutely the Manners & Intentions, the Characters in all their branches is the alone Wise or Sensible Man, & on this discrimination All Art is founded. I intreat, then, that the Spectator will attend to the Hands & Feet, to the Lineaments of the Countenances; they are all descriptive of Character, & not a line is drawn without intention, & that most discriminate and particular. As Poetry admits not a Letter that is Insignificant, so Painting admits not a Grain of Sand or a Blade of Grass Insignificant—much less an Insignificant Blur or Mark.

Translating such a dictum into a critical approach involves of course grave risks, and I am sensible of these. I hope only that I have been "Sensible" if not "Wise."

Some of the more elaborate explications are obviously products of my own admiration for Blake's remarkable craftsmanship; others are intended to justify my belief that certain well-known and admired poems fail, ultimately, to carry their burden. Just so, the final decision as to which poems ought to be dealt with in detail was based partly, I suppose inevitably, on my own taste, mostly on the importance of the individual poem's contribution to an understanding both of the whole multifaceted Blakean system and of the single, unified work,

Songs of Innocence and of Experience. I have omitted, then, several of the simpler songs, a few that I don't know how to read (like *The Fly*) and two (*London* and *The Tyger*) which I feel have been so fully and excellently commented upon elsewhere that I should be able to do little more here than quote at length from, particularly, Joseph Wicksteed, Mark Schorer, Alfred Kazin, Stanley Gardner, and Martin K. Nurmi. Some special comments on *The Tyger*, however, I have reserved for the last chapter.

The texts reproduced here of *Songs of Innocence and of Experience, The Book of Thel, The Marriage of Heaven and Hell*, and *Visions of the Daughters of Albion* are Blake's own engraved texts. Eccentric, even chaotic as the punctuation and capitalization are, I believe strongly that we must begin with what Blake wrote the way he wrote it. The text of *Tiriel* is what I believe to be the first accurate transcript of the unique manuscript in the British Museum. For permission to print it here I owe a great debt not only to the British Museum but to David V. Erdman, who kindly supplied me with the transcript, and to Gerald E. Bentley, Jr. for double-checking it. All quotations throughout the book from these works are from these originals. For all quotations to Blake's other works I have used the beautiful Nonesuch edition of *The Complete Writings of William Blake,* edited by Sir Geoffrey Keynes (1957). For easy access to all that Blake wrote, to the more familiar normalized punctuation, and to the invaluable variant readings, the Keynes book is indispensable. I have followed Keynes's practice of reproducing Blake's incorrect spelling throughout all quotations.

For their assistance and courtesy I am grateful particularly to the librarians and staffs of The Johns Hopkins University Library, the Library of the Peabody Institute of Baltimore, the Library of Congress, the University of Cincinnati Library, the Library of the Air University, Alabama, the University of Wisconsin Library, and the Wayne State University Library. To the University of Wisconsin Graduate School my thanks for a summer grant to provide for further research and writing on the manuscript.

It is a pleasure to acknowledge the encouragement and helpful criticism of Professor Earl R. Wasserman of The Johns Hopkins University throughout the entire period during which this study took shape. My thanks also to Professors Don Cameron Allen, George H. Ford, Helen C. White, and David V. Erdman for their careful reading of the manuscript in part or in toto in its early stages. My debts to numerous other Blake scholars I have tried to acknowledge, however inadequately, in my notes. For advice on bibliographical matters and for the use of an early transcript of their Census of Blake's Illuminated Books I wish to thank Geoffrey Keynes and Edwin Wolf II; also Leslie M. Oliver of the Harvard College Library for manuscript information, and George P. Solomos of the Wayne State University Press for his valuable suggestions and comments.

Sections of this book have been previously published in the following journals: *Philological Quarterly, Journal of Aesthetics and Art Criticism,* and *Bulletin of the New York Public Library.*

All page references in parentheses are to Keynes's *The Complete Writings of William Blake.* Also I have adopted often (in the text and notes) the simplified form, *Innocence,* to refer to the entire work, *Songs of Innocence,* and *Experience* to refer to the entire work, *Songs of Experience.*

R. F. G.

Detroit
September 1958

CONTENTS

PART I

SONGS OF INNOCENCE AND OF EXPERIENCE

Shewing the Two Contrary States of the Human Soul

PART II

PART III

PART IV

PART V

PART VI

PART VII

PART I

SONGS OF INNOCENCE AND OF EXPERIENCE

Shewing the Two Contrary States of the Human Soul

SONGS OF INNOCENCE

Introduction

Piping down the valleys wild
Piping songs of pleasant glee
On a cloud I saw a child.
And he laughing said to me.

Pipe a song about a Lamb;
So I piped with merry chear,
Piper pipe that song again—
So I piped, he wept to hear.

Drop thy pipe thy happy pipe
Sing thy songs of happy chear,
So I sung the same again
While he wept with joy to hear

Piper sit thee down and write
In a book that all may read—
So he vanish'd from my sight.
And I pluck'd a hollow reed.

And I made a rural pen,
And I stain'd the water clear,
And I wrote my happy songs
Every child may joy to hear

The Shepherd

How sweet is the Shepherds sweet lot,
From the morn to the evening he strays:
He shall follow his sheep all the day
And his tongue shall be filled with praise.

For he hears the lambs innocent call.
And he hears the ewes tender reply.
He is watchful while they are in peace.
For they know when their Shepherd is nigh.

The Ecchoing Green

The Sun does arise,
And make happy the skies.
The merry bells ring
To welcome the Spring.
The sky-lark and thrush,
The birds of the bush,
Sing louder around,
To the bells chearful sound.
While our sports shall be seen
On the Ecchoing Green.

Old John with white hair
Does laugh away care,
Sitting under the oak,
Among the old folk,
They laugh at our play,
And soon they all say.
Such such were the joys.
When we all girls & boys,
In our youth time were seen,
On the Ecchoing Green.

Till the little ones weary
No more can be merry
The sun does descend,
And our sports have an end:
Round the laps of their mothers,
Many sisters and brothers,
Like birds in their nest.
Are ready for rest;
And sport no more seen,
On the darkening Green.

The Lamb

Little Lamb who made thee
Dost thou know who made thee
Gave thee life & bid thee feed.
By the stream & o'er the mead;

Gave thee clothing of delight,
Softest clothing wooly bright;
Gave thee such a tender voice,
Making all the vales rejoice:
  Little Lamb who made thee
  Dost thou know who made thee

  Little Lamb I'll tell thee,
  Little Lamb I'll tell thee;
He is called by thy name,
For he calls himself a Lamb:
He is meek & he is mild,
He became a little child:
I a child & thou a lamb,
We are called by his name.
  Little Lamb God bless thee.
  Little Lamb God bless thee.

The Little Black Boy.

My mother bore me in the southern wild,
And I am black, but O! my soul is white;
White as an angel is the English child:
But I am black as if bereav'd of light.

My mother taught me underneath a tree
And sitting down before the heat of day,
She took me on her lap and kissed me.
And pointing to the east began to say.

Look on the rising sun: there God does live
And gives his light, and gives his heat away.
And flowers and trees and beasts and men recieve
Comfort in morning joy in the noon day.

And we are put on earth a little space,
That we may learn to bear the beams of love,
And these black bodies and this sun-burnt face
Is but a cloud, and like a shady grove.

For when our souls have learn'd the heat to bear
The cloud will vanish we shall hear his voice.

Saying: come out from the grove my love & care,
And round my golden tent like lambs rejoice.

Thus did my mother say and kissed me,
And thus I say to little English boy.
When I from black and he from white cloud free,
And round the tent of God like lambs we joy:

Ill shade him from the heat till he can bear
To lean in joy upon our fathers knee.
And then I'll stand and stroke his silver hair,
And be like him and he will then love me.

The Blossom

Merry Merry Sparrow
Under leaves so green
A happy Blossom
Sees you swift as arrow
Seek your cradle narrow
Near my Bosom.

Pretty Pretty Robin
Under leaves so green
A happy Blossom
Hears you sobbing sobbing
Pretty Pretty Robin
Near my Bosom.

The Chimney Sweeper

When my mother died I was very young,
And my father sold me while yet my tongue,
Could scarcely cry weep weep weep weep.
So your chimneys I sweep & in soot I sleep.

Theres little Tom Dacre, who cried when his head
That curl'd like a lambs back, was shav'd, so I said.
Hush Tom never mind it, for when your head's bare,
You know that the soot cannot spoil your white hair.

And so he was quiet, & that very night.
As Tom was a sleeping he had such a sight,

That thousands of sweepers Dick, Joe Ned & Jack
Were all of them lock'd up in coffins of black

And by came an Angel who had a bright key
And he open'd the coffins & set them all free.
Then down a green plain leaping laughing they run
And wash in a river and shine in the Sun.

Then naked & white, all their bags left behind,
They rise upon clouds, and sport in the wind.
And the Angel told Tom if he'd be a good boy,
He'd have God for his father & never want joy.

And so Tom awoke and we rose in the dark
And got with our bags & our brushes to work.
Tho' the morning was cold, Tom was happy & warm,
So if all do their duty, they need not fear harm.

The Little Boy Lost

Father, father. where are you going
O do not walk so fast.
Speak father, speak to your little boy
Or else I shall be lost,

The night was dark no father was there
The child was wet with dew.
The mire was deep. & the child did weep
And away the vapour flew.

The Little Boy Found

The little boy lost in the lonely fen,
Led by the wand'ring light.
Began to cry, but God ever nigh,
Appeard like his father in white.

He kissed the child & by the hand led
And to his mother brought.
Who in sorrow pale, thro' the lonely dale
Her little boy weeping sought.

Laughing Song,

When the green woods laugh with the voice of joy
And the dimpling stream runs laughing by,
When the air does laugh with our merry wit.
And the green hill laughs with the noise of it.

When the meadows laugh with lively green
And the grasshopper laughs in the merry scene,
When Mary and Susan and Emily.
With their sweet round mouths sing Ha, Ha, He.

When the painted birds laugh in the shade
Where our table with cherries and nuts is spread
Come live & be merry and join with me,
To sing the sweet chorus of Ha, Ha, He.

A CRADLE SONG

Sweet dreams form a shade,
O'er my lovely infants head.
Sweet dreams of pleasant streams,
By happy silent moony beams

Sweet sleep with soft down.
Weave thy brows an infant crown.
Sweet sleep Angel mild,
Hover o'er my happy child.

Sweet smiles in the night,
Hover over my delight.
Sweet smiles Mothers smiles
All the livelong night beguiles.

Sweet moans, dovelike sighs,
Chase not slumber from thy eyes,
Sweet moans, sweeter smiles,
All the dovelike moans beguiles.

Sleep sleep happy child.
All creation slept and smil'd.

Sleep sleep. happy sleep.
While o'er thee thy mother weep.

Sweet babe in thy face.
Holy image I can trace.
Sweet babe once like thee.
Thy maker lay and wept for me

Wept for me for thee for all,
When he was an infant small.
Thou his image ever see,
Heavenly face that smiles on thee.

Smiles on thee on me on all
Who became an infant small,
Infant smiles are his own smiles.
Heaven & earth to peace beguiles.

The Divine Image.

To Mercy Pity Peace and Love,
All pray in their distress:
And to these virtues of delight
Return their thankfulness.

For Mercy Pity Peace and Love,
Is God our father dear:
And Mercy Pity Peace and Love.
Is Man his child and care.

For Mercy has a human heart
Pity, a human face:
And Love, the human form divine,
And Peace, the human dress.

Then every man of every clime,
That prays in his distress,
Prays to the human form divine
Love Mercy Pity Peace.

And all must love the human form,
In heathen, turk or jew.
Where Mercy Love & Pity dwell
There God is dwelling too.

9

HOLY THURSDAY

Twas on a Holy Thursday their innocent faces clean
The children walking two & two in red & blue & green
Grey headed beadles walkd before with wands as white as snow
Till into the high dome of Pauls they like Thames waters flow

O what a multitude they seemd these flowers of London town
Seated in companies they sit with radiance all their own
The hum of multitudes was there but multitudes of lambs
Thousands of little boys & girls raising their innocent hands

Now like a mighty wind they raise to heaven the voice of song
Or like harmonious thunderings the seats of heaven among
Beneath them sit the aged men wise guardians of the poor
Then cherish pity, lest you drive an angel from your door

Night

The sun descending in the west,
The evening star does shine.
The birds are silent in their nest,
And I must seek for mine,
The moon like a flower,
In heavens high bower;
With silent delight,
Sits and smiles on the night.

Farewell green fields and happy groves,
Where flocks have took delight;
Where lambs have nibbled, silent moves
The feet of angels bright;
Unseen they pour blessing,
And joy without ceasing,
On each bud and blossom,
And each sleeping bosom.

They look in every thoughtless nest,
Where birds are coverd warm;
They visit caves of every beast,
To keep them all from harm;

If they see any weeping.
That should have been sleeping
They pour sleep on their head
And sit down by their bed.

When wolves and tygers howl for prey
They pitying stand and weep;
Seeking to drive their thirst away,
And keep them from the sheep.
But if they rush dreadful;
The angels most heedful,
Recieve each mild spirit,
New worlds to inherit.

And there the lions ruddy eyes,
Shall flow with tears of gold:
And pitying the tender cries,
And walking round the fold:
Saying: wrath by his meekness
And by his health. sickness.
Is driven away.
From our immortal day.

And now beside thee bleating lamb.
I can lie down and sleep;
Or think on him who bore thy name.
Grase after thee and weep.
For wash'd in lifes river,
My bright mane for ever,
Shall shine like the gold.
As I guard o'er the fold.

Spring

Sound the Flute!
Now it's mute.
Birds delight
Day and Night.
Nightingale
In the dale
Lark in Sky
Merrily
Merrily Merrily to welcome in the Year

Little Boy
Full of joy.
Little Girl
Sweet and small,
Cock does crow
So do you.
Merry voice
Infant noise
Merrily Merrily to welcome in the Year

Little Lamb
Here I am,
Come and lick
My white neck.
Let me pull
Your soft Wool.
Let me kiss
Your soft face.
Merrily Merrily we welcome in the Year

Nurse's Song

When the voices of children are heard on the green
And laughing is heard on the hill,
My heart is at rest within my breast
And everything else is still

Then come home my children, the sun is gone down
And the dews of night arise
Come come leave off play. and let us away
Till the morning appears in the skies

No no let us play, for it is yet day
And we cannot go to sleep
Besides in the sky, the little birds fly
And the hills are all coverd with sheep

Well well go & play till the light fades away
And then go home to bed
The little ones leaped & shouted & laugh'd
And all the hills ecchoed

Infant Joy

I have no name
I am but two days old.—
What shall I call thee?
I happy am
Joy is my name,—
Sweet joy befall thee!

Pretty joy!
Sweet joy but two days old.
Sweet joy I call thee;
Thou dost smile.
I sing the while
Sweet joy befall thee.

A Dream

Once a dream did weave a shade.
O'er my Angel-guarded bed,
That an Emmet lost it's way
Where on grass methought I lay.

Troubled wilderd and folorn
Dark benighted travel-worn,
Over many a tangled spray
All heart-broke I heard her say.

O my children! do they cry
Do they hear their father sigh.
Now they look abroad to see,
Now return and weep for me.

Pitying I drop'd a tear:
But I saw a glow-worm near:
Who replied. What wailing wight
Calls the watchman of the night.

I am set to light the ground,
While the beetle goes his round:
Follow now the beetles hum.
Little wanderer hie thee home.

On Anothers Sorrow

Can I see anothers woe,
And not be in sorrow too.
Can I see anothers grief,
And not seek for kind relief.

Can I see a falling tear.
And not feel my sorrows share,
Can a father see his child,
Weep, nor be with sorrow fill'd.

Can a mother sit and hear.
An infant groan an infant fear—
No no never can it be.
Never never can it be.

And can he who smiles on all
Hear the wren with sorrows small.
Hear the small birds grief & care
Hear the woes that infants bear—

And not sit beside the nest
Pouring pity in their breast,
And not sit the cradle near
Weeping tear on infants tear.

And not sit both night & day,
Wiping all our tears away.
O! no never can it be.
Never never can it be.

He doth give his joy to all.
He becomes an infant small.
He becomes a man of woe
He doth feel the sorrow too.

Think not, thou canst sigh a sigh,
And thy maker is not by.
Think not, thou canst weep a tear,
And thy maker is not near.

O! he gives to us his joy.
That our grief he may destroy
Till our grief is fled & gone
He doth sit by us and moan

SONGS of EXPERIENCE

Introduction

Hear the voice of the Bard!
Who Present, Past, & Future sees
Whose ears have heard,
The Holy Word,
That walk'd among the ancient trees.

Calling the lapsed Soul
And weeping in the evening dew;
That might controll
The starry pole;
And fallen fallen light renew!

O Earth O Earth return!
Arise from out the dewy grass;
Night is worn,
And the morn
Rises from the slumberous mass.

Turn away no more:
Why wilt thou turn away
The starry floor
The watry shore
Is giv'n thee till the break of day.

EARTH'S Answer

Earth raisd up her head.
From the darkness dread & drear.
Her light fled:
Stony dread!
And her locks cover'd with grey despair.

Prison'd on watry shore
Starry Jealousy does keep my den
Cold and hoar
Weeping o'er
I hear the father of the ancient men

Selfish father of men
Cruel jealous selfish fear

Can delight
Chain'd in night
The virgins of youth and morning bear.

Does spring hide its joy
When buds and blossoms grow?
Does the sower?
Sow by night?
Or the plowman in darkness plow?

Break this heavy chain.
That does freeze my bones around
Selfish! vain!
Eternal bane!
That free Love with bondage bound.

The CLOD & the PEBBLE

Love seeketh not Itself to please.
Nor for itself hath any care;
But for another gives its ease.
And builds a Heaven in Hells despair.

So sung a little Clod of Clay,
Trodden with the cattles feet;
But a Pebble of the brook,
Warbled out these metres meet.

Love seeketh only Self to please,
To bind another to Its delight;
Joys in anothers loss of ease,
And builds a Hell in Heavens despite.

HOLY THURSDAY

Is this a holy thing to see,
In a rich and fruitful land,
Babes reduced to misery,
Fed with cold and usurous hand?

Is that trembling cry a song?
Can it be a song of joy?

And so many children poor?
It is a land of poverty!

And their sun does never shine.
And their fields are bleak & bare.
And their ways are fill'd with thorns.
It is eternal winter there.

For where-e'er the sun does shine.
And where-e'er the rain does fall:
Babe can never hunger there,
Nor poverty the mind appall.

The Little Girl Lost

In futurity
I prophetic see.
That the earth from sleep,
(Grave the sentence deep)

Shall arise and seek
For her maker meek:
And the desart wild
Become a garden mild.

In the southern clime,
Where the summers prime,
Never fades away;
Lovely Lyca lay.

Seven summers old
Lovely Lyca told,
She had wanderd long,
Hearing wild birds song.

Sweet sleep come to me
Underneath this tree;
Do father, mother weep.—
"Where can Lyca sleep".

Lost in desert wild
Is your little child.

How can Lyca sleep,
If her mother weep.

If her heart does ake,
Then let Lyca wake;
If my mother sleep,
Lyca shall not weep.

Frowning frowning night,
O'er this desart bright.
Let thy moon arise.
While I close my eyes.

Sleeping Lyca lay;
While the beasts of prey,
Come from caverns deep,
View'd the maid asleep

The kingly lion stood
And the virgin view'd,
Then he gambold round
O'er the hallowd ground:

Leopards, tygers play,
Round her as she lay;
While the lion old,
Bow'd his mane of gold.

And her bosom lick,
And upon her neck,
From his eyes of flame,
Ruby tears there came;

While the lioness
Loos'd her slender dress,
And naked they convey'd
To caves the sleeping maid.

The Little Girl Found

All the night in woe,
Lyca's parents go:

Over vallies deep.
While the desarts weep.

Tired and woe-begone.
Hoarse with making moan:
Arm in arm seven days.
They trac'd the desart ways.

Seven nights they sleep.
Among shadows deep:
And dream they see their child
Starv'd in desart wild.

Pale thro' pathless ways
The fancied image strays.
Famish'd, weeping, weak
With hollow piteous shriek

Rising from unrest,
The trembling woman prest,
With feet of weary woe;
She could no further go.

In his arms he bore.
Her arm'd with sorrow sore;
Till before their way,
A couching lion lay.

Turning back was vain,
Soon his heavy mane.
Bore them to the ground;
Then he stalk'd around.

Smelling to his prey.
But their fears allay.
When he licks their hands;
And silent by them stands.

They look upon his eyes
Fill'd with deep surprise:
And wondering behold,
A spirit arm'd in gold.

On his head a crown
On his shoulders down.
Flow'd his golden hair.
Gone was all their care.

Follow me he said,
Weep not for the maid;
In my palace deep,
Lyca lies asleep.

Then they followed.
Where the vision led:
And saw their sleeping child,
Among tygers wild.

To this day they dwell
In a lonely dell
Nor fear the wolvish howl,
Nor the lions growl.

THE *Chimney Sweeper*

A little black thing among the snow:
Crying weep, weep. in notes of woe!
Where are thy father & mother? say?
They are both gone up to the church to pray.

Because I was happy upon the heath.
And smil'd among the winters snow:
They clothed me in the clothes of death.
And taught me to sing the notes of woe.

And because I am happy. & dance & sing.
They think they have done me no injury:
And are gone to praise God & his Priest & King
Who make up a heaven of our misery.

NURSES Song

When the voices of children. are heard on the green
And whisprings are in the dale:
The days of my youth rise fresh in my mind,
My face turns green and pale.

Then come home my children. the sun is gone down
And the dews of night arise
Your spring & your day. are wasted in play
And your winter and night in disguise.

The SICK ROSE

O Rose thou art sick.
The invisible worm.
That flies in the night
In the howling storm:

Has found out thy bed
Of crimson joy:
And his dark secret love
Does thy life destroy.

THE FLY.

Little Fly
Thy summers play,
My thoughtless hand
Has brush'd away.

Am not I
A fly like thee?
Or art not thou
A man like me?

For I dance
And drink & sing;
Till some blind hand
Shall brush my wing.

If thought is life
And strength & breath;
And the want
Of thought is death;

Then am I
A happy fly,
If I live,
Or if I die.

The Angel

I Dreamt a Dream! what can it mean?
And that I was a maiden Queen:
Guarded by an Angel mild;
Witless woe, was neer beguil'd!

And I wept both night and day
And he wip'd my tears away
And I wept both day and night
And hid from him my hearts delight

So he took his wings and fled:
Then the morn blush'd rosy red:
I dried my tears & armd my fears,
With ten thousand shields and spears.

Soon my Angel came again:
I was arm'd, he came in vain:
For the time of youth was fled
And grey hairs were on my head

The Tyger.

Tyger Tyger. burning bright,
In the forests of the night;
What immortal hand or eye,
Could frame thy fearful symmetry?

In what distant deeps or skies.
Burnt the fire of thine eyes?
On what wings dare he aspire?
What the hand, dare sieze the fire?

And what shoulder, & what art,
Could twist the sinews of thy heart?
And when thy heart began to beat,
What dread hand? & what dread feet?

What the hammer? what the chain,
In what furnace was thy brain?
What the anvil? what dread grasp,
Dare its deadly terrors clasp?

When the stars threw down their spears
And water'd heaven with their tears:
Did he smile his work to see?
Did he who made the Lamb make thee?

Tyger Tyger burning bright,
In the forests of the night:
What immortal hand or eye,
Dare frame thy fearful symmetry?

My Pretty ROSE TREE

A flower was offerd to me;
Such a flower as May never bore.
But I said I've a Pretty Rose-tree.
And I passed the sweet flower o'er.

Then I went to my Pretty Rose-tree:
To tend her by day and by night.
But my Rose turnd away with jealousy:
And her thorns were my only delight.

AH! SUN-FLOWER

Ah Sun-flower! weary of time.
Who countest the steps of the Sun:
Seeking after that sweet golden clime
Where the travellers journey is done.

Where the Youth pined away with desire.
And the pale Virgin shrouded in snow:
Arise from their graves and aspire,
Where my Sun-flower wishes to go.

THE LILLY

The modest Rose puts forth a thorn:
The humble Sheep, a threatning horn:
While the Lilly white, shall in Love delight.
Nor a thorn nor a threat stain her beauty bright

The GARDEN of LOVE.

I went to the Garden of Love.
And saw what I never had seen:
A Chapel was built in the midst.
Where I used to play on the green.

And the gates of this Chapel were shut,
And Thou shalt not. writ over the door;
So I turn'd to the Garden of Love,
That so many sweet flowers bore,

And I saw it was filled with graves.
And tomb-stones where flowers should be:
And Priests in black gowns, were walking their rounds,
And binding with briars my joys & desires.

The Little Vagabond

Dear Mother, dear Mother, the Church is cold.
But the Ale-house is healthy & pleasant & warm;
Besides I can tell where I am use'd well,
Such usage in heaven will never do well.

But if at the Church they would give us some Ale.
And a pleasant fire, our souls to regale;
We'd sing and we'd pray. all the live-long day:
Nor ever once wish from the Church to stray.

Then the Parson might preach & drink & sing.
And we'd be as happy as birds in the spring:
And modest dame Lurch, who is always at Church,
Would not have bandy children nor fasting nor birch.

And God like a father rejoicing to see,
His children as pleasant and happy as he:
Would have no more quarrel with the Devil or the Barrel
But kiss him & give him both drink and apparel.

24

LONDON

I wander thro' each charter'd street,
Near where the charter'd Thames does flow
And mark in every face I meet
Marks of weakness, marks of woe,

In every cry of every Man,
In every Infants cry of fear.
In every voice: in every ban.
The mind-forg'd manacles I hear

How the Chimney-sweepers cry
Every blackning Church appalls.
And the hapless Soldiers sigh
Runs in blood down Palace walls

But most thro' midnight streets I hear
How the youthful Harlots curse
Blasts the new born Infants tear
And blights with plagues the Marriage hearse

The Human Abstract

Pity would be no more,
If we did not make somebody Poor:
And Mercy no more could be.
If all were as happy as we;

And mutual fear brings peace;
Till the selfish loves increase.
Then Cruelty knits a snare,
And spreads his baits with care.

He sits down with holy fears,
And waters the ground with tears:
Then Humility takes its root
Underneath his foot.

Soon spreads the dismal shade
Of Mystery over his head;

And the Catterpiller and Fly.
Feed on the Mystery.

And it bears the fruit of Deceit.
Ruddy and sweet to eat;
And the Raven his nest has made
In its thickest shade.

The Gods of the earth and sea,
Sought thro' Nature to find this Tree
But their search was all in vain:
There grows one in the Human Brain

INFANT SORROW

My mother groand! my father wept.
Into the dangerous world I leapt:
Helpless, naked, piping loud:
Like a fiend hid in a cloud.

Struggling in my fathers hands:
Striving against my swadling bands:
Bound and weary I thought best
To sulk upon my mothers breast.

A POISON TREE.

I was angry with my friend;
I told my wrath, my wrath did end.
I was angry with my foe:
I told it not, my wrath did grow.

And I waterd it in fears,
Night & morning with my tears:
And I sunned it with smiles,
And with soft deceitful wiles.

And it grew both day and night,
Till it bore an apple bright.
And my foe beheld it shine,
And he knew that it was mine.

And into my garden stole.
When the night had veild the pole;
In the morning glad I see;
My foe outstretchd beneath the tree.

A Little BOY Lost

Nought loves another as itself
Nor venerates another so,
Nor is it possible to Thought
A greater than itself to know:

And Father, how can I love you,
Or any of my brothers more?
I love you like the little bird
That picks up crumbs around the door.

The Priest sat by and heard the child.
In trembling zeal he siez'd his hair:
He led him by his little coat;
And all admir'd the Priestly care.

And standing on the altar high.
Lo what a fiend is here! said he:
One who sets reason up for judge
Of our most holy Mystery.

The weeping child could not be heard.
The weeping parents wept in vain:
They strip'd him to his little shirt.
And bound him in an iron chain.

And burn'd him in a holy place
Where many had been burn'd before:
The weeping parents wept in vain.
Are such things done on Albions shore.

A Little GIRL Lost

Children of the future Age,
Reading this indignant page;

Know that in a former time,
Love! sweet Love! was thought a crime.

In the Age of Gold,
Free from winters cold:
Youth and maiden bright.
To the holy light,
Naked in the sunny beams delight.

Once a youthful pair
Fill'd with softest care:
Met in garden bright.
Where the holy light,
Had just removd the curtains of the night.

There in rising day,
On the grass they play:
Parents were afar:
Strangers came not near:
And the maiden soon forgot her fear.

Tired with kisses sweet
They agree to meet,
When the silent sleep
Waves o'er heavens deep;
And the weary tired wanderers weep.

To her father white
Came the maiden bright:
But his loving look.
Like the holy book,
All her tender limbs with terror shook.

Ona! pale and weak!
To thy father speak:
O the trembling fear!
O the dismal care!
That shakes the blossoms of my hoary hair

To Tirzah

Whate'er is Born of Mortal Birth.
Must be consumed with the Earth

28

To rise from Generation free:
Then what have I to do with thee?

The Sexes sprung from Shame & Pride
Blowd in the morn; in evening died
But Mercy changd Death into Sleep;
The Sexes rose to work & weep.

Thou Mother of my Mortal part.
With cruelty didst mould my Heart.
And with false self-decieving tears.
Didst bind my Nostrils Eyes & Ears.

Didst close my Tongue in senseless clay
And me to Mortal Life betray:
The Death of Jesus set me free,
Then what have I to do with thee?

The School Boy

I love to rise in a summer morn,
When the birds sing on every tree;
The distant huntsman winds his horn,
And the sky-lark sings with me.
O! what sweet company.

But to go to school in a summer morn
O! it drives all joy away;
Under a cruel eye outworn.
The little ones spend the day,
In sighing and dismay.

Ah! then at times I drooping sit,
And spend many an anxious hour.
Nor in my book can I take delight,
Nor sit in learnings bower,
Worn thro' with the dreary shower.

How can the bird that is born for joy,
Sit in a cage and sing.
How can a child when fears annoy,
But droop his tender wing.
And forget his youthful spring.

O! father & mother, if buds are nip'd,
And blossoms blown away,
And if the tender plants are strip'd
Of their joy in the springing day.
By sorrow and cares dismay.

How shall the summer arise in joy.
Or the summer fruits appear.
Or how shall we gather what griefs destroy
Or bless the mellowing year.
When the blasts of winter appear.

The Voice of the Ancient Bard.

Youth of delight come hither.
And see the opening morn,
Image of truth new-born.
Doubt is fled & clouds of reason.
Dark disputes & artful teazing.
Folly is an endless maze,
Tangled roots perplex her ways,
How many have fallen there!
They stumble all night over bones of the dead;
And feel they know not what but care;
And wish to lead others when they should be led.

P·A·R·T
·II·

CHAPTER I

THE STRUCTURE OF BLAKE'S POETIC

ॐ

Only treason to his own sense of the divine
can rob the new person of his creativity.
—LEWIS MUMFORD, *The Conduct of Life*

I

"What was written for children can hardly offend men."[1] Thus
wrote Swinburne in 1868 about Blake's *Songs of Innocence,* and many
readers today still subscribe to this dictum. Blake himself lent credence
to it by concluding his *Introduction to Songs of Innocence* with:

> And I wrote my happy songs
> Every child may joy to hear.

A number of editions of Blake's songs have been published especially
for the young reader, and one has little doubt that children do joy to
hear them read. But Blake's "child" is a very special child, with very
special qualities, and Blake was interested not only in the joy his visions
and poems afforded but in their elucidation. "I am happy," he writes
in 1799, "to find a Great Majority of my Fellow Mortals who can
Elucidate My Visions, & Particularly they have been Elucidated by
Children. . . ."[2] "It is pleasant enough," then, as Swinburne wrote, "to
commend and to enjoy the palpable excellence of Blake's work; but
another thing is simply and thoroughly requisite—to understand what
the workman was after."[3]

What *was* the workman after? Happy songs and sad songs, yes—

Songs of Innocence and *Songs of Experience*—but also a poetic description of "two contrary states of the human soul." The states are of course innocence and experience, and they have been approached, explained, and commented upon in terms of mysticism, antinomianism, occultism, neo-Platonism, psychology, sociology, and autobiography. In part, at least, all of these approaches are valid, but inevitably they come to represent some sort of system or structure imposed from without. Blake's system, on the contrary, evolved organically out of the poems themselves; and it was never a static concept. This cumulative systematizing, then, is the great problem with which we must deal: to see the *Songs* as individual poems in their own right, but also to see them as integral parts of a complete book (*Songs of Innocence and of Experience*) and contributions to the formulation of a system upon which their *full* meaning largely depends.

Swinburne cautioned the readers of Blake to heed this organic unity: "They will blunder helplessly if they once fail to connect this present minute of his work with the past and future of it: if they once let slip the thinnest thread of analogy, the whole prophetic or evangelic web collapses for them into a chaos of gossamer. . . ."[4] The explicatory chapters of this study are intended to unravel many of those analogical threads. One final problem: during the course of my analyses there will inevitably appear references to elements of Blake's system which cannot then be elucidated without undue awkwardness; further, Blake's symbols are so diverse and multivalent, his interlocking images so intricate, that occasionally one cannot see the system for the images. For these reasons, as well as to provide a general introduction to Blake's main ideas, I should like to telescope the main elements of the system, as I see them, into a bald statement of their interrelationships.

The basic conceptions of his system are ancient and elemental:[5] a supramundane and eternal world is assumed, and a fall and return are presupposed. The physical world resulted from the interaction of two elemental forces, one active and formative, the other passive and receptive; and these forces were often thought of as masculine and feminine, inner and outer. On these more or less commonplace suppositions Blake superimposed the idea that the imagination was a summation of all the members of the active, masculine series. Opposed to it he placed reason and selfhood.

In the beginning, then, before the universe appeared, was the Word or the Eternal Mind;[6]

> Earth was not: nor globes of attraction;
> The will of the Immortal expanded
> Or contracted his all flexible senses;
> Death was not, but eternal life sprung. (*Urizen*, 223)

In this primordial essence the substance of all things was contained, and from it by division and evolution each separate identity or being came into existence. Christ is that essence; all the "Eternals" "in him & he in them / Live in Perfect harmony, in Eden the land of life."[7] One of the "Eternals" is Albion, similar in conception to Swedenborg's "Grand Man, who is heaven" and the Cabbalistic Adam Kadmon. He is the symbol of all mankind as well as the universe, which has the organic unity of a man. In Eden, the eternal realm, Christ and Albion are identical for all practical purposes; their separateness is only a matter of point of view:

> Then those in Great Eternity met in the Council of God
> As one Man, for contracting their Exalted Senses
> They behold Multitude, or Expanding they behold as one,
> As One Man all the Universal family. . . . (*Zoas*, 277)

Only as a result of a fall does the materiality of Albion constitute a distinguishable entity. Of this fall Blake will

> Sing,
> His fall into Division & his Resurrection to Unity:
> His fall into the Generation of decay & death, & his
> Regeneration by the Resurrection from the dead. (*Zoas*, 264)

This then is Blake's starting point, a unity from which all creation emanates in some way and to which all creation strives, or should strive, to return.

Albion, the "human form divine," or Man, "anciently contain'd in his mighty limbs all things in Heaven & Earth."[8] His oneness is destroyed when, like the Gnostic man, he descends into and becomes the world of matter; but, like the Gnostic man, he collects up "the

35

scatter'd portions of his immortal body / Into the Elemental forms
of every thing that grows" and reascends (*Zoas*, 355). Significantly
Albion is the human form divine as opposed to the sexual or the human
form human, as I have chosen to call it: "The Sexual is Threefold:
the Human is Fourfold," wrote Blake.[9] "Humanity is far above / Sexual
organization" (*Jerusalem*, 721); humanity and all life are one:

> Each grain of Sand,
> Every Stone on the Land,
> Each rock & each hill,
> Each fountain & rill,
> Each herb & each tree,
> Mountain, hill, earth & sea,
> Cloud, Meteor & Star,
> Are Men Seen Afar.[10]

Since this Grand Man is endowed, then, with potential Being, he
might be called more correctly the Grand Family or the Eternal Family, united as one man by common participation in eternal life.[11] Eternity is sundered when one of the eternal family usurps for himself the
role of eternal man:

> If Gods combine against Man, setting their dominion above
> The Human form Divine, Thrown down from their high station
> In the Eternal heavens of Human Imagination, buried beneath
> In dark Oblivion, with incessant pangs, ages on ages,
> In enmity & war first weaken'd, then in stern repentance
> They must renew their brightness, & their disorganiz'd functions
> Again reorganize, till they resume the image of the human. . . .
>
> (*Zoas*, 366)

The fundamental usurpation in Blake's cosmos is that of Urizen, the
rational element. His act is an act of will, which "is always Evil."[12]
With this assertion of individuality, and hence of personal omniscience
and omnipotence, Urizen created the world:

So he began to form of gold, silver & iron
And brass, vast instruments to measure out the immense & fix
The whole into another world better suited to obey

His will, where none should dare oppose his will, himself being King
Of All, & all futurity be bound in his vast chain. (*Zoas,* 317)

This is the natural world of generation, strife, and death, from which
Urizen himself soon cringes and finally flees. Yet the division is not
thus limited: Urizen's self, like the human form divine from which he
came, divides against himself and produces the female emanation. The
ultimate result of this act is the war of the sexes:

> When the Individual appropriates Universality
> He divides into Male & Female, & when the Male & Female
> Appropriate Individuality they become an Eternal Death.
> (*Jerusalem,* 737)

Thus the active power is set into motion by two contrary forces, male
and female, positive and negative, physical and spiritual; and this
power transfers the cosmos from the plane of eternal ideal (Eternal
Mind, Man, Family) to that of finite manifestation, from the noumenal
to the phenomenal.

The theme of sex is prominent here of course. In the occult tradition,
as Denis Saurat has pointed out, "The Demiurge creates the world or
becomes the world by an act which, more or less vaguely . . . is a cosmic
parallel to the sexual act. In its extreme expression we find the her-
maphrodite God, who divides himself and whose parts fecundate each
other."[13] Blake posits sexual union as the one valid method of reachiev-
ing the eternal oneness. Of the two separated halves of our sexually divided self woman, the emanative passive contrary, is restrained. Even
though she is the emotional element in life, once separated from the
rational or intellectual element, she is afraid of passion; she is chaste,
jealous, and intolerant, given to secrecy and guile. Most of the women
in *Songs of Experience* embody these traits. The active contrary, man
or spectre, is intellectually uncertain instead of aggressive, fearful and
inhibited instead of experimental. Theotormon in *Visions of the
Daughters of Albion* is a good example of this. In his impotence the
male contrary is, like Arthur, "Woman-born / And Woman-nourish'd
& Woman-educated & Woman-scorn'd!" (*Jerusalem,* 698) An effort
of will cannot unite Urizen again with the human form divine; only
a denial of self and the concomitant selfless, creative union with his
emanation can accomplish this.

Separated from the divine One, Urizen becomes Reason incarnate, the emanations become feeling or emotion, and each desires the other but tries to conquer rather than yield to the other's dominion. On the human level this takes the form of sexual strife, and it is always severance from spiritual life which precedes the separation of emanation from body. "Rent from Eternal Brotherhood we die & are no more" (*Zoas,* 293). Only when spiritual life is regained can reunion take place. So long as there is separation, the struggle for predominance goes on, the dependent part or emanation developing for the purposes of contention a will of its own, the "female will." "In Eternity Woman is the Emanation of Man; she has No Will of her own. There is no such thing in Eternity as a Female Will" (*Last Judgment,* 613). The reunion, therefore, can only be consummated by an imaginative act, a creation, which involves at once the denial of reason and emotion individually and the acceptance of both. Without the requisite denials there is only the repetitive rape of Oothoon by Bromion (*Visions of the Daughters of Albion*), each a reassertion of the fact of division.

The world created by this division is, as I have said, one of generation, strife, and death. Urizen—or popularly Jehovah—institutes the iron-clad law to rule his subjects, to keep them in a state of subservience to himself:

> Lo! I unfold my darkness, and on
> This rock place with strong hand the Book
> Of eternal brass, written in my solitude:
> Laws of peace, of love, of unity,
> Of pity, compassion, forgiveness;
> Let each chuse one habitation,
> His ancient infinite mansion,
> One command, one joy, one desire,
> One curse, one weight, one measure,
> One King, one God, one Law. (*Urizen,* 224)

The cleverness of Urizen's propagandistic approach is worth noting: the appeal of the virtues, and their complete submergence under one law, Urizen's. But such a bearing of indisputable rule brings with it continual revolt and further restraint—the laws of society, morality, religion, science, marriage, the laws which strangle the human and perpetuate the original fall into ultimate non-entity, the depths of division. In effect Urizen loses control of the creation because of the very method of control which he has imposed upon it.

At this point the creation is assumed by the hand of the human form divine. A limit is placed on the fall to prevent utter annihilation and a reversion to chaos, Boehme's "eternal Abyss."

> Thus were the stars of heaven created like a golden chain
> To bind the Body of Man to heaven from falling into the Abyss.
> (Zoas, 287)

The limit is Adam, the natural world. "Creation," said Blake, "was an act of Mercy" (*Last Judgment,* 614).

> For the Divine Lamb, Even Jesus who is the Divine Vision,
> Permitted all, lest Man should fall into Eternal Death. (*Zoas,* 287)

Thus, while the fall was originally Urizen's responsibility, dictated by a rational act of will, the creation of man himself was the province of the divine imagination; man was created so that he could rise from the fall, overcome blind reason, and reachieve the imaginative realm. With the arrest of the retrogressive effect of the fall by the formation of man's corporeal, mortal body, which Blake calls the "limit of contraction," man becomes bound to the realm of time and space. Nevertheless, though fallen through Urizen's revolt, he is still a spark of the divine: "Human nature is the image of God"; "God is a man."[14] But caverned in his body of five senses, man fails to perceive that the reality underlying everything is a portion of eternity and therefore infinite:

> The Visions of Eternity, by reason of narrowed perceptions,
> Are become weak Visions of Time & Space, fix'd into furrows of death.
> (Jerusalem, 679)

"The roaring of lions, the howling of wolves, the raging of the stormy sea. and the destructive sword. are portions of eternity too great for the eye of man."[15] To regain the ability to perceive eternity is prerequisite to reunion or, popularly, salvation.

2

That in briefest outline is Blake's cosmic system. To relate it to the world of the *Songs of Innocence and of Experience* we must restate the outline in several different terms, the progression of those terms leading us from the cosmic plane eventually to the plane of child, man, woman in the states of innocence and experience. To return to the primal unity, then, the Eternal Family which makes up the Eternal Man is composed of what might be called unconscious selves, all parts of a greater, all-embracing self, the human form divine. In these terms Urizen's revolt is a separation of the individual self from the divine selfhood, the latter being a positive good, the former, evil in the sense that it is intrinsically negative.[16] Thus individualized, Urizen's self arranges and governs the world as if he were the human form divine and everything were a part of him. The creation is for his profit, and to his self accrues all its benefits. In this situation the way to reunion lies in recognizing the existence of one's selfhood and then denying it by merging with another self, the emanation. Or, as Blake put it in *A Vision of the Last Judgment*, "Whenever any Individual Rejects Error & Embraces Truth, a Last Judgment passes upon that Individual" (613). Or again, in terms Blake establishes in *The Marriage of Heaven and Hell* (155), whereas selfhood is all-devouring, the denial of self is prolific. The union (not the reconciliation) of self with self, on selfless terms, can then reinstitute the condition of unconscious selfhood which preceded Urizen's revolt.

This cosmic myth, however, also includes the fall and rise of the imagination. Again, to paraphrase St. John, "In the beginning was the Eternal Mind." It alone is real. It is also "the most Prolific of All Things & Inexhaustible" and hence is identified with "Imagination, which is Spiritual Sensation" or the "Spiritual Perception" Sir Joshua Reynolds was so anxious to disprove.[17] This spiritual perception constitutes the Divine Vision of "what Eternally Exists, Really & Unchangeably."[18] In fact, Imagination is eternity. Within this dialectic the fall is a process of contraction in which the clarity of imaginative vision is obscured by ratiocination. With each successive division from the primal unity of imagination or the human form divine, eternal or fourfold vision becomes darker and darker, and man, though still a portion of the eternal, is enclosed more tightly in the prison of the five senses "till he sees all things thro' narrow chinks of his cavern" (*Marriage,* 154). His "senses unexpansive in one stedfast bulk remain" and cannot penetrate beyond the bounds of self, "As the tree knows not what is outside of its leaves and bark" (*Zoas,* 305, 314). This is what Blake called single vision, the limit of opacity, Ulro, complete darkness. "Natural objects always . . . weaken, deaden & obliterate Imagination," he said; "The Natural Body is an Obstruction to the Soul or Spiritual Body." "I assert for My Self that I do not behold the outward Creation & that to me is a hindrance & not Action; it is as the Dirt upon my feet, No part of Me."[19] The dichotomy between the natural man and the imaginative man is made most clear in Blake's tractate, *There Is No Natural Religion,* etched before the *Songs of Innocence*:

> *The Argument.* Man has no notion of moral fitness but from Education. Naturally he is only a natural organ subject to Sense.
>
> I. Man cannot naturally Percieve but through his natural or bodily organs.
>
> II. Man by his reasoning power can only compare & judge of what he has already perciev'd.
>
> III. From a perception of only 3 senses or 3 elements none could deduce a fourth or fifth.
>
> IV. None could have other than natural or organic thoughts if he had none but organic perceptions.
>
> V. Man's desires are limited by his perceptions, none can desire what he has not perciev'd.
>
> VI. The desires & perceptions of man, untaught by any thing but organs of sense, must be limited to objects of sense.
>
> *Conclusion*: If it were not for the Poetic or Prophetic character the Philosophic & Experimental would soon be at the ratio of all things, & stand still, unable to do other than repeat the same dull round over again.

This is Ulro and Generation. The return from these lower depths to imaginative vision is hinted at in the "Second Series" of this same tractate:

> I. Man's perceptions are not bounded by organs of perception; he percieves more than sense (tho' ever so acute) can discover.

II. Reason, or the ratio of all we have already known, is not the same that it shall be when we know more.

III. [This proposition is lost.]

IV. The bounded is loathed by its possessor. The same dull round, even of a universe, would soon become a mill with complicated wheels.

V. If the many become the same as the few when possess'd, More! More! is the cry of a mistaken soul; less than All cannot satisfy Man.

VI. If any could desire what he is incapable of possessing, despair must be his eternal lot.

VII. The desire of Man being Infinite, the possession is Infinite & himself Infinite.

Application. He who sees the Infinite in all things, sees God.

He who sees the Ratio only, sees himself only.

Therefore God becomes as we are, that we may be as he is.

But with the fallen imagination contracted into the five senses, how does one ever see the infinite in all things? Blake answers the question in *The Marriage of Heaven and Hell:* "This will come to pass by an improvement of sensual enjoyment" (154), that is, through the imagination who is Jesus Christ, the Saviour. "Therefore God becomes as we are, that we may be as he is." This is the key to all of Blake's poetry. In this concept of salvation the rise from division, the denial of self, the reachievement of imaginative vision, and the descent and resurrection of Christ are all merged.

The first step toward such salvation is the recognition of self as the great evil, as error incarnate, and the consequent denial of it for a place in the greater self. "One Error not remov'd will destroy a human Soul" (*Jerusalem,* 676); "to be an Error & to be Cast out is a part of God's design" (*Last Judgment,* 613). Parallel to this denial or casting out is the realization that a rational approach to life gives only a ratio rather than the whole picture; man's vision, instead of being directed outward, is turned in upon itself by the walls of the five senses and he "sees himself only."[20] Hence, Blake's insistence upon an *improvement* of sensual enjoyment. This does not mean, as many have believed, free

42

love or anything of the sort, but rather a breaking of the mundane shell of the five senses, a conscious violation of the moral, religious, and social law which exists for its own or Urizen's sake, and which stifles energy and life at every turn. Promiscuity is not the answer, but neither is chastity. This is one of the points on which Blake and Swedenborg very nearly agree. For the former, chastity was anathema since it presupposed a restrictive law, not necessarily ethical, but restrictive to action; the latter believed more or less the same thing although he stated it in somewhat different terms. Still those terms do express more clearly than any of Blake's prose approximately what he meant by ideal sexual union:

> . . . Love truly conjugial is chastity itself. The reasons are these: (1) Because it is from the Lord, and corresponds to the marriage of the Lord and the church. (2) Because it descends from the marriage of good and truth. (3) Because it is spiritual, just in the degree that the church is with man. (4) Because it is the fundamental love, and the head of all loves, celestial and spiritual. (5) Because it is the true seminary of the human race, and thence of the angelic heaven. (6) Because it therefore exists also among the angels of heaven, and with them spiritual offspring are born of it, which are love and wisdom. (7) And because its use is thus pre-eminent above all the other uses of creation. From this it follows that love truly conjugial, viewed from its origin and in its essence, is pure and holy, so that it may be called purity and holiness, and therefore chastity itself.[21]

For Blake, however, action, not the bond of marriage, was the one solution, for all act is good and virtuous and all prohibition of action, whether in others or in the self, is evil or vicious.

In other words, life must be positive according to Blake, and this is impossible as long as any kind of restraint invokes an everlasting nay. To act in terms of the self alone is to prevent action on the part of another; to act according to reason is to limit sensual enjoyment; to act for one's own good according to one's own individual preference is to isolate the self completely from the all-inclusive self of the human form divine. Hence Blake's equation of reunion, revivification of imaginative vision, and Christ's sacrifice. He became as we are—that is he denied his self to *produce* action in men; once on earth he acted not from the rules but from impulse[22] so that his life was the epitome of improved sensual enjoyment. And he acted for the good of all to reorganize the human form divine.[23] This is the main reason, of course, why Blake can unite the imagination, the poetic or prophetic character, and man himself all in the person of Jesus Christ. He is the human form *divine* just as man, fallen, is the human form *human,* and man, reunited in the Eternal Man or Family, is the human form *divine.*

Blake's use of Christ's relationship to Mary is also pertinent here, especially in view of the doctrine of the virgin birth. A chaste ethics, of course, was synonymous in Blake's mind with the moral law, natural religion; and yet "Christ's very being," as Milton O. Percival says, "is a repudiation of the religion which engendered him." Mary stands at once "for the chastity of a restrictive ethics and, by having given birth to an illegitimate child, for a forgiveness which defies chastity."[24] She represents the law and freedom from the law. As the former, she is that humanity which Christ must put off eternally "Lest the Sexual Generation swallow up Regeneration" (*Jerusalem,* 737). Out of the cruelty of dark religions, just as out of experience, come the forgiveness of sins and the higher innocence.

The recreative union of the separate selves has a corollary in imaginative creation, as that act applies to man's attempt to reachieve eternity. As we have seen, the division into male and female was a direct result of the initial cosmic fall. Reuniting these two contraries demands the greatest of human acts, sexual union. "In Eternity the lover and loved are literally one," said St. Matthew. But it is a very special kind of sexual union of which Blake wrote, one which involves his concepts of prolific and devourer, spectre and emanation. The mere reconciliation of the two is not the solution; indeed Blake believed that earthly "Religion is an endeavour to reconcile the two" and "whoever tries to reconcile them seeks to destroy existence." "Without Contraries is no progression" (*Marriage,* 155, 149). To join the two and yet maintain their respective "contrariety," Blake introduced the idea of creation as opposed to mere copulation, Swedenborg's scortatory love; the latter, however defined, is not what Blake meant by an improvement of sensual enjoyment. It is lust, a debasement of sensual enjoyment. The male must at once give and take to satisfy Blake's conditions, and the female must at once take and give. The former gives of the seminal fluid in the process of creation, but at the same time he "devours" the woman's body; the woman gives herself while at the same time devouring the seed. In these terms the sexual act is tacit recognition of the eternal union and the personal participation in that union; the proof lies in the creation—in this case the child, in the poet's case a poem. In either case, the senses per se are penetrated by the light of vision and the act becomes what Blake calls a last judgment, the final reunion.

But what of the child, the creation itself? For this we must turn to Blake's conception of innocence, experience, and a higher innocence.

3

In the *Songs of Innocence* the child is the symbol of primal unity, for all practical purposes a God. He is an unconscious self; or, in other words, innocence is the Eternal Family united in God by common participation in eternal life. But it is not quite the same. Blake has lowered the frame of reference from the cosmic to the human; fourfold vision in eternity, the unified imagination, has given way here to its approximation on earth, the highest plane which mortal man can reach. Blake calls it Beulah, the realm of the sun's reflection, the realm of the moon, the realm of threefold vision. In Beulah the child is born, and for him it is a paradise on earth; for the parents it is the ultimate step (creation) before reunion with the human form divine. The characteristics of innocence are those of eternity: perfect happiness in ignorance of evil and the self; freedom and energy without restrictive law; unhindered communion between the child's life and the lives of animals and the surrounding universe; and the clear vision (which is love) of the divine world. The child revels in all of this and is protected from premature division by the earthly mother and the spiritual father, for the child is part human, part divine. The time must come, however, when the child achieves adolescence, the mind begins to develop, and the senses mature. At this point experience must be entered without the guiding hand of an earthly mother or spiritual father. Given the world of contraries, both must be experienced to achieve the ultimate union in Beulah, and finally Eternity. Those contraries we have already seen as prolific and devourer; here they are innocence and experience, unconscious selfhood and conscious selfhood.

In these human terms Blake's fall is a movement from pristine unconsciousness into selfconsciousness; the child becomes aware of his separate impulses and their conflicts. The transcendence of experience (or separation) lies in reintegration and, as Schorer put it, "in the achievement of a higher consciousness that is without the strife of the middle state but is also aware as the first was not."[25] Every child is born a self, despite Swedenborg's denial of a "proprium" for him, but in innocence that self is unrecognized as such, even while it is being indulged promiscuously. As long as this ignorance obtains, the primal unity is not threatened. Yet infantilism is not what Blake was after. He envisioned an organized innocence, an "Innocence [that] dwells with Wisdom, but never with Ignorance." Childhood is the realm of ignorance. To know implies first of all self-knowledge, and self-knowledge can only be gained by realizing one's own corporeal existence in relation to the rest of the universe. It is self-identification. At this point the crisis of the child's life has been reached—to see the self as the great evil contrary in the world and to deny that contrary in favor of the over-all self which is the human form divine. As Bronowski expressed it in striking language, "The child must take and must murder experience; it must become father and hypocrite; and it will have found itself if that iron cruelty has rewritten innocence."[26] Now it should be especially clear why Blake thought of the creation—or experience—as an act of mercy: within experience and only within experience can the spark of divine light be enlarged and brightened to grow into a higher innocence. "Experience," as Percival says, "is remedial."[27] In cosmic terms the child divides itself into self and self-less, into the reasoning spectre and the affectionate emanation. The two must be rejoined in an imaginative creation like that which unites prolific and devourer.

In experience of course this is particularly difficult because there all freedom, energy, desire, and vision are throttled by the man-made law of father, priest, and king. These three, a composite Urizen, must be conquered. Collectively they are experience, and they produce the harlot (Blake's "virgin"), religion, morality, and jealousy. Yet they are not the real enemy, for they are basically symbolic manifestations of the perversities of all human nature. The real enemy is the individual self, through which father, priest, and king can reach the individual soul, and it is the self which must be recognized as experience and ultimately denied. The ministering mother of the state of innocence is no longer there for protection—indeed, if she is there she is a tyrant; but the father *is* there and he is a Urizen or a Tiriel. The only way to overcome him is by an improvement of sensual enjoyment, by thwarting law, by cleansing the windows of perception, and by achieving a vision of the eternal unity that can be achieved only through selfless creation. This is the state Swedenborg described as "The innocence of wisdom . . . genuine innocence . . . it is eternal: for it belongs to the mind itself."[28] Precisely how Blake meant this state to be reached lies within the province of the prophetic books and hence not within the limits of this discussion. The present state of the soul was the subject of the *Songs*.

<h2 style="text-align:center">4</h2>

In the progression from childhood to maturity and marriage, from innocence to experience to a higher innocence in wisdom, there are two main ideas which predominate, joy and love. They are by no means mutually exclusive ideas and they are not strictly definable; yet, their interdependence provides the reader with the key to what Blake meant when he wrote, "Generation, Image of regeneration" (*Jerusalem*, 626). At the core of his system, they encompass Christ and the child, the father and mother, imagination and vision.

The happiness of the child in innocence is by nature selfish and instinctive, although, as we have seen, that selfishness is not a conscious attitude. The child lives for itself in much the same fashion that eternity exists for itself. On the other hand, Blake wrote, "Eternity is in love with the productions of time" (*Marriage*, 151), and "The Ruins of Time builds Mansions in Eternity" (Letter to Hayley, 797). It is with time that both innocence and experience have to do. To continue the selfish and instinctive life results in the pseudo-joy of the vales of Har and Heva, a joy predicated on the fact of the self's existing only for the self. This was Har's error in creating his race of men in *Tiriel*, the race of Tiriels which makes up this world. Actually, at maturity—or from the advent of experience on—man can experience a happiness much greater than can ever be known by the child, for it is no longer selfish and instinctive but inclusive and imaginative.

47

Hence the state of experience is at once a state of disillusionment and the origin of a potential guiding light for all mankind; individuation and unity go hand in hand. Blake's general symbol of experience is the grave, and the voice of the grave at the end of *The Book of Thel* is his most explicit and concise description of the state. The soul is on the horns of a dilemma: to share the joy which it has so happily and irresponsibly reveled in alone in innocence, or to keep the joy as its own and retreat with it to the vales of Har. But Blake makes unmistakably clear in *Thel* and *Tiriel* that the soul is not self-sufficient. Indeed it was not self-sufficient even in innocence, for the earthly mother helped to keep innocence inviolate, and the spiritual father was there to restate the fact of innocence at crucial moments like that in *The Little Boy Found*. Man must pass out of innocence; there is no real choice if imagination and the higher innocence are to be reached.

Vaguely similar to a "fortunate fall," the Blakean fall from innocence to experience is necessary so that each of us, through a last judgment, may live eternally. F. C. Prescott has put it in a more modern context: "Even this garden has been but a stopping-place for the human mind; however longingly we look back to it we cannot return; when we have once taken our departure the path leading toward it is fatally regressive."[29] In other words there is actually a difference between the cosmic fall and the human fall, though Blake does merge them constantly in his system. Urizen's fall was a result of willful revolt and hence an unnecessary "accident"; with the subsequent creation of humankind the fall became a necessity so that man could recognize the selfhood of error that is his legacy from Urizen. If the self persists in its ways beyond childhood and innocence, without self-consciousness, it will be unable to know the joy of brotherhood or any other kind of unity. Without imagination, which links his life with all that is beyond his life, man remains in the grave of memory,[30] stagnant from here to eternity. That stagnation was called by Blake the joyless moral law, which imposed general form upon the inherently individual human form divine. For his salvation, man ironically does not look outside himself but within, not to the self which is man's approximation of the divine, but to his essential humanity which *is* divine. Urizen was divine to begin with, but he felt he had to usurp divinity to assert that fact before the cosmic audience. "God is no more," said Blake in *The Ever-*

lasting Gospel (750); God is Jehovah, the very "without" that imposes the iron-clad law. "Thine own Humanity learn to Adore," for "where is the Father of men to be seen but in the most perfect of his children?"[31]

> I am not a God afar off, I am a brother and friend;
> Within your bosoms I reside, and you reside in me.
>
> (*Jerusalem, 622*)

When man can see that, as the child does in *A Little Boy Lost* for example, the windows of the morning have once again been opened.

Vision, of course, precludes restraint. "Thou shalt not" is the form restraint takes in this world; instinct and passion are banned in favor of reason and abstinence. Spiritual purpose is completely denied to instinctive life by earthly morality. Thus, the purpose of experience in Blake's system is, in Max Plowman's phrase, the "imaginative redemption of instinct."[32] Then and only then will the five senses appear as inlets to the soul.

Love has much the same history as joy-instinct, for Blake saw God as love. Hence man, too, is love. In innocence love is as selfish as joy has been seen to be, both founded on ignorance. With the advent of experience, however, love must find an object. There are many, of course, but all of them ultimately come under the headings of love of another and love of self. Swedenborg, for example, divides love into two groups of two: "There are in heaven two distinct kinds of love— love to the Lord, and love towards the neighbor." The former is celestial love, the latter spiritual. "But . . . Man is not born to those two Kinds of Love, but to their Contraries, viz. to Self-Love and the Love of the World. . . ."[33] Though Blake could not agree with this idea of original sin, he did agree wholeheartedly with the basic dichotomy. To pursue the love of self even after innocence recedes into the past is to turn to the past and memory, to go the way of Thel when she fled the grave in horror. To love others is to love God. "The worship of God is. Honouring his gifts in other men each according to his genius, and loving the greatest men best, those who envy or calumniate great men hate God. for there is no other God."[34] "Thine own Humanity learn to Adore." Love is a process of becoming one, but like the prolific and devourer, it is not complete self-abnegation. The fulfillment of two desires is necessary: the prolific is also devouring, as we have seen, and the devourer is prolific. Man cannot give himself until he possesses himself through self-assertion; imagination cannot function except through the individual who has realized himself. Similarly, love without sensual enjoyment is sterile, and sensual enjoyment, redeemed from lust by imagination, thus becomes neither selfishness nor self-denial but a marriage of the two.

So far from free love is Blake's "improvement of sensual enjoyment," then, that we may read his phrase with equal correctness as "an improvement of spiritual enjoyment." For soul and body are always one in Blake's system. When the senses are enjoyed as the true inlets of the soul through which spiritual perceptions (multifold vision) can be made, then matter can no longer hamper soul, the doors of perception will be clean, and everything will appear as it is, infinite.

5

Despite this threefold scheme I have been outlining, Blake's system actually breaks down into four steps. I insist on three here only because the fourth and lowest is seldom mentioned in connection with the songs, and indeed has very little significance, for our purposes, beyond what we would call chaos. As we have seen, Blake called it Ulro, the lowest state of the cosmos after Urizen's revolt, or single vision, which sees the self only. Above Ulro's darkness is what I have been calling experience, Blake's Generation, the realm of the flesh, this world, within which there is potentially double vision. With double vision man can see beyond the self and the mere facts of existence to recognize the human. But experience is also the world of "goodness," which "is the passive that obeys Reason" (*Marriage*, 149), and of the moral law, under which the sacredness of all life is denied and an ethics of repression superimposed on it. With the divine world hidden, the worship of God takes the form of man-made law in empty, hypocritical ceremony. Jealousy stalks the battlefield between the warring contraries, and fear is the only password. Natural religion enmeshes all life and the highest vision attainable is man. God is no more.[35]

God returns in Beulah with its threefold vision, in which the divine is visible in the human. This as we have seen is the realm of the highest union on earth, the union which approaches in all respects a final reintegration with eternity and the human form divine. Blake's choice of the name, Beulah (which means "married"), to symbolize the felicitous relationship of the two main contraries, man and woman, is thus most apt. In the ideally married state the jealousy of experience has no place, the outer and inner worlds are in harmony (Swedenborg's "equilibrium") and at peace, for no portion of life is denied. As Blake wrote in *Jerusalem*:

Embraces are Cominglings from the Head even to the Feet,
And not a pompous High Priest entering by a Secret Place (708),

as is the case in Generation, where forgiveness has been lost sight of in the mysteries of the moral law.

The final reintegration is Eden, fourfold vision, the innocence of wisdom, where all is love and all is one. Mercy, pity, peace are all included here in the Divine Man, Adam Kadmon, the Imagination. It is Blake's Heaven.

With these manifold—and shifting—patterns in mind, we can undertake a detailed analysis of each contributive element as it evolved in Blake's mind and poetry; but before that can be done we must examine Blake's method of presenting those elements.

CHAPTER II

THE IMAGINATION

The stuff of inspiration is living images.
—AUSTIN FARRAR, *The Glass of Vision*

Blake's view of the imagination as both a religious and a poetical concept can be examined best by seeing it in terms of the very system that spawned and comprehended it. The main difficulty in any approach to his view of course is the fundamental one of definition, since nowhere in his works is there a systematic exegesis of what he meant by the term. Generally he uses "imagination" rather loosely to mean the highest faculty available to man for his salvation—or, in other words, for the practice of art.[1] For this faculty he found a convenient symbol in his own peculiar conception of Jesus Christ. This is hardly sufficient to explain poetic technique, but within the dialectic of Blake's system it does provide a clue to the first step in the creative process, perception.

Perception is debilitated in the fall from primal unity in the same way that the human form divine is fractured to produce the splinter, man; the loss of imagination is the loss of the ability to perceive the divine because of the wall of nature intermediated by the mundane world. Since Blake was not a pantheist this interposition of the world was intensely obscuring. Although the creation of the world and of man included the equipment of man with five senses for directly perceiving that world, Blake believed that these were not so much the perceptive agents themselves as the windows through which a mental or imaginative or divine grasp of reality is possible. If soul (or mind) and body are the same, as Blake insisted they were, the act of perception is relative in that the pragmatic reality of the natural, phenomenal world is at best a partial reality. The real is only that portion of the perception conceived to be real by the mind which beholds it. The passive acceptance of the validity of Reynolds' "General Nature" or general reality Blake could not tolerate. "To Generalize is to be an Idiot," he wrote; "General Knowledges are those Knowledges that Idiots possess." To particularize, which "is the Alone Distinction of Merit" (Annotations to Reynolds, 451), is to contribute something from one's own mind to the act of perception. "Every Man's Wisdom is peculiar to his own Individuality" (*Milton,* 483), for "Every Eye Sees differently" (Annotations to Reynolds, 456). The imaginative eye of the wise man or the poet sees more of the reality of the perceived object than that of the fool, who, seeing "the Ratio only, sees himself only" (*No Natural Religion,* 98). The former, in Northrop Frye's words, "throws his entire imagination behind his perception" instead of cautiously pruning "away different characteristics from that imagination [to] isolate one."[2] Since the mind is free, far from being a tabula rasa upon which sense impressions create their own existence, the imagination operates unbounded to unify the total experience of perception. This is not unlike Coleridge's idea of the Reason, the spark of the Logos in man which, by uniting outer and inner life, enables man to recognize genuine universals or eternal verities. As opposed to imagination, sense experience is limited by its very sensuality and by the dimensions of tangibility, just as the fallen man is restricted in vision to the narrow chinks of his bodily cavern. "The bounded is loathed by its possessor," wrote Blake in *There Is No Natural Religion*: "The same dull round, even of a universe, would soon become a mill with complicated wheels" (97).

This does not mean, however, that the data of sense experience are ignored, "for it is impossible to think without images of somewhat on earth" (Annotations to Lavater, 88). Again it does not mean that the senses must be controlled by a guiding reason. It does mean that they are to be employed by the imagination, acted upon, so that the latter may create out of the chaotic tabula rasa data a mental form. "All

Forms are Perfect in the Poet's Mind," Blake wrote in his copy of Reynolds' *Discourses,* "but these are not Abstracted nor Compounded from Nature, but are from Imagination" (459). The late eighteenth century idea of "coalescence" operated in a similar manner, though its ultimate application to the presentation of a wholly new creation was a development Blake did not permit his idea to take. His creation already existed in eternity, and the conscious "coalescence" of present sensation was only to facilitate a presentation of that creation in concrete form. The form in its smallest unit is the image; more complicated and more complete it is the symbol; totally unified it is the poem. At this point the perceptive imagination becomes creative.

Man in his creative acts, as well as in his perceptions, is a god; the world of imagination is one of creators and creatures. But if perception is a godlike act, God Himself cannot be perceived except as He exists in the perceiver. Confusion on this point, Blake observes in *The Marriage,* was the cause of the mistake of the ancient poets, who "animated all sensible objects with Gods or Geniuses" and then, for the purposes of worship, attempted "to realize or abstract the mental deities from their objects." "Thus men forgot that All deities reside in the human breast" (153). Since true perception has been seen to be mental creation, God cannot be created by less than God: "Man can have no idea of any thing greater than Man, as a cup cannot contain more than its capaciousness. But God is a man" (Annotations to Swedenborg, 90). Similarly, the ultimate in perception, which is vision, is the realization "of what Eternally Exists, Really & Unchangeably." "There Exist in that Eternal World the Permanent Realities of Every Thing which we see reflected in this Vegetable Glass of Nature" (*Last Judgment,* 604, 605). This latter statement, like some others by Blake, seems to involve a basic contradiction in his thought. Basil de Selincourt noted it in his book, *William Blake*: "It will be observed at once . . . that Blake's description of the rising sun as 'a round disc of fire, somewhat like a guinea' is a pretty piece of evidence, were any such evidence needed, that he could when he chose, see through the corporeal eye as clearly as anyone; and that his statement, 'for myself, I do not behold the outward creation,' means no more than the conscious study of natural forms had ceased to be a part of his artistic or spiritual activity."[3] Out of its context and applied here to the *Songs of Innocence and of Experience,* de

Selincourt's surmise is too extreme (actually he is basing it on Blake's later artistic work). But it does seem to prove, despite Blake's quoted thought to the contrary, that he certainly did see the natural world and did not merely invent a fiction to circumvent it. The important thing to remember is that Blake looked at the world, as he says, *through* not *with* the eye. De Selincourt's confusion on this point is inherent in his casual use above of the phrase, "see through the corporeal eye." Blake's distinction is perhaps somewhat analogous to that suggested by the popular saying, "to see the world through rose-colored glasses." In each case the vision is colored, but while the glasses reflect only a state of mind, Blake's vision reflects the whole mind. Having made this distinction in modes of seeing, Blake could thus say in apparent contradiction, "Natural Objects always did & now do weaken, deaden & obliterate Imagination in Me" (Annotations to Wordsworth, 783), and "To Me This World is all One continued Vision of Fancy or Imagination" (Letter to Trusler, 793). This is far from mere perversity. By the first Blake meant simply that the natural world hindered perception of the eternal realities; by the second that the world was a "continuing" source of poetic metaphor with which to communicate his vision of the eternal realities. De Selincourt's conclusion, then, is valid: Blake did fail "to distinguish between the visualizing and the creative imagination."[4] To see the eternal realities through the vegetable glass was the job of the former; to unite the vegetable glass with the realities was the job of the latter.

An adequate presentation of this relationship demanded a more subtle, complex tool than image or similitude. "Demonstration, Similitude & Harmony are Objects of Reasoning. Invention, Identity & Melody are Objects of Intuition."[5] Symbolic poetry has seldom had so concise a definition. "I will not Reason & Compare," wrote Blake: "my business is to Create" (*Jerusalem*, 629). Reason comprehends but the ratio of things; imagination encompasses, and then presents, the totality. Imagination is art.

I have said that imaginative perception is creation. To create a simile involves, in the final analysis, little imagination. The basic qualities of two objects are abstracted and some similarity is noted. As an aid to the clarification and enrichment of the quality insisted upon the figure is invaluable; yet it is hardly representative of eternal reality.

Largely for this reason Swedenborg's theory of correspondences per se (as well as Boehme's doctrine of signatures) could not satisfy Blake's needs. Beyond the basic idea of macrocosm visible in microcosm Swedenborg's system was a vast, endless analogy or allegory. All natural things Swedenborg believed to have spiritual meanings, and the arbitrary meanings assigned made the theory of correspondences the *reductio ad absurdum* of the symbolic method. The system inevitably strangled itself. Blake approached the mystic's analogical penchant only in his interpretation of the Bible; but though he read it in singular fashion, there is little reason to believe his approach was dictated or even suggested by Swedenborg's theory. Blake had more fundamental reasons for contemplating a "Bible of Hell."

In view of the patent inadequacy of similitude, then, Blake turned to metaphor and more particularly to symbol. To create a symbol, and then a poem, requires invention, identity, and melody; these, Blake said, are produced by intuition, not analysis. This is the real basis for his vague definition of the highest poetry, "Vision or Imagination," as opposed to "Fable or Allegory." The latter are the progeny of the "daughters of Memory" (*Last Judgment,* 604), and "Imagination has nothing to do with Memory" (Annotations to Wordsworth, 783). To see completely a chair, a house, or a sunrise, one must raise the power of his senses to an imaginative level. As de Selincourt explains, "The object is, in effect, thus raised by . . . the mind which provides for it such a context as the mere sense impression has not of itself the means of summoning up."[6] The mind draws from its own resources images to add to the sensuous image actually before it. "The Imaginative Image returns by the seed of Contemplative Thought" (*Last Judgment,* 605). Thus Blake could say with absolute conviction, "In my Brain are studies & Chambers fill'd with books & pictures of old, which I wrote & painted in ages of Eternity before my mortal life" (Letter to Flaxman, 802). From this reservoir of what Yeats might have called the eternal mind or great memory the poet draws to his perception both image and emotion of eternal reality to complete, unify, and clarify the sense experience of the isolated moment. "All of us on earth," Blake wrote in his copy of Lavater, "are united in thought" (88).

It is obvious, then, that although Blake wrote almost always of what I have called the perceptive imagination and the dangers of unalloyed sense experience—in *There Is No Natural Religion, All Religions Are One, The Marriage,* the annotations to Reynolds, and later prose writings—the creative artist in him instinctively recognized the need for communication. That involved the unification of experience, the revelation of the eternal realities behind the vegetable glass of nature by means of that glass itself. It demanded the symbol and the poem, and they are the evidence we must study here.

Blake's concept of the imagination, then, was at least threefold, more strictly speaking fourfold. On the lowest level is the imagination of the fool, single vision; then double vision or imaginative perception; then the creative imagination; and finally the all-inclusive Body of the Imagination, the ultimate union of creator and creature. They correspond precisely with Blake's fourfold division of the cosmos into Ulro, Generation, Beulah, and Eden:

Now I a fourfold vision see,
And a fourfold vision is given to me;
'Tis fourfold in my supreme delight
And threefold in soft Beulah's night
And twofold Always. May God us keep
From Single vision & Newton's sleep! (Letter to Butts, 818)

With these various versions of the imaginative faculty in mind we can now more accurately determine the place the imagination occupies in Blake's system.

Since both the primal and ultimate unity of the cosmos are called Imagination, it must necessarily have some relationship to the fall into division and the rise to reintegration. "All Things," as Blake wrote, "are comprehended in . . . Eternal Forms in the divine body of the Saviour, the True Vine of Eternity, The Human Imagination" (*Last Judgment,* 605-606). In addition to these forms, however, there is another eternal which apparently has little connection to eternal forms but which provides much of the basis for Blake's poetic technique. "From Essence," wrote Blake, "proceeds Identity & from one Essence may proceed many Identities" (Annotations to Swedenborg, 91). With the disruption of this essence, two kinds of imagination appear in the place of one. They are perhaps analogous to the spectre and emanation of the cosmic myth, certainly comparable to the contraries reason and emotion. These two are, of course, sense perception and imaginative perception, the same dichotomy we examined earlier in *There Is No Natural Religion*. The intimate connection of this division with the system outlined in Chapter I is exemplified by the allusion to self and nonself (or God) in the "Application" of the tractate: "He who sees the Infinite in all things, sees God. He who sees the Ratio only, sees himself only." To reorganize this duality of perception Blake, as we have seen, relies upon the creative imagination which is always equated with Christ and the Poetic Genius.

The division of Imagination has further ramifications in the idea of "states," and it is here that imagination and essence find their common denominator. Blake may have derived the term "state" from his reading of Swedenborg, who recognized three main states through which man progressed: damnation (inherited), reformation, and regeneration. In addition to these, however, Swedenborg conceived of many states from which man cannot extricate himself—states like fear, insanity, and ignorance. Blake's states, on the contrary, are at once eternal and annihilable to differentiate them from individuals who are eternal and unannihilable. States owe their existence to separation from Imagination. For example, Blake writes, "Affection or Love becomes a State when divided from Imagination." Thus states are a part of the creation, "Created to be Annihilated" (*Milton*, 522). The annihilation comes about when an individual, moving toward reunion with Imagination, enters a state and assumes its quality; that is, he becomes the state momentarily. To continue his journey he must annihilate the state in himself. In this sense "States Change, but Individual Identities never change nor cease" (*Milton*, 521). At the same time "States remain for Ever" (*Last Judgment*, 606) for others to enter, become, and annihilate. Man "passes thro' them like a traveller who may as well suppose that the places he has passed thro' Exist no more, as a Man may suppose that the States he has passed thro' Exist no more" (*Last Judgment*, 606). From this it is obvious that Blake took Swedenborg's teaching and developed it along very different lines. Not the condition of man in them, as Swedenborg supposed, but the states themselves are eternal in Blake's system. Blake spoke of man's salvation in terms of man, not in terms of the state called Satan from which he was to be rescued: "Christ . . . Comes to deliver Man, the Accused, & not Satan, the Accuser" (*Last*

Judgment, 615). The journey through the states involves, of course, the fall from innocence to experience and the ascension to a higher innocence, for these realms are Blake's main states. To present, or to represent, them in all their peculiarities required something more than mere perception, whether that perception were sensual or imaginative. The diverse particulars of the *Songs of Innocence* and *Songs of Experience* mean little in terms of the system without some unifying element to give them a meaning. That element is the symbol. In the *Songs of Innocence* the symbol is a child (and mother), in the *Songs of Experience* the father-priest-king.

Now, as the state is but a portion of the eternal imagination, so the symbol of the state is only a part of the divine essence. It is identity as opposed to similtude, to use Blake's terms; it is more familiarly the individual self, though as yet unrealized, which is a part of the divine self. But where does the symbol originate? Did Blake merely make a haphazard guess? The answer lies in the nature of the system itself: unity to division to unity conforms to the pattern of the child's growth to wise maturity, or more universally, conforms to the eternal cycle of birth, life, decay, and death (rebirth). Similarly, the state of disunity or experience is symbolized by the father-priest-king, and the final reintegration by Christ, Albion-Jerusalem, and Milton. Thus Blake could say when describing one of his paintings: "It ought to be understood that the Persons, Moses & Abraham, are not here meant, but the States Signified by those Names, the Individuals being representatives or Visions of those States as they were reveal'd to Mortal Man in the Series of Divine Revelations as they are written in the Bible; these various States I have seen in my Imagination; when distant they appear as One Man, but as you approach they appear Multitudes of Nations" (*Last Judgment,* 607). In a similar vein Blake also wrote, "Where man is not nature is barren" (*Marriage,* 152); "Time & Space are Real Beings" (*Last Judgment,* 614); and the famous passage in his copy of Swedenborg: "Think of a white cloud as being holy, you cannot love it; but think of a holy man within the cloud, love springs up in your thoughts, for to think of holiness distinct from man is impossible to the affections. Thought alone can make monsters, but the affections cannot" (90). Thus, as always in Blake, the concrete is preferred to the abstract, the symbol to mere personification.[7] In eternity these symbols—child, father, Christ—these identities never change (*Last Judgment*, 606-607); but in the world of division they must change insofar as passage through the states constitutes what we on earth think of as change. Actually the change in Blake's system is not so much a change as it is a cumulative development, for the final reunion takes into account all states. The child of innocence can only be said to change in that he recognizes himself for what he is, a self that must be denied; that knowledge of experience he uses as a springboard to the wisdom of the higher innocence. There the doors of his perception are cleansed and the Imagination lies open before him. In symbolic terms, the symbols merge progressively, just as they develop progressively: the child in his passage through the states becomes more and more the imagination itself until, at his own individual last judgment, he is the saviour and the saved.

Between the perception and the creation, however, there is a tremendous gap. To present the reintegration of the divided Imagination, the poet or bard must be imbued with the very wisdom which his characters or symbols yet seek. He is Christ to their fallen man. His problem, then, is the presentation of the symbolic experience in such a way that it adumbrates the cosmic reunion. The poem is that adumbration. Yet each poem can only be a partial victory, for innocence as well as experience is a multifarious state made up of many lesser states. The act of creation precludes the separate existence of such states; it encompasses all states, and all symbols, in the Imagination. These symbols have their existence from the system, within the frame of reference invoked by the creator, Blake. So man has no reality, in the eternal sense, outside of the divine, and it is no accident that a continuation of Urizen's revolt would have led to "Non-Entity." What eternally exists, really and unchangeably, goes on existing outside the immediate frame of reference; the poet pulls the eternal down to the temporal so that the temporal may rise to the eternal. It is Christ's sacrifice. When the higher innocence is reached, the mundane shell, as Blake calls it, falls away in the clear perception of the infinite, for the child merges with father, innocence with experience, to reachieve essence and God. This is what Frye aptly calls "the unified synthesis of experience."[8] It is vision and wisdom.

Even if his poetry is not all that Yeats believed it to be,[9] it is symbolic in the sense that its frame of reference is one myth, one Bible, one Word. Some eighteenth-century mythographers, like Bryant and Davies, interpreted that myth historically, or according to what they conceived history to be;[10] Blake interpreted it poetically and philosophically. His interpretation is his system, the product of the unifying creative imagination. Tradition could not supply him with all the elements, for salvation is an intensely personal problem; besides, Blake's imagination would not admit of fetters. To cope with the ancient heroes and cosmic myths would involve the careful exclusion of all association foreign to his central theme. He took some but left most; what he took was transformed in the process. Even Christ. With somewhat different emphasis D. G. James, in *The Romantic Comedy,* explains that process this way: "Blake uses the old myths; but as myths proper he will have nothing to do with them, except to express his violent hostility to what they were originally intended to convey."[11] The religion of imagination could not be conceived without imagination as its main symbol. And there was no such symbol before Blake wrote.

CHAPTER III

BLAKE'S SYMBOLIC TECHNIQUE

> Above all let us not do him the violence of reading him on one plane.
> —W. B. YEATS, *A Vision*

Within Blake's system the imagination has been seen to occupy a central place. Although I believe that an understanding of how the creative imagination presented that system in poetic form is possible only in the context of explication, an introduction to the prevailing structure of the poems will be valuable here as an aid to understanding my method of explication in succeeding chapters.

Basically Blake's method is simple, its roots lying in his concept of states and their symbols. These states are innocence, experience, and a higher innocence, their symbols the child, the father, and Christ. I shall call them major symbols for they provide the context for all the minor symbolism of the poems. These minor or contributory symbols are obviously too numerous for categorical analysis even if precise definition were always possible; moreover, such a procedure would reveal neither their *modus operandi* in the poems nor the fundamental reason for their use at all. My purpose is not to define each symbol but rather to suggest a method of approach applicable to all the symbols.[1]

Each of Blake's song series (or states or major symbols) is comprised of a number of smaller units (or states or symbols), so that the relationship of each unit to the series as a whole might be stated as a descending progression: from the states of innocence and experience to the *Songs of Innocence and of Experience,* to each individual song, to the symbols within each song, to the words that form the symbols. Conceivably ignorance of or indifference to one word can prohibit the imaginative perception and understanding of the whole structure. "Every word and every letter is studied and put into its fit place," Blake wrote in the preface to *Jerusalem;* "the terrific numbers are reserved for the terrific parts, the mild & gentle for the mild & gentle parts, and the prosaic for inferior parts; all are necessary to each other" (621). Though such precision may legitimately be doubted in regard to *The Four Zoas, Milton,* or *Jerusalem,* a recognition of Blake's punctiliousness in the songs is indispensable to a correct, full reading of each song as well as to a comprehension of his major states. Helen White has written of his symbolism:

> At first it seems too complicated, so obscure, so incoherent, so utterly unrelated to any world of meaning with which the reader is familiar, that his first impulse is to dismiss it as mad nonsense. But the more the . . . writings are studied, the clearer it becomes that, however fragmentary and even inconsistent a particular "song" or "vision" or "book" may be, its symbolism comes out of the same body or world of symbol as that out of which the rest of Blake's work comes. In other words, even if the system revealed in these writings is neither logically exact nor well-articulated, it is fundamentally organic.[2]

The serious reader of Blake's songs, then, must be constantly aware of the context or state in which each individual poem appears; and since each state is made up of many poems, other poems in the same state must be consulted to appreciate the fullest possible significance of any one poem.

Yet the necessity for a cumulative reading of Blake's songs should in no way detract from his artistry in each individual song; the hundreds of comments on the songs, the countless anthologized segments of his work, and the universal praise accorded the songs are all eloquent testimony to their fundamental self-sufficiency. Yet out of its context each song means a great deal less than Blake expected of his total invention; and occasionally it may be taken to mean something quite different from what he intended. Since innocence and experience are vital parts of Blake's system, to deny to the *Songs of Innocence* the very background and basic symbology it helps to create is as wrong as reading *The Rape of the Lock* outside the epic tradition. Without an awareness of his design Blake is the simplest of lyric poets. But with very little study the child of innocence can be seen to be radically different from the child of experience; and the mother of innocence is scarcely recognizable in experience. The states are separate; they are the two contrary states of the human soul, and the width of the hiatus is spanned by the poems which appeared after the engraving of the *Songs of Innocence* and before the *Songs of Experience—The Book of Thel, Tiriel, Visions of the Daughters of Albion, The Marriage of Heaven and Hell.*[3] These poems are the products of a transition in Blake's own thinking. With the *Songs of Innocence* behind him, he had as yet no vehicle, no ready plan, and no completely formulated major symbol for experience. *Thel, Tiriel,* and the *Visions* were his experiments to find that form, the "reinforced lyric," and that symbol, the father-priest-king. Outside the context of this half-light between the states, these three poems are susceptible to facile misunderstanding, simply because the controlling symbols and their milieu are ignored or unrecognized. Other poems especially subject to erroneous reading for the same reasons are *The Chimney Sweeper, The Little Boy Lost,* and *Night* in *Innocence;* and *Nurses Song, The Little Girl Lost, The Little Girl Found, A Little Boy Lost, The Chimney Sweeper,* and *Holy Thursday* in *Experience.*

Closely related to the necessity for reading each song in terms of its state is the vital importance of point of view. Usually it is so unobtrusive as to elude the casual reader's eye, but many times a faithful interpretation of a poem depends upon a correct determination of speaker and perspective. That this element should carefully be considered is evidenced by the introductory song to each series: one is sung by the Piper, the other by the Bard. Superficially there seems to be little to distinguish one from the other since the Piper clearly exhibits imaginative vision and the Bard sees present, past, and future. Yet for the Piper the past can only be the primal unity, for the present is innocence, and the immediate future is experience; while for the Bard the past is innocence, the present experience, the future a higher innocence. Accordingly it is natural to expect the Piper's point of view to be joyful, happy; he is conscious of the child's essential divinity and assured of his present protection. But into that joyous context the elements of exper-ience constantly insinuate themselves, and a note of sorrow is never completely absent from the Piper's pipe. In experience, on the other hand, the Bard's voice is solemn, serious, and more deeply resonant, for the high-pitched joy of innocence exists now only as memory or as a degenerate, hypocritical smile. Within experience, though, lies the ember which can leap into flame at any moment to light the way to the higher innocence. What joins the two voices together is that both singers are imaginative; they are the poetic and/or prophetic charac-ters. Because of this Blake demands that his reader always consider the imaginative point of view no matter who is speaking, seeing, or acting in the poem. The inexplicit, he said, "rouzes the faculties to act" (Letter to Trusler, 793). And though one singer uses "mild and gentle numbers" and the other the more "terrific" tones, the reader must rouse his faculties to realize that both Piper and Bard see the spiritual, im-aginative significance of the terrestrial, sensational activity in all the songs.

Both singers are William Blake. And since he, or they, sing all the songs, the fact that they are identifiable or not identifiable with a character in a poem contributes most importantly to the total meaning of that poem. For example, in *The Chimney Sweeper* (*Innocence*) the angel is equated at one point with the Piper, but in *Infant Sorrow* it is vital to recognize the speaker to be quite separate from the Bard, the former's myopia only being discernible through the Bard's greater vision. Similarly, in *The Little Vagabond* the reader must discover at least four points of view: that of the mother, who is the direct anti-thesis of the mother Blake wrote of in *Songs of Innocence;* that of the parson, who is equated as always by Blake with the major symbol of experience; that of the vagabond himself, who must be viewed as a child of experience, not the carefree, irresponsible, thoughtless child of innocence; and that of the Bard, through whose vision each of the other points of view can be studied and evaluated. Without an aware-ness of this complexity in *The Little Vagabond,* the reader fails to grasp an essential part of the poem's structure, the very element which rescues it from the limbo of sentimental drivel. Other good examples of Blake's manipulation of point of view may be seen in *A Dream,*

Holy Thursday, The Chimney Sweeper, The Little Black Boy, and *The Blossom* in *Innocence; Thel* and *Visions of the Daughters of Albion;* and *Earth's Answer, Nurses Song, The Little Girl Lost, The Little Girl Found, A Little Girl Lost, The Human Abstract, The Chimney Sweeper,* and *Holy Thursday* in *Experience.*

One of the several ways to ascertain the point of view is to observe various characters' reactions to the same symbol, for ultimately that symbol resolves itself into one aspect of the major symbol governing that particular poem. It is to both kinds of symbol, the major and the minor, that we now turn.

In all of Blake's poetry acts, objects, and characters can be symbolic, the determination of their value and association depending upon whether they contribute to the structure of the controlling symbol. For example, the mother of *Songs of Innocence* is symbolic to the extent that her protective solicitude for the child contributes to his status as the major symbol of the state of innocence. And since most of Blake's symbols are recurrent throughout the poetry, the pattern or incidence of their recurrence will reveal the technique by which Blake achieved the intensive richness of each individual poem. This is perhaps what Yeats meant when he wrote that "all art is . . . a monotony in external things for the sake of an interior variety, a sacrifice of gross effects to subtle effects."[4]

To illustrate the way in which such a symbol gathers the moss of association and connotation within Blake's self-created "poetic tradition," I shall trace briefly the recurrence of the staff or rod or, in its most easily recognizable form, the sceptre. It appears first in unsymbolic context in the *Poetical Sketches* with little more than a literal or "traditional" meaning—sovereignty, power, rule:

O Winter! bar thine adamantine doors:
The north is thine; there hast thou built thy dark
Deep-founded habitation. Shake not thy roofs,
Nor bend thy pillars with thine iron car.

He hears me not, but o'er the yawning deep
Rides heavy; his storms are unchain'd, sheathed
In ribbed steel; I dare not lift mine eyes,
For he hath rear'd his sceptre o'er the world. (*To Winter,* 3-4)

In *Gwin, King of Norway* cruelty and tyranny are added to the sceptre's significance, foreshadowing the hypocrisy of the secular, religious, and domestic rulers of *Songs of Experience* as well as the selfishness of Tiriel:

> Come, Kings, and listen to my song:
> When Gwin, the son of Nore,
> Over the nations of the North
> His cruel sceptre bore,
>
> The Nobles of the land did feed
> Upon the hungry Poor;
> They tear the poor man's lamb, and drive
> The needy from their door! (11)

In *Holy Thursday* (*Innocence*) Blake varies the symbol for the first time and establishes the more modern version of authority and cruelty —the rod or staff or wand:

> Twas on a Holy Thursday their innocent faces clean
> The children walking two & two in red & blue & green
> Grey headed beadles walkd before with wands as white as snow
> Till into the high dome of Pauls they like Thames waters flow.

The beadle wielding the authority is a representative of the organized church of "natural religion" which Blake hated so violently. The wand itself represents not merely authority but an act of restraint which forces the children to act according to rule rather than their inherently divine impulses. The whiteness of the wand suggests the frigidity of man-made moral purity as opposed to the warmth of young, energetic, exuberant innocence. And finally, its usage here suggests the worldly concept of duty (and its corollary, harm), the duty of worship which clashes with all of Blake's ideas of freedom and spontaneity.

Following this context of ecclesiastical authority, in *Tiriel* the symbol appears as purely secular rule, personified by the king and the father. Tiriel himself is both, and Har is the father of Tiriel. Upon entering the false innocence of the vales of Har, Tiriel, who has been thrown out of his castle and apparently deposed by his sons and daughters, glozingly intreats a welcome from the pitiful Har and Heva and their protectress, Mnetha:

> I cast away my staff the kind companion of my travel
> And I kneel down that you may see I am a harmless man.

The staff is symbol of the man. All that the poem reveals Tiriel to be has gone into the associative formation of that staff: the cruelty of his curse upon his children, the tyranny of his expulsion of his brothers, the selfishness of his reign and his parenthood, the hypocrisy of his approach to Har, Heva, and Ijim, and the error of his entire life. "There is not an Error," Blake wrote, "but it has a Man for its Actor"; then in manuscript he changed "Actor" to "Agent" and added, "that is, it is a Man" (*Last Judgment,* 615). Tiriel is the actor, agent, and man of error; the staff is his heraldic device. Taken with the reference to harm it also suggests a variant of staff or rod, the scourge. Denying the real existence of harm since it depends upon the efficacy of physicality, Blake recognized only harm to the soul, to the divinity of man, and that had nothing to do with corporeal punishment or material rewards. Hence Tiriel's curse on Har, who formed a whip to "rouze the sluggish senses" of Tiriel "to act,"

> And scourges off all youthful fancies from the new-born man
> Then walks the weak infant in sorrow compelld to number footsteps
> Upon the sand. &c
> And when the drone has reachd his crawling length
> Black berries appear that poison all around him. Such was Tiriel
> Compelld to pray repugnant & to humble the immortal spirit. . . .

Tiriel's "harmless" gesture to Har and Heva, then, is blatantly hypocritical in view of Blake's attitude toward harm; yet on earth the act of disarmament brings results, for the earth is fallen and harmlessness has become the equivalent of love. The fact remains, though, that the staff is only the symbol of the man. Kneeling or not, Tiriel never for a moment relinquishes his devotion to or grasp of earthly power. He takes back his staff when he leaves the vales, and on his return visit he heralds his approach with an emphatic assertion of his omnipotence.

Such worldly dominion is carefully related by Blake to the concept of self: a denial of self, which is prerequisite to attaining the higher innocence, is equal to a denial or surrender of personal power. The circumstances of self-denial provide the context of the sceptre's next appearance, in *The Book of Thel:*

> Does the Eagle know what is in the pit?
> Or wilt thou go ask the Mole:
> Can Wisdom be put in a silver rod?
> Or Love in a golden bowl?

The silver rod is, of course, Thel's symbol of sovereignty: she is queen of Har. The poem recounts her attempt to retain physical immortality and youth and still pass through the state of experience. That is, she hopes to gain the wisdom of the higher innocence without relinquishing her silver rod. In Blake's system this is impossible, since the self must be denied in favor of participation in the greater self; recognizing none greater than herself, Thel flies the prospect of an ugly existence which would deny to her her beauty, youth, power, and (she believes) her happiness.

So the process of symbolic accumulation goes, until in *The Four Zoas* we can find a sceptre redolent with meaning in the hands of Urizen as he plots the initial fall into division:

> "Thou Luvah," said the Prince of Light, "behold our sons & daughters
> Repos'd on beds; let them sleep on; do thou alone depart
> Into thy wished Kingdom, where in Majesty & Power
> We may erect a throne. . . .
>
>   "I . . .
> Will lay my scepter on Jerusalem, the Emanation,
> On all her sons, & on thy sons, O Luvah, & on mine
> Till dawn was wont to wake them; then my trumpet sounding loud,
> Ravish'd away in night; my strong command shall be obey'd. . . ."
>   (277-278)

Finally, in *Jerusalem* the sceptre and scourge of Tiriel join forces with the iron chain, another of Blake's great symbols, to produce the following:

> O Divine Spirit, sustain me on thy wings,
> That I may awake Albion from his long & cold repose;
> For Bacon & Newton, sheath'd in dismal steel, their terrors hang
> Like iron scourges over Albion. . . . (635)[5]

Though a study of *The Four Zoas* and *Jerusalem* is outside the scope of this book, it is important to understand that Blake did not discard all the tools of his lyric trade when he took up the prophetic instrument. Rather he took those tools—and images, incidents, and characters—and expanded them immensely. Two instances of that expansion I have quoted above. In the second, which appears the more cryptic, the reader need know nothing of Bacon and Newton if he has made a careful reading throughout Blake's poetry of the sceptre-chain-scourge symbols. With the manifold associations of restriction, tyranny, cruelty, reason, conventional morality, natural religion, selfish oppression, myopic vision, and so on, Newton and Bacon both become metamorphosed, through the medium of their iron scourge, into a Tiriel, a father, a priest, and a king (the fool is innate). Or, the other way around, if Newton is appreciated in his symbolic role of single vision incarnate ("Newton's sleep"), all of the associations of the symbol gather about his figure. Such symbolic reciprocity is constantly employed by Blake, but it is effective only if we are aware of the full, cumulative power of each symbol in a given context. In the Bacon and Newton passage, for example, we need to know also about the chain image.

Like the sceptre, it too developed from a humble beginning, in *King Edward The Third*:

> The enemy fight in chains, invisible chains, but heavy;
> Their minds are fetter'd; then how can they be free? (18)

In *The Marriage of Heaven and Hell* Blake describes Milton as "a true Poet and of the Devils party without knowing it" because he "wrote in fetters when he wrote of Angels & God, and at liberty when of Devils & Hell." Also in *The Marriage* the chains which seem to bind the "Giants who formed this world into its sensual existence" are described as "the cunning of weak and tame minds. which have the power to resist energy." Thus,

> Deceit to secresy confind
> Lawful cautious & refind
> To every thing but interest blind
> And forges fetters for the mind. (Rossetti MS., 175)

In *Earth's Answer* the fallen Earth cries out to the "Selfish father of men":

70

> Break this heavy chain.
> That does freeze my bones around
> Selfish! vain!
> Eternal bane!
> That free Love with bondage bound.

In *The Garden of Love* the chain becomes briars, nonetheless strong and cruel and oppressive:

> And I saw it [the garden] was filled with graves.
> And tomb-stones where flowers should be:
> And Priests in black gowns, were walking their rounds,
> And binding with briars my joys & desires.

London recalls the passages from *The Marriage* and the Rossetti manuscript poem, hints at religious restriction ("ban"), and gives the chain symbol its most characteristic and famous form:

> In every voice: in every ban.
> The mind-forg'd manacles I hear.

In *A Little Boy Lost* the priest binds the child "in an iron chain" after the latter proves himself a "fiend" by recognizing his own essential divinity. And in *A Divine Image* the "Human Dress" (that is, the human form human), the condition of being man, is described as "forged Iron." And so on into the prophetic books.

But the associative function of Blake's symbols does not cease with the physical appearance of the words "sceptre," "rod," "wand," "staff," "chain," "scourge," and "briar." The symbols can appear with equal effectiveness, perhaps even more effectiveness, by implication. For example, in *Visions of the Daughters of Albion* Blake describes Bromion and Oothoon as bound back to back in Bromion's den, and in the Rossetti manuscript he writes of being bound down by his "mirtle tree" (169). Bondage is chain is Tiriel is priest is religion is reason, and so on. The process is almost interminable, but the resultant richness of the poetry more than justifies the reader's search.

From the above truncated equation it should be clear that acts too may be symbolic. As Gardner points out, "Just as symbol and symbolic action are, in writing of the highest quality, related to dramatic conflict and theme, so the figures of myth and allegory are identifiable from the symbolism of their actions."[6] For Blake every experience became a person. The priests in *The Garden of Love,* Har in *Tiriel,* the father in *A Little Girl Lost,* and Tirzah, among others, are fused in the act common to all, bondage. Similarly, since the priests are ecclesiastical authority, Har and Tiriel monarchical authority, the father domestic authority, and Tirzah natural—or even cosmic—authority, the sceptre admirably symbolizes all of their acts. The object, act, and actor can all be classified under the major symbol of experience, the father-priest-king. Just so, the protective action of the mother in innocence contributes to the symbolic significance of the child. And the attempt by "the little boy lost" to seize his "father" bodily is as wrong in Blake's world as the weeping of "the little boy found" is right. Both acts substantiate the symbolic value of *the* child of innocence, and a knowledge of both acts is prerequisite to a correct interpretation of, say, *The Chimney Sweeper* and *A Little Boy Lost* in *Experience.* In the same way the raising of voices in song (both *Holy Thursday* poems), the sharing of sorrow (*On Anothers Sorrow, A Cradle Song*), the nibbling of lambs and the preying of wolves and tigers (*Night*), shading another from the sun (*The Little Black Boy*), whispering (*Nurses Song* in *Experience*), sulking (*Infant Sorrow*), drinking ale (*The Little Vagabond*), and killing a fly (*The Fly*) are all symbolic acts. And each act takes on a different significance as it is viewed from different points of view.

Perhaps the most important and certainly the most interesting act in the *Songs* and allied poems is that which involves the transition from innocence to experience. In *The Little Black Boy,* for example, Blake translates the transitional act into several symbols—light and shade, the sun and the tree, the sun and the cloud. Learning to "bear the beams of love" is the act, and around it Blake builds an ironic contrast between the apparent blackness of the black boy and the apparent whiteness of the white boy. This contrast is emphasized by the former's unselfish shading of the latter until he too can bear the beams of love. Tiriel, of course, is already in experience, but his "fall" is powerfully summarized in his final curse on his father Har. It foreshadows the voice of the grave in *The Book of Thel,* perhaps Blake's most powerful presentation of the way to experience. The transition in *Thel* is in terms of a denial of self, a surrender of earthly dominion, and the entry into the grave. If we have read carefully *The Little Girl Lost,* Thel's crucial error and her reason for fleeing the grave in terror become most clear. In *The Little Girl Lost* Lyca's approach to experience is voluntary and self-sacrificing. It is the right way. Thel's approach is fearful and selfish and proud. The fundamental significance of both poems and the key to correct interpretation of the transitional act depend heavily on the points of view involved.

As with the symbolic object (like the sceptre, chain, scourge), Blake again did not discard the symbolic act when he came to write the prophetic books. So in *Milton* we can find the transition from innocence to experience expressed as follows:

And Milton said: "I go to Eternal Death! The Nations still
Follow after the detestable Gods of Priam, in pomp
Of warlike selfhood contradicting and blaspheming.

  .   .   .   .

I will arise and look forth for the morning of the grave:
I will go down to the sepulcher to see if morning breaks:
I will go down to self annihilation and eternal death,
Lest the Last Judgment come & find me unannihilate
And I be siez'd & giv'n into the hands of my own Selfhood.

  .   .   .   .

I in my Selfhood am that Satan: I am that Evil One!
He is my Spectre! in my obedience to loose him from my Hells,
To claim the Hells, my Furnaces, I go to Eternal Death."

And Milton said: "I go to Eternal Death!" Eternity shudder'd,
For he took the outside course among the graves of the dead,
A mournful shade.   (495-496)

With such care in his use of point of view, recurring symbols, and symbolic action, Blake leads the reader to see the gradual merging of many of his characters. The final product of the merger is what I have called the major symbol. In other words, kindred points of view tend to unite the holders of those points of view; characters who are associated continually with the same or similar recurring symbols tend to melt into each other; and a similar pattern of action reveals a fundamental affinity among the actors. In these ways the symbolic value of any one character in any one poem is intensified and expanded beyond the bounds of the immediate context. The identity may shift, but the symbolic character remains the same. When the beadle's wand in *Holy Thursday* is recognized as a part of the basic sceptre motif, the beadle's identity, while being retained as representative of church law, merges with that of Tiriel and the father. Within the single symbol are inherent all the others which go to make up the major symbol of the context. Similarly, in innocence the child merges with the lamb, which in turn merges with the figure of Christ in *The Lamb;* the angel merges with the Piper in *The Chimney Sweeper* of *Innocence;* and the earth of *Earth's Answer* merges with Oothoon of the *Visions of the Daughters of Albion.* Once he has established a character like Tiriel, Blake will use him over and over again, always being careful to provide for him a different context, different associates, and a different object or act upon which to exert his particular symbolic influence. This poetical peregrination occasionally changes to some extent the character's outward form, but the rudimentary outline stands sure, bringing with it the myriad associations it has absorbed from many contexts. All the associations are valid and even necessary as explicatory aids in Blake's poetry.

Perhaps the finest example of shifting identity is the major symbol of experience. The very fact that Blake often refers to it in the aggregate—father-priest-king—demonstrates the close connection among the three principles. When he speaks of them as a unit he calls them "hypocrite." Though it is doubtful he had this early broken it down, Blake first refers to the group in his 1788 annotations to Lavater's *Aphorisms,* where he denounces the "hypocrite" with great vigor (68, 73, 74-75). Though this is little more than the facile device of personification, close upon writing the notes to Lavater Blake was creating *Tiriel* and the *Songs of Innocence.* In the *Songs* both the beadle and the father appear, the latter in emphatically negative form: "No father was there" (*The Little Boy Lost*). In *The Chimney Sweeper* the father sells his son into virtual servitude, and in *Tiriel* he becomes a gigantic figure for there he is also a king. In *Thel* Thel herself is the queen of Har, a ruler who refuses to renounce her sovereignty and her self. In

A Song of Liberty the starry king promulgates the ten commandments to control the flaming energy of the Christ-like newborn babe, an act reminiscent of Har's scourging of Tiriel's "youthful fancies"; and *A Song* ends with a chorus about the "Priests of the Raven of dawn" who "curse the sons of joy." In *The French Revolution* the king enacts his traditional tyrannical role, while in the *Visions of the Daughters of Albion* Bromion's power, the power of natural religion, is universal and in his "religious caves" lie the enslaved subjects of the moral law. In *America* the guardian prince of Albion (here England) squeezes America beneath his heel until revolutionary forces flame into life.

In the *Songs of Experience* the major symbol, of course, appears in many forms: the "selfish father of men" (*Earth's Answer*), the pebble (*The Clod and the Pebble*), the "cold and usurous hand" (*Holy Thursday*), God (*The Chimney Sweeper*), the dreamer (*The Angel*), the earth implicit in *Ah! Sun-Flower,* the priest (*The Garden of Love*), the mother, parson, and "Dame Lurch" (*The Little Vagabond*), "Cruelty," "Humility," and the "Human Brain" (*The Human Abstract*), and Tirzah (*To Tirzah*). And finally the father-priest-king is recognizable in Enitharmon and Urizen in *Europe,* in "the primeval priest" in *The First Book of Urizen,* Urizen again in *The Book of Ahania, The Book of Los,* and *The Song of Los,* Urthona, Tharmas, Luvah, and Urizen in *The Four Zoas,* Satan in *Milton,* and Albion's spectre in *Jerusalem.*

In each of these figures is all the others. The priests of *The Garden of Love* bind with briars love and desire, but they do so because they are selfish like Tiriel and the father of men in *Earth's Answer,* because their hands are cold and usurious like those in *Holy Thursday,* because they represent this world, the earth implicit in *Ah! Sun-Flower,* because they are the gods of this world with all the cruelty, humility, and hypocrisy of which the human brain of *The Human Abstract* is capable. The priests are as much the major symbol as the father, just as the lamb, sheep, grasshoppers, birds, "the divine image," etc. are all the major symbol of innocence—the child.

But how does one distinguish among all these characters, especially the ones in the prophetic books? "The point is," as Schorer says, "that the individuality of these creations lies not in their rich diversity but in the outline that separates them from their backgrounds."[7] That is, each individual identity in its specific context is at once a part of the whole context and the whole of which it is a part. Both the priests of *The Garden of Love* and the birds of *Night* are self-sufficient for an understanding of the poems. Blake simply asked his reader for more than understanding: that is "corporeal" activity. He wanted them to imagine as he imagined, to see as he saw, even to recreate as he created; only then does the symbolic method make sense, only then can one see the minor symbols as parts of a major symbol, only then can the song take its place as a song of innocence or of experience.

For a lesser poet all of this would have been enough to insure the richness, depth, and complexity necessary for a presentation of the state of experience. But Blake went even further—to develop in the songs a most difficult and subtle device, one which is not entirely divorced from any of the technical aspects described above; indeed it is so inextricably bound up with these other elements that the resultant intricacy all but defies systematic analysis. This intricacy, this subtlety I shall call ambiguity, though I am not at all happy about the term.

At any rate this ambiguity is invariably related to point of view; usually its context is experience, though that is not a rule. It may consist in two different views of the same symbol (for example, the two views of "sleep" in *The Little Girl Lost* and *The Little Girl Found*); it may consist in the relative truth or falsity of a dream as in *The Little Girl Found;* it may consist in grammatical "confusion" whereby two or more speakers can logically be connected with the same speech, as in the *Introduction* to *Experience;* it may consist in the polarity of spiritual and earthly significance of an act, as in *Holy Thursday* of *Experience;* or it may consist in the simple contradiction of adjectives applied to the same subject, as in *The Sick Rose.* The ambiguous relationship of the fundamental elements in all these poems is technically identical, although the elements themselves obviously differ radically from poem to poem. In *The Little Girl Lost* and *The Little Girl Found,* for example, the mother considers the girl's sleep to be merely the sleep of innocence, in which the child is protected by the mother, angels, and Christ. This kind of sleep, as it is presented in *A Cradle Song,* for example, is only the prelude to a new day of innocence. To the titular character of *The Little Girl Lost* and *The Little Girl Found,* however, sleep is the passage of the soul into experience and is associated with the kind of "death" presaged by the grave's voice in *Thel*. In these terms the girl will awake to the darkness of error and the terror of this world (as in *Infant Sorrow*), not to a continuation of play on the echoing green. If the ambiguity of "sleep" is not seen, both *The Little Girl Lost* and *The Little Girl Found* fail as songs of experience: the girl's point of view becomes the same as that of her parents and the poems become foolishly redundant. The problem of evaluating the parents' dream in *The Little Girl Found* is the same. They accept their dream as true within the context of their own lighted world of innocence, in which the darkness of experience appears only as a horrible dream, not yet a reality. They are frightened by their dream to the extent that they search for their lost child to try to snatch her back from the darkness. To the poet, and to the reader, however, their vision of experience is a true vision of what has actually happened, not a warning about the future. Lyca is *in* experience. She cannot be snatched back. She has already fallen asleep and her lostness is infinitely more final than any temporary lapse from innocence, like that in *The Little Boy Lost*, for example. The little boy never really "leaves" innocence except in ignorant desire. Lyca *has* left, and the parents' attempt to "rescue" her is doomed to failure since their protective function ceases at the border of experience. Without the multiple significance of the dream, the girl remains an innocent and the two poems develop into long-winded variants of *The Little Boy Lost* and *The Little Boy Found*.

Another excellent example of ambiguity founded upon point of view is in the *Introduction* to *Songs of Experience*. Both the Bard and the holy Word of the first stanza speak the words in the other stanzas. If the Word is considered the only speaker in the poem, the advice given fallen Earth is both false and hypocritical, for in experience God is Jehovah, the lawgiver, tyrant, and father. On the other hand, if the stanzas are interpreted as a speech simultaneously by the Bard and by the holy Word, the poem is at once an invitation (the Word's) to eternal imprisonment by natural religion and a statement (by the Bard) of the way to a higher innocence beyond nature. In experience there is always some sign of the higher innocence; and in this poem Blake merely combines the two in the same words. Without both speakers the holy Word's preaching is of a strange kind of redemption, unaccountably repeated by the Bard; and symbols like the starry pole, the fallen light, the dewy grass, and the watery shore are buried in a traditionally Christian, un-Blakean religious mold.

This, then, is Blake's ambiguity—troublesome, often obscure, but an indispensable part of his poetic technique. By it he achieves what I have already called intensive richness, alluding to two completely different symbolic structures by means of one symbol. The resultant pattern of contrasts not only clarifies the central idea of the poem but provides a framework around which Blake can construct the whole poem. In the final analysis, that coherency within the poem and within the song series is the method's *raison d'être*. Blake used the method as early as *Holy Thursday*, which appeared first in *An Island in the Moon*, but the real importance of ambiguity lies in the fact that it solved his problem of finding a vehicle for the state of experience. That vehicle was the lyric after all, not the form of *Thel* or *Tiriel* or the *Visions of the Daughters of Albion*, but the lyric enriched and structurally reinforced to support the great weight of experience. Blake realized after his intermediate experiments in more expansive forms that expansion was not what he needed but contraction and intensity and precision. Even the *Songs of Innocence* approached this goal but rarely.

Before actually turning to the songs to see Blake's symbolic technique in operation there remains one other point to consider—his use of traditional symbolism. (By "tradition" I mean here not only those symbols, like the cross, which are a part of a systematic myth from which they draw their associative sustenance, but also the symbols which have accumulated common-sense connotation throughout the centuries, whether from a body of myth or not, symbols like the sceptre or the pebble.) Blake used traditional symbolism, as I have said earlier, for his own special purposes, and although he did not necessarily transform the symbol itself, he frequently bent its traditional associative *galbe* to fit the exigencies of his system. Thus the sceptre of tyranny becomes associated with the dominance of reason, with the spectre and selfhood. And the rose is not merely love but a very special kind of love thriving only in Blake's state of experience. Perhaps his use of tradition can be made most clear if we examine *Ah! Sun-Flower*, a universally admired poem.

Its main symbol is traditional, the flower rooted in the earth but turning its blossom toward the heavens and the moving sun. All well and good. But the earth in Blake's world is experience; in it the youth and virgin pine away in desire because their enjoyment is prohibited, not by the earth, but by the laws and restrictions of earthly morality. In a sense then, the earth is Blake's church, the priests of the raven of dawn who bind with briars joy and desire. Similarly, the sun is not God in the traditional sense, nor is it heaven; it is Eden, the higher innocence suffused with the spiritual warmth of love, the realm in which energy is eternal delight and an improvement in sensual enjoyment is one's pass through the gates. The sunflower and the young couple are thus in the grave of experience, the same grave from which Thel fled. The death implied is spiritual, not physical; the youth and maid are physically alive, but in Blake's eyes they are fundamentally, imaginatively dead. Without some such reference to Blake's modification of traditional symbols in this poem, it becomes little more than a trite analogy for aspirations of immortality, something like Thel's desire for gentle sleep in her attempt to bypass experience and achieve the higher innocence instantaneously.

Blake's use of the traditional symbol, however, was to become increasingly erratic and arbitrary as he waded into his prophetic works. He never again achieved the brilliance he demonstrated in the complex *A Cradle Song,* in which shifting symbol, merging identity, recurring symbols, traditional symbols, and ambiguity all contribute to the apparently simple, polished surface. It is to those surfaces that we now turn, to examine in detail the operation of Blake's techniques as he evolved his system in the *Songs,* and in *Tiriel, Thel, The Marriage,* and the *Visions of the Daughter of Albion.*

PART
III

CHAPTER IV

INTRODUCTION TO INNOCENCE

ॐ

I . . . was once delighted every morning,
I . . . was once the musique of these vallies.
—SIR PHILIP SIDNEY, *Arcadia*

I

One of the most puzzling things about Blake is the way he continually changed the order of the songs in the *Songs of Innocence* and the *Songs of Experience*. His persistence is almost perverse and yet he seemed to be trying to establish a pattern or system of transition within each state which would have some meaning for the astute reader over and above that of each individual song.[1] After careful study, however, I have found no such pattern. Still it is obvious that in whatever order we read them the poems do light up each other, to use Yeats's phrase, and if we read the two songs series as integrated books, as we should, rather than as haphazard collections, it matters little which poem was written first or last. For the purposes of this study, however, in order to examine more fully and carefully this contributory function of individual songs, I have separated the *Songs of Innocence* into three groups. Within each group certain symbols, characters, and/or acts constitute the common denominator. In the first group, the one to be examined in this chapter, the irresponsible gaiety of the child at play, and his relationship to the lamb and Christ, maintain the coherence. The second group, though more amorphous, delineates the difficult midway point between the primal unity and the approach of experience by means of a basic symbolic contrast of black and white and the use of dreams or visions. The final group reveals most clearly the encroachment of the night of experience as well as the omnipresence of a saviour who foreshadows the prospect of a higher innocence. I have imposed no pat labels upon the groups and have made no effort to read a meaning or significance into the more or less arbitrary order. When the situation seems to warrant it, I will refer to the relative position of the song in the over-all arrangements Blake made of the *Songs of Innocence and of Experience*. For this purpose I will consider only those copies known to have been paginated or foliated by Blake himself. In all cases Keynes's *Bibliography* along with Keynes and Wolf's recent census of *William Blake's Illuminated Books* will be the final authorities.

2

A discussion of the *Introduction* to *Innocence* can best be introduced by an interesting Biblical passage, Luke vii.31-35: "To what then shall I liken the men of this generation? And what are they like? They are like children sitting in the market place, calling to one another and saying, 'We have piped for you, and you have not danced; we have sung dirges and you have not wept.'" The close relationship between this verse and Blake's poem cannot be accidental. The antithesis between "men of this generation" who do not dance or weep to the pipe and the song (that is, who are spiritually bankrupt) and the children who do dance and sing is remarkably close to the contrast between Blake's states of innocence and experience. In addition, the passage from Luke suggests Blake's insistence that the shadow of experience constantly impinges upon the sunlit area of innocence. Though the state of experience which is dramatized in *Songs of Experience* probably did not exist in any detail in Blake's mind when he wrote of innocence, he certainly was conscious that the world around him evinced little of the carefree gaiety the *Songs of Innocence* were to display. Consequently we ought to expect to find inherent in these songs an otherwise unexpected subtlety and complexity. In the *Introduction* such complexity is due largely to Blake's artful use of the Biblical quotation.

It is a different Blake here from the one who wrote in *Samson,* "O white-robed Angel, guide my timorous hand to write as on a lofty rock with iron pens the words of truth, that all who pass may read" (37). With less pomposity and infinitely more meaning, Blake in the *Introduction* guides the reader through Beulah, one step below the Edenic realm of four-fold vision and the eternal imagination. But since to understand Beulah one must also know something of Generation *and* Eden, Blake carefully included in his poem of innocence references to experience and a higher innocence as well.

On the simplest level the poem properly concerns itself with the state of innocence: "wild," "pleasant," "merry," "happy," and full of "joy." These words occur in the poem in this sequence so that they not only characterize this state but suggest a progression of states through which the soul of the "infant joy"[2] must pass to attain the higher innocence. Though Blake would probably disagree, the progression is somewhat reminiscent of Wordsworth's "natural education" of the child in *Tintern Abbey,* from the "coarser pleasure of . . . boyish days" to "a feeling and a love" to the hearing of "the still, sad music of humanity."

The setting in the first stanza is most vivid though it is sketched in with only a few bold strokes. Blake conjures up not all the familiar trappings of pastoral poetry but more the atmosphere of that tradition, a carefree abandon, a kind of aimless delight unburdened by restriction, destination, or vision. The glad animal spirit revels in its innocence, for it knows and wants nothing else. Its world is a child's dream-world where everything is alive and speaks, and the mere shape of a cloud does not preclude its being a laughing child; its world is a valley where the tangled labyrinth of dark forest neither obscures the sun nor obstructs the gay piper's wanderings; its world is sensuous and "pleasant."

But following the visionary child's peremptory command in stanza 2 we move a vision deeper into the folds of Blake's mind: the song is no longer aimless, the wandering has stopped for a moment, and piping of *one* song, "about a Lamb," is made "with merry chear." The song is still without words but it is now about *a* lamb, an animal known for its mildness, pleasantness, softness, brightness, perhaps its aimlessness, and above all its innocence:

Little Lamb who made thee
Dost thou know who made thee
Gave thee life & bid thee feed.
By the stream & o'er the mead;
Gave thee clothing of delight,
Softest clothing wooly bright;
Gave thee such a tender voice,
Making all the vales rejoice.

But at the same time this is also, of course, the Lamb of God; in Blake's threefold vision of innocence, the child, the lamb, and Christ:

For he calls himself a Lamb:
He is meek & he is mild,
He became a little child:
I a child & thou a lamb,
We are called by his name.

By thus deepening and expanding his vision Blake begins to systematically outline the steps from the first light of this world to the eternal light of the eternal world. The path so delineated does not necessarily lead from life to death, it is to be remembered, but rather from "infant joy" through "infant sorrow" to a state Blake might have written of as "infant love." The infant's steps cannot be directly upward, as we have seen in Chapter I, because without self-identification one continues to pipe aimlessly down the valley wild or one sings in a cage like Har (*Tiriel*). The achieving of selfhood is at once the greatest evil and the greatest good in Blake's system. It can be both because error or evil is annihilable only if it is recognized in human form.[3] That recognition constitutes vision, the greatest good. Thus, simply, to go up one must go down, and the way down is characterized by restrictions upon the wild abandon of the innocents. This descent has been called the awakening of thought, and certainly that is part of its meaning; but most of all it involves a contraction before an infinite expansion,[4] a saddening before infinite joy. In the *Introduction,* then, the child on a cloud is laughing as he commands the song to be played; and he weeps after it is played the second time. The thought of the Lamb of God is essentially a vision of loveliness, but one also tinged with sorrow. The figure of Christ, which always carries over-tones of tragedy, contracts from the divinity and innocence of the child in the manger to the man on the cross of experience. And the song is, if not a dirge as in Luke, a recognition of the existence of tigers as well as lambs, and a hint that innocence is a temporary state from which one must either advance to a higher innocence or retreat to infantilism.

This reading is supported by a subtle change in the movement of the verse. In the first line of the second stanza the lilting beat of the regular trochees is reinforced by the initial anapest of the second line. In the third line, however, there are two important variations. Though the line is apparently trochaic, the substitution of "that song" for "a song" not only stresses the demand for one particular song about a lamb but also commands an accent greater than either *a*'s in the first line. The accent is further strengthened by the preceding caesura. As a result there is a distinct braking in the line: "PIPer // PIPE THAT SONG aGAIN—" Perhaps the most important prosodic device here is the dash at the end of the line. It is Blake's favorite indication of a heavy pause and one of the few marks of punctuation he uses con-sistently and with meaning.[5] In this poem, for example, it is used only in one other place:

> Piper sit thee down and write
> In a book that all may read—
> So he vanish'd from my sight,

where the pause is unmistakably abrupt and emphatic. The last line of stanza 2, then, begins slowly, breaks abruptly, and then continues on with "wept" receiving major emphasis. The change of pace is clearly deliberate; without it the last two lines are enigmatic, even facetious: "So I piped, he wept to hear." The entire second stanza is at once an indication of the intimate consociation of innocence and experience, and, as I shall point out below, two modes of poetry and perception.

In view of this interpretation of stanza 2, the first line of the third stanza seems now to present an insurmountable problem: how can the pipe be called "happy" if it has just played a dirge? Blake's point is that the song played by the happy pipe, though the same song about a lamb, is heard imaginatively on two levels. The Piper's tune is no longer simple sensuous sounds played to the sensuous ear, but a song about a lamb played to the spirit as well. The latter knows that the lamb must die at the hands of the tiger in order to live in eternity, fourfold vision, Imagination unsullied by mundane, corporeal things.[6] Though happy the pipe must be dropped in favor of a human voice which sings the same song. It will evoke neither laughter nor tears but joyful weeping. "The living voice is ever living in its inmost joy," wrote Blake (*Zoas,* 289). "Joy" is a key word in his poetry, as we have seen; within it mirth and tears meet in perfect harmony, each retaining its characteristic essence, yet having no identity separate from the other. In effect happiness and sorrow no longer exist; it is not a question of human voices waking us and we drown, as Eliot has it, but rather the human voice divine waking us so that we may live. The pipe has its place, but the severe limitations of that place must be admitted and the pipe discarded sometime. Only the divine human is eternal.

The glad animal sounds of the *Introduction* thus give way to the voice of divine humanity through a recognition of experience and its concomitant woe. That recognition provides the self with identity and leaves the new-formed will a choice: to direct feeling, thought, and life to the self or to others. If the former obtains, vision is lost and the only salvation possible lies in the fact that one cannot fall lower than the limit of contraction, Adam. The love of otherness constitutes the rejection of error anthropomorphized in self and the attainment of the greater joy. "Excess of sorrow laughs," Blake wrote in *The Marriage;* "Excess of joy weeps." That is, innocence is a perfectly ordered and satisfactory state until it becomes self-indulgence. On the other hand selflessness is synonymous with the eternal joy of the higher innocence, which is achieved through a sympathetic vision of the sorrows of experience. The progression in the *Introduction* therefore is from laughter to weeping to joyful weeping to joy. But Blake also wrote, "Joys impregnate. Sorrows bring forth" (*Marriage*). Though the visionary inspiration (like the child on a cloud) be lovely, creation involves a knowledge of both ugliness and loveliness, joined with the imaginative ability to fuse both into a larger and higher loveliness.[7] This cannot be done with aimless infantile piping; it must be done by means of mature conceptual creation in which both joy and sorrow are present, yet do not exist independently.

The last two stanzas of the poem form the introduction proper to the *Songs of Innocence*. The visionary child has vanished, though only "from . . . sight," for as the divine human is eternal, so the child's presence is eternal too—the child Christ, the child imagination, the child inspiration. As Wicksteed aptly put it, "We can only sing when we cease to pipe, we can only write when we wake from dream."[8] And it is significant that when he does write, Blake utilizes the tools of his pastoral innocence, the reed and the magical water, to compose songs that "Every child may joy to hear."

The *Introduction* is also a song about poetry, imagination, and vision. Wicksteed suggests that the Piper is a human soul (Blake) descending into a valley (earth), discovering through the aid of heaven the Lamb of God, and being inspired to a mission of joy.[9] This is at least partly correct, for Blake unquestionably thought himself divinely inspired, even to the point of claiming automatic writing and designing.[10] Yet another reading is possible and, I think, more satisfactory. As the beginning of the poem concerned itself with the aimless, irresponsible, pleasantly gleeful wandering of innocence, so the poetry of the first stanza has no "intention." It is music, pleasant sound. Almost immediately, however, a vision is added, not Christ, not the heavenly muse, but precisely what Blake says it is, a child on a cloud laughing. The point is extremely important if Blake is to be understood correctly when he writes of vision and imagination or the poetic genius. The Piper sees not merely a cloud, or a tree, or Whitman's blade of grass (though it is more like the latter than the former two); he sees a child *on* a cloud, as corporeal as you or I. And the child and the Piper in the valley are as far apart spatially as possible, one defying the laws of the physical universe, the other existing and reveling, substantially, in that same universe. Somehow in the poem the gulf between the two is bridged. And since the gulf is epistemological rather than physical, the bridge is sight, twofold vision. Single vision would have only a cloud. This is what provides direction for the aimless song of the wandering Piper: the child demands with magnificent impertinence a song about a specific and meaningful subject. Still only the sensuous quality of the song is apparent, despite its revelation of a double attitude toward the lamb. It is the third stanza that once again provides the added fold to triple the meaning of the song the third time it is heard.

The pipe is dropped and to the music is added the human word, the embodiment of the idea of a lamb which is so beautifully expressed in *The Lamb* and its counterpart, *The Tyger*. The coexistence of joy and weeping in the last lines of stanza 3 adumbrates the relationship between these two lyrics, symbols of the states of innocence and experience respectively.

At this point in the *Introduction* the Piper, the child, and the lamb are in effect one—poet, inspiration, and song. The progression has gone from Piper to vision and inspiration to the poet to the song; from unalloyed laughter to weeping to joyful weeping to joy; from Eden to Ulro and Generation to Beulah and Eden; from innocence to experience to marriage to the higher innocence; from the simple ignorance of single vision to double vision and its view of the human, to triple vision and its view of the divine in the human, to fourfold vision and union of human and divine. "Pipe a song"; "So I piped." "Sing thy songs"; "So I sung." "Sit thee down and write"; "So he vanish'd." "And I wrote."

The last two stanzas, then, graphically represent creation, the most divine act the human can perform, a process which involves the union of poet, inspiration, song, and most important of all for Blake, Christ. This creation is not a selfish act (as is the wandering of the first stanza), nor is it aimed at one child or listener (as is the song of the second and third stanzas); it is meant for all. The necessity for such a sacrifice of self can only be learned by experiencing the tears of stanza 2. With the abrupt disappearance of the child, the Piper must choose between two alternatives, returning to his selfish glee or crystallizing his vague feelings of change in a creation (stanza 5).

With the child's vanishing and the concomitant revelation of the way out of experience and selfhood, the highest state of Blake's imaginative cosmos is reached. And the step-by-step process of creation leading to this state is summed up in the closing lines of the poem:

> And I pluck'd a hollow reed.
> And I made a rural pen,
> And I stain'd the water clear,
> And I wrote my happy songs. . . .

The first of these is almost a thoughtless act, for the reed might be made into something or not; the second imparts direction to the apparent aimlessness, for a choice is made and a pen is formed; the third adds imagination or magic (as Yeats called it), just as the imaginative human voice raises the song to a level higher than the pipe alone could do; and the fourth line is the selfless creation so that "Every child may joy to hear." A child piping to children; Christ becoming as we are so that we may be as he is; Blake writing poetry so that we, the readers, may listen to him rather than to the cacaphonous clanking of Urizen's iron book of laws.

3

In innocence Blake's poetry echoes the play of the children, the joyous sounds of spring, the laughing chatter of birds, as well as the ominous rumblings of distant thunder which will eventually drown out the happy sounds. Almost as much as the *Introduction* itself, then, *The Ecchoing Green* presents the background and some of the main actors of the state of innocence.[11] It has been said, truly, that *The Ecchoing Green* is not only the history of a day but of all human life. But it also includes a view of the inevitable darkness of experience without which the life cycle presented here is little more than dilettantish philosophy. Considered within Blake's system, that life cycle may be seen as his "circle of destiny," innocence, experience, and the higher innocence. *The Ecchoing Green* is concerned with infancy (or innocence) and maturity (either experience or the higher innocence) in relation to physical energy (by nature selfish) and spiritual energy (by definition selfless). It is also concerned with the spiritual sterility of living in the past, the sterility of memory which is given such powerful voice by Har and Heva in *Tiriel*. The *Green* is Blake's first attempt to present his idea of memory[12] and it is bungled because it is not clear, not fully documented, not completely thought out. Largely because of this the poem fails as a poem, but its manifold elements pertinent to Blake's system make analysis mandatory in such a study as this, especially since many of these elements recur throughout the songs.

In view of Blake's prevailing belief in the visibility of macrocosm in microcosm, it is not surprising that the poem may be read simply as an account of a day in the life of a child—its cheerful sounds, its abounding energy, its romping sport, its carefree merriment. But such a reading ignores both the macrocosm and several key details in the poem itself: the subdued poignance of the second stanza, the shift from happiness, merriment, and cheer in the first stanza to laughter in the second, the subtle change in movement in the third stanza, and the final substitution of "darkening Green" for the title-line chorus.

The sun that rises in the first stanza is the spiritual or eternal sun of the state of innocence, from which emanate the beams of love "the little black boy" must learn to bear. The rejoicing bells are analogous to the song of praise in *The Shepherd* for the creation and continuation of this state of irresponsible gaiety. "Oh Lord, open thou our lips, And our mouth shall show forth thy praise." Universal happiness reigns from the birds of the heavens (the skylark and thrush) to the birds of the earth (the bush), from the skies to the green. The welcome to spring, with its implications of renascence (spiritual and physical) is peculiarly apt here since this is not just any spring day but *the* day of innocence, the perennial school vacation universalized. It is this very traditionalism and simplicity that make the change of subject in stanza 2 even more abrupt than it might have been otherwise.

Yet that abruptness is not wholly without transition. Blake merely makes the shift first, to emphasize the contrast between stanza 2 and stanza 1, and then inserts the transition in the fifth line. The stanza begins with the picture of Old John, in whom spring finds its complement, the winter of man's life with its white hair, old age sitting in the shade of an oak tree. The tree will become an extremely important symbol in *The Little Black Boy,* but here it is tantalizingly vague. Blake neither resolves nor develops his few hints at a deeper meaning, but we must try to piece it together by referring to other works and to Blake's major themes.

For Old John the green echoes only memories, memories which in themselves imply the Blakean man's greatest tragedy, lack of vision. John cannot now sport on the green in the brilliant sun because, except for the brief span of his childhood, he has not learned, as the black boy does learn, to bear its beams of love. Unable to accept and sublimate experience, he and the other "old folk" have become bogged down by the cares of the natural world. When seen aright, these are only joys bound, energy curbed, vision clouded, but without the vision contingent upon a selfless act like that of the mother at the end of the poem, memory is all that is left. It provides John with a momentary, vicarious respite from the inner darkness that is symbolized by the external shade of the tree. But that respite is indicative of the depths of John's spiritual poverty, an emptiness suggested in the effective line, "Such such were the joys," with its hesitant note of pitiable helplessness.[13] John's laughter confesses his lack of a mature substitute for innocent sport. Blake's repetition of the word "laugh," associated with single vision in the *Introduction*, underscores the contrast. Whereas the Piper turned his back on his "valleys wild" and advanced into the body of imaginative creation, Old John returns vicariously and ignorantly to his youth and consequently remains merely a natural creature without a creation. To live vicariously is as impossible as vicarious vision is a contradiction in terms. Experience cannot be laughed away. An improvement in vision, in sensual enjoyment, is the only cure, but in the shade of the tree, which is for the protection of the innocent, vision remains the same.

After this indictment, which gains added effectiveness by following immediately after the lilting first stanza,

> . . . the little ones weary
> No more can be merry.

Literally these lines reflect the physical weariness of the child home from play. Symbolically the end of the day finds the children spiritually weaker as well (soul and body being the same in Blake) as worldly cares approach, as the long night of experience slowly but inevitably eclipses the sunshine of innocence. So the nurse cries out to the children laughing on the hill in *Nurse's Song (Innocence)*:

> Then come home my children, the sun is gone down
> And the dews of night arise
> Come come leave off play. and let us away
> Till the morning appears in the skies.

As the light fades away, the carefree merriment that Old John persists in trying to recapture is impossible. The sun descends, the sports end.

But the cycle is not yet complete. The data of sense experience have not yet been unified in creation by the poet. Blake thus recalls the first stanza. The birds which were singing so loudly to the joyous bells are now identified with the children as they seek the last refuge remaining to them before experience takes over: maternal love, care, and protection, the same protection the nurse affords in *Nurse's Song,* the shepherd provides in *The Shepherd,* the angels in *Night,* the earthly bosom in *The Blossom.* The mother, then, contrasts sharply with the old folks under the tree. Whereas they can only sit hidden from the very sun which should be their rightful province and try vainly to feel the warmth through memory, she fulfills her role in Beulah as the selfless protector, refuge, and teacher[14] for the children who have yet to venture forth in the forests from which she has already emerged.

The final couplet gives the poem its ultimate impact, while at the same time echoing the futility of Old John's attempt at the consolation of memory:

> And sport no more seen,
> On the darkening Green.

These lines have been read as if "sport" were the verb following the subject "Many sisters and brothers." Blake is careful, however, to make a distinct break before the last two lines,[15] and I think it clear that the couplet is a general summary designed to contrast sharply with the end of the first stanza: "While our sports shall be seen / On the Ecchoing Green." With the end of innocence no sport is seen by anyone except in the dim halls of memory. Sport is a part of the state of innocence, and hence the green echoes it; but it has no place as such in the higher innocence where wisdom reigns instead of selfish ignorance. The green no longer is echoing because it is dark and deserted, and echoes cannot penetrate the forests of experience. It is a most succinct and powerful way to signify the death of a part of life; the sporting children will find not rest but a need for greater energy than ever, an energy which must burn through "mind-forg'd manacles" and earthly mother love as well, an energy which leads to eternal delight only after error is made to assume concrete form so that it might be destroyed forever. To hide that error, that evil if you will, by turning one's eyes inward toward childhood is eternal death; to recognize its existence, to grapple with it, to destroy it, is eternal life.

4

The connection between *Spring* and *The Ecchoing Green* is obviously very close despite the fact that Blake persistently kept the two apart in his issues of the songs.[16] Apparently he used *Spring* many times as a contrasting poem, for in fifteen issues before 1815 it appears in connection with *On Anothers Sorrow, The Blossom, The School Boy* (before its transference to *Experience*), *The Little Black Boy, Holy Thursday,* and *The Chimney Sweeper;* after 1815 it follows *Night.* In none of these poems does springtime play a major role except as a contrasting element. But *Spring* is more than merely an element in the contrast between happiness and sorrow, despite its apparent insouciance. Its more serious purpose is comparable to Blake's implied drama in the second stanza of *The Ecchoing Green.*

The anonymous command opening the poem ("Sound the Flute!") may be read simply as the breaking of the dark silence of the long night, the awakening of spring after winter's sleep, the revival of sport on the green after a night in the earthly mother's warm, protective bosom.[17] In any case the rest of the stanza Blake devotes to a favorite subject, the birds of the air and the "bush," just as the next stanza belongs to the boy and girl, and the third to the lamb and "I." This type of Blakean progression also forms a prominent part of the structure of *Night* and the *Introduction,* and it is a good example of the way in which various symbols contribute to the formation of a major symbol, as well as of the process I have called shifting identity. In *Spring* the birds welcoming in the new year are the same birds that sing in *The Ecchoing Green,* that laugh in *Laughing Song,* that sport in the sky in *Nurse's Song,* that seek their nests in *Night,* that smile and cry in *The Blossom.* But they are also, specifically, a nightingale and a lark, a bird of the bush and a bird of the air, a bird of the night and a bird of the day. Blake thus establishes a dichotomy while at the same time maintaining the essential unity of the opposites in their identical response to the flute. Both birds sing, both delight, both welcome in the year. The joy of heralding spring is thus universalized so that the idea of renascence, as in *The Ecchoing Green,* can be applied equally well to divinity, humanity, and the animal world.

In the second stanza the dichotomy is translated into human terms, the boy and girl, a technique used also in *The Ecchoing Green, Nurse's Song,* and *The Blossom.*[18] Both boy and girl echo the welcome of stanza 1 with what Blake now calls infant noise, something undoubtedly like "the sweet chorus of Ha, Ha, He" in *Laughing Song.* There is nothing articulate as yet except insofar as joy is inherent in a word-less cry of ecstasy. Infancy in all its innocence and animality is another way to welcome in the year, to celebrate the awakening not merely of spring but of the human body (and soul), to commemorate the birth of the infant joy into the long day of sport on the green. The last stanza then goes beyond the simple, obvious comparison to unify the whole poem by resolving the two dominant images or "sets of characters," and synthesizing the diverse particulars which make up the universal welcome.

Though the last stanza begins on the same note as stanza 2, Blake introduces two new characters, the lamb and "I." If the comparison already in force between bird and child is expanded to include these lines, the poem resolves itself into something of an epic simile: as the birds delight and the boy and girl "crow" with infant noise, so we, the lamb and I, welcome in the year. Yet the "I" is not identified, except possibly as Blake himself, the lamb's appearance is unprepared for, and the mode of welcome in the last stanza differs greatly from those of the first two stanzas. This latter difference is due to the dichotomy already established between nightingale and lark, boy and girl: the first pair "delight," the second "crow" with "Merry voice." And capitalizing on the awakening of the body and soul in stanza 2 and the existence in the poem of male and female, the unmistakable tactile quality of the third stanza particularizes the random joy of the first two stanzas in the idea that "we" *love* to welcome in the year, love in the very limited sense applicable to ignorant, instinctive inno-cence. The tumult of the first two stanzas has now ceased, and in its place Blake evokes the sensuality of tongue on white neck, the softness of white wool, and the physical excitement of a kiss. In other words renascence is essentially a physical phenomenon in innocence. After having heard the herald and joined their infant sounds to the paean, the children become articulate in the awakening of physical desire. It is not necessary to read Freud into the lines but merely to recognize, as Blake did, that children's sport is physical as well as selfish. "Thoughtless" is Blake's word.[19] Just as the song of a bird and the cry of a child is expended energy unrestrained, so the expression of bodily contact is divine energy in another form, the "sensual enjoy-ment" that must be "improv'd" before regeneration is possible. Blake's choice of the nightingale in the first stanza is therefore most apt: the male sings during the breeding season, the "energetic" season one might say. The entire last stanza concerns action, not contemplation, gratified desire not rationality.

The use of the first person, finally, shows Blake at his subtle best, in the reunification of what he has broken in two. "I" is at once the voice of both birds and both children, the latter now articulate; and the voice can be only one, the Piper's. In fact the entire structure of *Spring* is similar to that of the *Introduction:* the aimless piping in the latter parallels the birds' song in *Spring;* the piping of a song about a specific subject parallels the human voices of stanza 2; the addition of words to the Piper's music as the human voice replaces the pipe parallels the entire last stanza of *Spring;* and finally the union of inspiration, poet, Piper, and lamb also parallels the last stanza here. The parallels are inexact, of course, but the similarity goes even further. The command of stanza 1 in *Spring* is fundamentally the same as that delivered by the child on a cloud to the Piper; and *Spring* as a whole can easily be considered as the song about a lamb. This is precisely why Blake introduced the lamb into this poem at all. Where else could he have turned for a more appropriate symbol of rejuvenation and renascence than to the Lamb of God? Reawakening, then, is spiritual as well as physical. For Blake the two were identical, an improvement in sensual enjoyment being synonymous with regeneration.

The summary identification or resolution of the symbolic figures in *Spring* is the basis of *The Lamb:*

> He became a little child:
> I a child & thou a lamb,
> We are called by his name.

In stanza 3 of *Spring* the lamb encompasses the nightingale and lark, the boy and girl; the "I" includes the Piper of the song, both children, and both birds. In a sense the children celebrate themselves: they are spring, they are the lamb, they are awakened. Hence Blake's change in the last line from "to welcome in the Year" to "we welcome in the Year." All creation welcomes the Christ: he causes the renascence and he is the renascence. Through the mouth of the Piper, his voice tuned to the notes of pipe or flute, he announces his coming.

97

CHAPTER V

LOST AND FOUND IN INNOCENCE

> I'm only lost until I see
> I'm lost because I want to be.
> —W. H. AUDEN, *The Labyrinth*

I

This second group of *Songs of Innocence* is generally concerned with the symbolic action of becoming lost and being found, though the widely different actors Blake places in the same situation sometimes obscure their fundamental similarity. The group also approximates the state of the innocent soul at a slightly more advanced age than that of the "infant joy." The quality of innocence does not change, nor does the child's essential character: he is still the symbol of instinctive, thoughtless life, and if the joyousness of innocence is not immediately apparent, it is simply because the child ventures, or is thrown, beyond his depth. That is, he becomes lost. To be found again depends upon his instinctive reversion to his rightful role, that of thoughtless child—and that reversion comes about through tears, vision (or dream), and divine guidance. They are all one and the same to Blake. The basic motif is established best in *The Little Boy Lost* and *The Little Boy Found*.

The two poems are usually treated, for various reasons, as if they were one. The most convincing evidence for such a treatment is that the poems seem to develop a systematic contrast between false and true light: the boy is lost chasing the former and found by the latter.[1] Treated separately, however, *The Little Boy Lost* can be seen as a "tragedy" of innocence, somewhat akin to that in *The Chimney Sweeper*. But it is not irrevocable tragedy. A little boy who wanders away is a far cry from the lost boy of *Experience,* who is not found. If we refuse to believe, as many do, that Blake could want to keep the poem in *Innocence,* and if we read it therefore as a song of experience, there is little reason for having another boy lost in *Experience* (*A Little Boy Lost*). Such a reading ignores the important fact that inherent in innocence is the seed of experience, selfhood, which becomes the greatest evil if reason once seizes upon its significance. Self-indulgence in physical pleasure is the innocent's natural milieu; self-analysis and self-assertion are his tickets to experience. The little boy of this poem is ignorant of the very quality that characterizes the state of innocence; he is a child who seeks his father in the realm of earthly motherhood. Similarly, in *The Little Girl Found* the parents seek in vain for an innocent child in the realm of adulthood.

As in almost all of his poems, Blake provides a key to correct interpretation in the first line of *The Little Boy Lost*. Instead of being cradled in the lap of his mother dreaming dreams, the child is having what amounts to a nightmare, similar to that the parents have in *The Little Girl Found*. He calls for an earthly father, who only assumes poetic stature for Blake as the earthly law-giver of experience; and he questions, the second cardinal sin. He should be acting and being what he is, an "infant joy," a laughing bird, not usurping the rational powers of another realm. Actually, of course, the boy is incapable of reason; in his distress he should be seeking light and vision to assuage and dispel his fear or distress. As Blake wrote in *Auguries of Innocence,*

> God Appears & God is Light
> To those poor Souls who dwell in Night. (434)

The last line of the first stanza points up the exquisite irony of the whole poem. Confused and lacking the knowledge gained only through experience, the boy feels he "*shall be* lost" (my italics) if he doesn't get help from his father. The line is comparable to that in *The Chimney Sweeper* in which the Piper-angel ironically admonishes the sweeper to be a good boy and do his duty in order to avoid harm. The point is that if the boy did find the father, the decalogue of fatherhood, as pronounced by its creator (Urizen), would imprison him forever in the forests of the night.

The darkness of the night in stanza 2, then, is not the darkness of experience. Blake is most definite on that point. He deliberately does not say *his* father, but *no* father; no father is ever there in innocence. At this point the child instinctively realizes the futility of his search, and in a state of near collapse, he drops a tear, the vapor suddenly vanishes, and the climax of the poem is reached. Single vision, the way of the rationalist, is swept away and multiple vision dawns upon the boy in his instantaneous, tearful reversion to innocence, to the care of the mother, the angels, and Christ. They all will recognize the tear as "an Intellectual Thing" (*The Grey Monk,* 430), "a Babe in Eternity" (*Auguries,* 432), and they will sit by the child in sympathetic grief. This is the scene Blake creates in *Night,* with its unobtrusive reference to the "thoughtless" nest,

> Where birds are covered warm;
> They [angels bright] visit caves of every beast,
> To keep them all from harm;
> If they see any weeping.
> That should have been sleeping
> They pour sleep on their head
> And sit down by their bed.

Similarly in *On Anothers Sorrow* the child is told:

> Think not, thou canst weep a tear,
> And thy maker is not near.
>
> O! he gives to us his joy.
> That our grief he may destroy
> Till our grief is fled & gone
> He doth sit by us and moan.

The idea of father is gone, the questioning is gone, only action and being remain; and so the child is "found" in the sense that he finds himself. He is no longer lost the moment the vapor flies away. It was

not a light, either false or true, that the child was following, but a
father who did not exist although he was "thought" to be there. The
spiritual father is vision, not vapor. "A Spirit and a Vision are not,
as the modern philosophy supposes, a cloudy vapour, or a nothing:
they are organized and minutely articulated beyond all that the mortal
and perishing nature can produce" (*Descriptive Catalogue*, 576). And
it is this articulation of vision that Blake dramatizes in *The Little Boy
Found*. Lost like the boy of the previous poem, this boy makes no cry
(at least at first), he is apparently searching for no one, and he does
not question. In simple terms this being lost meant to Blake being
separated unaccountably from the protection which innocence provides against being lost, the protection of the mother. Real "lostness"
is impossible in innocence: it is appearance, not reality. If the little
boy were really lost, he would be in experience, and this poem would
be in *Songs of Experience*.

The most important divergence from the situation in *The Little
Boy Lost* is the unequivocal statement that there is a "light" here; in
the other poem there was no light at all, not even false light. The concept of a false light, in any case, is an unresolvable paradox, since truth
and falsity for Blake are non-existent: there is light or there is darkness, no dusk or half-light. The little boy follows the light, but unable
to reason whether it is real or false or what, he cries. God simultaneously appears. This is not merely a temporal sequence of events—
crying, then God appearing—but an instantaneous transfiguration or
metamorphosis of light to God.

Blake means, then, that the light is God from the very beginning,
the God of "wand'ring" innocence. But since neither the sunlight of
vision nor a dream-vision is possible to the child separated from its
mother, the tear is necessary for the revelation of what transcends instinct or mere corporeal sight. *The* father is there where *no* father can
be on earth. The anomaly is impressed upon us in the last line of the
stanza, in which God "Appeard *like his father* in white" (my italics).
The simile and its implicit reference to a dark father, a spectrous
father as opposed to a visionary lucent father, are irrefutable evidence
of Blake's intention. His intention comes even clearer if we look ahead
to *The Chimney Sweeper* of *Innocence*. There little Tom too is lost,
separated from his "father," and eventually he cries. "That same night".

a vision or dream of innocent delight is unfolded to him. The lost boy cries and is "found" in vision by the human form divine.

In the second stanza of *The Little Boy Found* the father in white brings the boy to his weeping mother because that is his rightful place in innocence, not chasing the light that really cannot be caught except through experience.[2] The mother is weeping, sorrowful, and pale as she seeks her child in vain. Blake deliberately avoids their reunion because the sentimentality of it surely would have obscured the importance of the mother's inability to find her son. She cannot because she is incapable of the vision that exists only in Eden. If she had reached that realm, it would have been she that was led to the boy, for then her union with Imagination would have enabled her to *be* the light in human form. Indeed her child would never have been lost then at all.

The title of the poem, therefore, is most apt, applicable to the entire mother-father-child relationship. The child can never find the earthly father in innocence, but by *being* innocent he can always find his heavenly father. The earthly mother can never find the child, but she is always there to be found by the child in vision. Loneliness, just as night and the vapor and the earthly father, is a fallacy to "those who Dwell in Realms of day" (*Auguries,* 434).

This then is the basic pattern of the two symbolic acts, being lost and being found. In innocence both are possible, which amounts to saying that in innocence one cannot really be lost. This fact is underscored by Blake's insistence in *Songs of Experience* that there one is never found. The one attempt made, in *The Little Girl Found,* is by its very nature a failure, for experience is the state of being lost.

In the state of innocence, however, apparent lostness takes several forms: the regimentation of the children in *Holy Thursday,*[3] the sooty servitude of "the chimney sweeper," the simple fact of being white in *The Little Black Boy.* Similarly the way in which the lost child is found also varies, though at the basis of each is the efficacy of the tear as the key to vision. In all cases, to be found depends upon the child's instinctive vision of his own essential innocence, a thoughtless, non-rational percept. Thus "the chimney sweeper" in his dream of the angel romps once again on the green, and the children in *Holy Thursday* achieve their vision in spontaneous song, which takes them out of themselves, so to speak, out of their apparent, restricted, non-innocent existence.[4]

2

In only one of the poems of this group does Blake look forward to the method by which one is finally found beyond experience. The key to this is a selfless act, the poem *The Little Black Boy,* in which the titular character shades the white boy so that the latter may learn, as the black boy has already learned, to bear the beams of love. In experience the tear, and the vision it gives shape to, are no longer efficacious; in fact, the tear is an agent of further division. If the child lost in experience weeps over his plight, he pities himself, and "pity divides the soul / And man unmans."[5] This is not to be confused with divine pity, tears for another:

> Pitying, the Lamb of God descended thro' Jerusalem's gates
> To put off Mystery time after time. . . .[6]

As the "mighty Fallen One" asks Enitharmon,

> "Why dost thou weep as Vala & wet thy veil with dewy tears,
> In slumbers of my night-repose infusing a false morning" (*Zoas,* 271),

so might the cloud, the lily, or the clod have asked Thel why she sheds tears for her own plight. Those tears only reveal more clearly her inability to enter the grave of experience and the inevitability of her retreat to the "false morning" and the pseudo-joy of the vales of Har. So, too, Theotormon's tears in *Visions of the Daughters of Albion* prohibit both his clear vision of Oothoon's essential divinity and their consequent union. And finally, the fact that *A Little Boy Lost* weeps in his predicament precludes his being found.

Closely related to this changed significance in experience of Blake's symbols is the inability of the mother (and father) to prevent the child from becoming lost; in experience she is out of her element, while the father is in his. In other words the father-priest-king is the agent of lostness: Earth is lost at the hands of God in *Earth's Answer,* the speaker of *The Garden of Love* is lost at the hands of the priests, the girl in *A Little Girl Lost* is lost at the hands of her father, and "the little vagabond" at the hands of his mother. To be free of the father-priest-king, the lost soul can rely no longer on an angel of innocence, or a father in white. Having achieved self-identification and self-realization, he must rely on himself to perform a selfless act, the greatest one being the surrender of self openly in sexual intercourse. To be found, Oothoon in the *Visions* had only to convince Theotormon that she had not given herself to Bromion, and that Theotormon should surrender himself to his erstwhile restrained passion for her. The tree in *My Pretty Rose Tree* and the queen in *The Angel* need only dispense with female wiles and yield to their respective lovers. The girl in *A Little Girl Lost* must pursue her love affair, not clandestinely but openly, and must cut the paternal cord if she is to be free. Only such acts can find the lost soul; only by means of them can the soul "rise from Generation free" (*To Tirzah*).

3

With these considerations in mind, let us proceed to several of Blake's other lost characters. Though *The Little Black Boy* is actually related to this theme only tangentially, I include it here because its symbols recur throughout other poems of this group and the third group. The most important one, perhaps, is shade, which Blake already used, somewhat obscurely, in *The Ecchoing Green*. And since being shaded is, in effect, a hallmark of innocent existence, the idea of being found, instinctively recognizing one's own innocence, never could have been very far from Blake's mind as he wrote the poem.[7]

Although the precise quality of the obvious opposition in the poem of black boy and white boy is not fully revealed by Blake until the last two stanzas, their respective roles are foreshadowed in the first stanza. Also in stanza 1 is an important allusion to the *Song of Solomon,* upon which more of this poem is based than has heretofore been noted. The first set of opposites proposed comprises the polar localities from which each boy comes, the "southern wild" and England; and without these the significance of the more obvious black-white contrast becomes almost banal. The southern wild is much the same as the valley wild through which the Piper wandered, both radically different from England, from the chartered streets of London, where

> In every cry of every Man,
> In every Infants cry of fear.
> In every voice: in every ban.
> The mind-forg'd manacles I hear. (*London*)

In this London of experience, the "home" of the children in *The Chimney Sweeper, Holy Thursday,* and *The School Boy,* "the youthful Harlots curse"

> Blasts the new born Infants tear
> And blights with plagues the Marriage hearse.

Having evoked such association, Blake then turns to the external contrast of black and white boy. The latter *seems* like an angel to the former; the former is *apparently* black, "as if bereaved of light." With the element of doubt clear in the last line of the stanza, it is not unreasonable to assume that there is also some element of doubt in the previous simile, "White as an angel." In any case, Blake is content at this point to leave the relationship of black boy to white boy on a superficial basis. His suggestion of the falsity of this basis he reserves for the third stanza and its equation of light and comfort. If we look back, then, from the third stanza to the first, it becomes clear that the black boy has an excess of comfort because of his absorption of the light; on the other hand, the white boy lacks that comfort because the "shades of the prison house" deny it to him. The second line of stanza 1 emphasizes this point in view of Blake's insistence that body does not exist separate from soul. As Solomon's song says, "I am black but comely, O ye daughters of Jerusalem, as the tents of Kedar, as the curtains of Solomon" (i.5). (And it is not too fanciful to suggest here that the curtains of Solomon, when removed, reveal the essential whiteness of the "tent of God.") The *Song* then continues: "Look not upon me, because I am black, because the sun hath looked upon me: my mother's children were angry with me; they made me the keeper of the vineyards; but mine own vineyards have I not kept" (i.6). Similarly the English child, born of the same mother, Earth, does not understand the meaning of the sun's looking upon the black boy. His only reaction, which is logical and right, is the simple and ignorant one of indifference to someone who is apparently "different" from himself; that person is consequently relegated to a position commensurate with his lower standing in the world. It is not a crime of reason but of instinct; it is a result of mere sense perception. Even in a child, when brought up in a shackled society, that crime is the highest crime of all in Blake's scale of values. It is lack of vision. Once this dichotomy is seen in the first stanza, and the later difference between light and heat, comfort and joy, is appreciated, the rest of the poem takes on a much deeper, more universal meaning than antislavery propaganda or the roles of mother and child in society.

After the introductory stanza of *The Little Black Boy,* Blake proceeds with his use of the *Song of Solomon* and another aspect of motherhood. Already in the first line of the poem Blake has recalled the fifth verse of the eighth chapter: "Who is this that cometh up from the wilderness, leaning upon her beloved? I raised thee up under the apple tree: there thy mother brought thee forth; there she brought thee forth that bare thee." Now, as the Bride says to the Bridegroom, "I would lead thee, and bring thee into my mother's house, who would instruct me" (viii.2), so Blake writes in his second stanza:

> My mother taught me underneath a tree
> And sitting down before the heat of day,
> She took me on her lap and kissed me.

Here is the same "apple tree among the trees of the wood" that is "my beloved among the sons. I sat down under his shadow with great delight, and his fruit was sweet to my taste" (ii.2). The tree, then, is both a source of the shade imagery and of at least part of Blake's concept of protective motherhood. Shady tree becomes body becomes cloud and then returns at the end of the poem as a grove of trees to unite all the shade images. In addition, the tree is a symbol of generation, the image of regeneration. And finally, the tree or shade is Christ insofar as the creation was an act of mercy to provide a way toward regeneration. Necessary but extremely temporary, the tree can without harmful consequences shield the soul from the sun for a while; the mother's protection is desirable. But if the shade is utilized inordinately, regeneration is impossible, for the beams of love can never then be borne. Love generates eternal joy; it is heat, energy. Physical comfort generates eternal servitude (like John's in *The Ecchoing Green,* like Thel's in *The Book of Thel*) in a "mirtle shade" (169); it is restraint of energy. Correspondingly the mother's capacity for instruction and protection is severely limited. If she pursues her role beyond the state of innocence, her love becomes as selfishly restrictive as the child's love for mother is selfish in its desire for self-protection. The longer the soul rests in the shade of the tree, the more difficult it is to deny the body's comfort for the soul's warmth.[8] That is Thel's great tragedy.

The third stanza of *The Little Black Boy* takes up the corollary to all of this, the difference between comfort and joy, and re-echoes the mother's care to sit under the tree *before* the heat of day. To the English child comfort is most welcome, but the noonday joy of soul is denied him because he has not been prepared for it by the shade. That preparation involves the self—that is, in terms of this poem, dispensing with physical comfort. By so doing the emancipated soul can act the role of shade, the body, and the grove for others. This is the responsibility which the power of love entails, that it be directed always outward; if it is hoarded to self, it becomes, as in the white boy, apparently lovely but inwardly dead. Once the soul has experienced the pain and terror of experience and the beams are bearable, its vision becomes multifold; and it is seen not as a black or white body, not even as a black or white soul, but as a lamb sporting around the "golden tent" of the sun. The cloud of the *Introduction* vanished to reveal the child within; then the child vanished to merge with the lamb. Only at this point may the soul be ordered by the spiritual father out from the same grove into which the earthly mother brought it for shelter. The transfiguration into lambs in stanza 5 of *The Little Black Boy*, of course, draws to the scene all the association of *The Lamb* and its Creator.

In these four stanzas (2 through 5) Blake has apparently lost sight of the little English boy while recounting the teachings of the black boy's mother. The point is that the black boy will pass on that teaching to the English boy. Here difficulty is encountered if the poem is allowed to remain on the social level, or even on the level of light and shade as we have already seen it. In stanza 5 the clouds of the body are said to vanish when the sun becomes bearable; in stanza 6 the clouds do vanish for both boys as they gambol like lambs around God's tent. It comes as something of a surprise, then, when in the last stanza the white boy is still unable to approach God, still unable to bear the heat. In his ignorance he has accepted the *light* of the sun as its most important quality and has thus assumed the inferiority, or at least the difference, of the black boy. With appearances stripped away, however, though the white boy skips with joy around the tent of God, it is clear that his joy is without knowledge and hence nothing. He still looks like an angel but he is not an angel. The black boy, on the other hand, is comely and worthy of the "Garden of Love" and can act as the shade. He has learned to bear the heat of love by bearing it for another. The white boy's childish ignorance and false self-assurance have left him in the comfort of the shade only to make him realize too late that he, too, must face the east and the rising sun, must himself become black before he can become white.

This is the significance of the oft-misread last two lines. When the white boy, singed by the heat of God's presence, realizes the black boy is really like him, he turns his love away from his own angelic body to the angelic form of the black boy's soul. With this act, he too can achieve that selflessness which lets us "lean in joy upon our father's knee." Then all children are lambs and the Lamb.

Though the little black boy in the final analysis is never really lost, the circumstances of his life and the images Blake employs in presenting his characteristic significance form a solid basis for describing the lostness of another little boy, the chimney sweeper.

Like *The Little Boy Lost* and *Holy Thursday, The Chimney Sweeper* is usually interpreted as a song of experience, many times because it has been read, like *The Little Black Boy,* as a social document. It is true that the mother here has died, that the earthly father presages the law-givers and hypocrites of experience, and that the child, not afforded the usual protective lap, is catapulted beyond his years into an experience not yet his due, into a bosom of soot. But since this is a song of innocence, the experience of *Songs of Experience* is not applicable here; the decalogue wielded by the earthly tyrants, mother and father, priest and king, has not yet been invoked. Instead Blake evokes a kind of freedom, though obviously not of the same quality as that of *The Ecchoing Green,* the Piper, or the shepherd's flock. It is more like the freedom of *The Little Black Boy,* a freedom of imagination. That is Blake's central theme in *The Chimney Sweeper.*

The first stanza portrays the anonymous speaker as a child whose feeble cry is far different from the "lambs innocent call" and the "ewes tender reply" (*The Shepherd*). He sleeps in soot instead of the earthly mother's bosom or lap. But just as the mother shields the child from the intense beams of God's love until he is able to bear them alone, so the sweeper's soot is ironically his shield. Blake pursues this idea in the next stanza, where Tom Dacre bemoans his shaven head and is comforted by the speaker:

> Hush Tom never mind it, for when your head's bare,
> You know that the soot cannot spoil your white hair.

The relationship thus created is identical to that of the black boy and white boy. Tom is like the English boy who had no fear that his hair would be spoiled, but on the contrary thought the black boy was spoiled because of *his* color. In *The Chimney Sweeper* the white hair cannot be spoiled because it is not there substantially; yet to the imagination the hair *is* there, unspoiled and in a sense protected. The reference to the lamb in this stanza intensifies the contrast, since God gave the lamb (and thus any child) "clothing of delight, / Softest clothing wooly bright." The stanza, then, is a remarkable parallel, significantly reversed, to the white boy's joy at his apparent whiteness in *The Little Black Boy.*

In Tom Dacre's dream or vision the sweepers, locked in black coffins which are at once their soot-covered bodies and the clouds of *The Little Black Boy,* are released by an angel with a bright key into the land of innocence in which they really dwell. The land of imagination Blake might have called it, where the sweepers' faces are clean, Tom has his lamb's hair, and naked souls rise "upon clouds" and shine in the comfort and light of the sun. The soot-bags are left behind. It is, in fact, the same vision the white boy finally experiences, the same vision that the black boy had all along of his white soul, the same vision the boy in *The Little Boy Found* evokes with his tears. The sweeper's place is in innocence, then, but vision is the only means of realizing it. The sooty protection from the beams of love must be imagined away.

The angel may be the angel of death,[9] a precursor of the land of eternal joy beyond innocence and experience, but to see only this compromises Blake's concept of the imagination within the realm of innocence itself. The angel here is similar to the child on a cloud of the *Introduction* but he does not go as far. More like the white-clad father of *The Little Boy Lost,* he unlocks the prison of the five senses and opens the eyes to the delight of childhood; but he points no further. There is no union of inspiration and child; there is merely direction, for this is all that can be achieved in innocence. Tom himself has yet to meet experience face to face. Only its shadow falls across his path, and as such it can be transcended merely by two-fold vision.

In the last stanza the anonymous speaker returns, the singer who has unaccountably been excluded from the dream and yet knows all about it. Indeed he is in reality the instigator of it, or perhaps the inspiration. I cannot see Tom as the speaker, as so many critics seem to, but I can see Blake as the speaker in the guise of the Piper of *Songs of Innocence*. In the moment of creation the Piper of the *Introduction* is united with the child on a cloud, with the song, and with Christ; he becomes one with his vision and thus achieves the higher innocence. In other words, he *knows*. Similarly the speaker of *The Chimney Sweeper* also knows, a fact revealed already in stanza 2; and in stanzas 3, 4, and 5 he fulfills his function of creating visions every child may joy to see and hear. The sweeper's dream is his whether he appears in it or not. But is he really absent from the dream in the context of visionary logic, the only logic Blake would have? Is he not also the angel? In these terms the bright key is his visionary picture of the true innocence of the sweepers, and the soot becomes a kind of shade under which the white hair or soul lies protected.

> And so Tom awoke and we rose in the dark
> And got with our bags & our brushes to work.
> Tho' the morning was cold, Tom was happy & warm.

Now Tom, as well as the Piper-angel-chimney sweeper, realizes that his rising "in the dark" is an imaginative sunrise; he is happy and comfortable in its light, warm in its rays. He is learning to bear the beams of love.

The last line of the poem, which causes so much embarrassment to Blake enthusiasts, now presents no difficulty. The Piper simply states a Blakean truism. Since there is no duty on earth except to attain the power of vision, "if all do their duty," if all dream dreams, if all retain the power of vision despite the stultifying atmosphere of this world, they need not fear harm because harm will not then exist. If "Fear is the Parent of Earthly Love," as Blake wrote (*Jerusalem*, 725), vision is the parent of eternal love.

4

Though relatively simple, the final poem of this group, *A Dream,* serves admirably as a transition to the last group of *Songs of Innocence* to be considered. On the one hand, it is intimately related to other lost and found poems by virtue of its unusual application of that theme to the mother rather than the child. On the other hand, its detailed account of what the mother must *not* do in innocence allies *A Dream* to *On Anothers Sorrow, A Cradle Song, The Blossom,* and *Night,*[10] in all of which the mother's positive role is amplified and clarified.

"Unorganiz'd Innocence: An Impossibility," Blake wrote on a manuscript page of *The Four Zoas* (380); in *A Dream* he dramatized that dictum by means of his special kind of allegory. In one issue of the songs *A Dream* appears in *Experience*[11]—apparently with good reason, for it recounts an excursion into the fringe of experience similar to that by "the little boy lost." But Blake quickly realized his error and returned the poem to *Innocence* in all other copies. As a dream poem and, most important of all, a child's dream, in *Innocence* it forms a distinct and powerful contrast with the dream poem of *Experience, The Angel.*

In *A Dream* the dreams of *A Cradle Song* form a shade over the "lovely infants head," who is guarded by the bright angel of the world of innocence. But the shade is tinged with tragedy, for an emmet-mother[12] has lost her way in the dream. Ostensibly a curious reversal of *The Little Boy Lost,* the poem is in fact Blake's first full definition of the mother's role in innocence, where her presence heretofore has been only tacitly accepted as part of his system.

The first two stanzas carefully explain the ramifications of "lost-ness." That it is night is essential, but unlike the night of most of the other "lost" poems, this is the rapidly encroaching night of experience, of this world. This is the fundamental reason for the poem's being in the form of a dream. If Blake had actually intended to dramatize the night of experience, he would have included *A Dream* in *Songs of Experience.* By using the dream device, as he does in *The Little Girl Lost* and *The Little Girl Found,* he can present certain elements of experience while retaining the fundamentals of the state of innocence. An implicit comparison is made immediately, then, between experience and innocence: the speaker is a child of innocence in a night of innocence dreaming a dream of innocence which only foreshadows the night and stark reality of experience.

The emmet in the dream is troubled and "wilderd," having lost her way and come upon a scene where she has no place, a scene forlorn. She is "dark" and "benighted," physically and intellectually blinded to her own condition. She is "travel-worn" after stumbling without vision through the tangled sprays of a life foreign to her, a life that is little more than death. A curious spectacle: the wayward mother denied her divinely appointed task and venturing wilfully into a darkness she cannot comprehend, a darkness that envelops her and summarily abolishes her divine right, as well as her ability, to rock the cradle of the sleeping child. She is not inexorably damned, however. The lost boy, we recall, was found. But in order to preclude dark oblivion, the mother must experience an impulsive, instinctive reversion to her rightful state —that of being an earthly mother, just as the lost boy had to cease the pursuit of the father physical and revert to characteristic tears (and the father spiritual) for his salvation.

The abruptness of the mother's reversion is reinforced by the stanza break: she cries out, "all heart-broke,"

> O my children! do they cry
> Do they hear their father sigh.
> Now they look abroad to see,
> Now return and weep for me.

The instantaneous reaction to the thought of her children is the proper one, worry and care and sympathetic grief. The second line of this stanza, however, is not quite so clear. Blake's point can be seen only if we read the line in conjunction with the one that follows: the children must "look abroad" to listen for their father's sigh; he is not in the home at all. Blake, I think, is trying to reinvoke by implication the situation in which "the little boy lost" cried: "No father was there." The pathetic irony of "Do they hear their father sigh" merely emphasizes the implicit negative answer to the question. Deserted by the mother, the children in effect have no home, no protection; if they look abroad, they see no father either. They are as lost as the mother is. All that is left is to return and weep just as the boy of *The Little Boy Lost* wept. Blake's blending of themes from the earlier poem into those of

A Dream constitutes a graphic revelation of "unorganiz'd innocence"; that it is an impossibility the rest of the poem points out.

The pity of the dreamer and the now-normal mother's grief produce the light, the epiphany. For, as Blake wrote in *Auguries of Innocence,*

> God Appears & God is Light
> To those poor Souls who dwell in Night. (434)

In *Night* protective angels appear; in *A Dream* a "glow-worm" (actually a female beetle) lights the ground for the watchman of the night, who "looks in every thoughtless nest" and sits down by the bed of those who weep (*Night*). The wandering emmet can now resume her rightful role, and innocence is restored in all its splendid "organization" for the infant dreamer.

But there may be additional significance in Blake's dream structure. According to his system the mother must be separated from the child at some point; otherwise innocence becomes self-destructive. It is possible, then, that Blake intended this dream of lostness to foreshadow the separation of the innocent dreamer and his mother. When that occurs, tears will effect no reunion; but the light of the glow-worm will be represented by the eternal light of vision and imagination, which will guide the wandering soul home to Eden.

CHAPTER VI

NIGHT AND THE PROSPECT OF DAWN

৯৶

> I cannot stay by now and watch.
> My time has come to move.
> —LILLIAN HELLMAN, *Watch on the Rhine*

I

Night has already made inroads into the *Songs of Innocence,* but less in substance than in shadow. Similarly the mother's act of protecting the child from those inroads has only been foreshadowed by her brief appearance at the end of *The Ecchoing Green,* by her teaching in *The Little Black Boy,* and by the necessity of her being found in *A Dream.* Finally, joy and sorrow have been seen to be mixed fine in the *Songs,* from the relatively unalloyed laughter of the first group, with its more sober overtones, to the apparent sorrow of the second group in which the essential existent joy of innocence is revealed through vision. In this third group the vision is intensified. In the *Introduction,* after the child on a cloud weeps to hear the Piper's second rendition of the song about a lamb, he weeps with joy to hear the third. That third version is, in effect, the third group of songs as I have organized them. Innocence has been established, experience has been alluded to; now, despite the earthly mother's greatest efforts, experience is close upon the child, and in it lies the key to a higher innocence beyond.

It is appropriate, then, to introduce this group with *A Cradle Song* since it concerns not only impinging experience but maternal protection in its most familiar form and the instinctive assurance of a new dawn on the part of both mother and child. The basis for that assurance is the eventual regeneration inherent in the figure of Christ; and this is perhaps one of the reasons that Blake, after 1815, usually followed *A Cradle Song* with *The Divine Image* in the sequence of *Songs of Innocence*.[1]

In addition to being one of the finest poems Blake ever wrote, *A Cradle Song* is one of the most complex structurally. Ideas and images subtly interlock to make up an exquisite network-unity of mother, child, and Christ, the unity without which Blake could not conceive of innocence. And finally, there is no finer exposition in the *Songs* of the state of Beulah, which came to be a central concept in all of the prophetic books. In *The Four Zoas*, for example, the scene that opens *A Cradle Song* is repeated in mythological form:

> There is from Great Eternity a mild & pleasant rest
> Nam'd Beulah, a soft Moony Universe, feminine, lovely,
> Pure, mild & Gentle, given in Mercy to those who sleep.
>
> .   .   .   .
>
> The daughters of Beulah follow sleepers in all their Dreams,
> Creating spaces, lest they fall into Eternal Death. (266-267)

In *Milton*

> There is a place where Contrarieties are equally True:
> This place is called Beulah. It is a pleasant lovely Shadow
> Where no dispute can come, Because of those who Sleep.
>
> .   .   .   .
>
> But Beulah to its Inhabitants appears within each district
> As the beloved infant in his mother's bosom round incircled
> With arms of love & pity & sweet compassion. (518)

And most meaningful and significant of all, in terms of the difference between the apparent sorrow of innocence and the very real grief of experience, is the following, again from *The Four Zoas*:

> ... The Moon has chambers where the babes of love lie hid,
> And whence they never can be brought in all Eternity
> Unless expos'd by their vain parents. (339)

In addition to these later amplifications of the first stanza of *A Cradle Song,* there is the usual interconnection between this song and others in *Songs of Innocence,* a poetical reciprocity which does not so much provide clues to a full understanding of this particular poem as it reinforces the over-all picture of the state to which all the songs contribute. For instance, abundant echoes rebound to the words of the first stanza: the dream of the chimney sweeper and the poem called *A Dream,* in which

> Once a dream did weave a shade.
> O'er my Angel-guarded bed;

all the "lovely infants" of the *Songs* and the "pleasant streams" in which the chimney-sweepers bathed and which "run laughing by" to join in the *Laughing Song;* and the "moony beams" of *Night,* in which

> The moon like a flower,
> In heavens high bower;
> With silent delight
> Sits and smiles on the night.

The dream of *A Cradle Song,* then, is a shady asylum from the blackness of the night, much the same as, in reverse fashion, the shade of the tree screened the black boy from the brilliance of the sun. That asylum is pleasant, suffused with "happy silent moony beams," which may be a suggestion that the dreams themselves reflect the love, peace, and joy of God as the moon reflects the sun's rays. And the lullaby-like repetitive structure of "sweet dreams," "sweet sleep," "sweet smiles," "sweet moans," not only suggests the elements which comprise the child's protection and love, but also constitutes the main line of development from pleasantness and happiness to sorrow. That structural unity is broken in stanza 5, which provides the transition, through the medium of the child's sleep, from suggestions of Christ's presence to a dramatization of his actual presence. The point that Blake is making in these early stanzas is that for the child, night and darkness do not exist; the dream is the reality. The rest of the poem, from stanza 5 on, is concerned with the universalization of that fact as it is applied to the child, the mother, and all creation.

In the second and third stanzas the basic simplicity of the song is immensely enriched. The shade of dreams has now come to rest on the infant's head in the shape of an "infant crown" woven of "soft down." The genius of this transformation can be seen only by examining the fine complexity inherent in the apparently unburdened guilelessness of the mother's song. Though Blake's mention of down may suggest the child's cradle (or pillow) itself, "soft down" also heralds the later advent of the dove and thus of God in the form of Holy Ghost. In addition, the infant crown unmistakably forebodes the tragedy of experience[2] which ever remains an aura around Blake's Christ-child, here as the crown of thorns. Both of these associations are later fused with the "Angel mild" hovering over the child. To Blake, as to Swedenborg, angels were children or men, so that the three-fold union of child-mother-Christ toward the end of the poem is carefully prepared for here. Almost magically, like the colors in a Renoir, the words of these two stanzas (2 and 3) shade off into others and then reassume their identity, until out of the literal kaleidoscope a form arises all the more brilliant because delineated in Blake's "minute particulars." For example, "Sweet sleep" is not only the infant crown of down but also an "Angel mild" hovering "o'er my happy child"; and in stanza 3 the hovering angel is joined by "sweet smiles," which also "Hover over my delight." Here the smiles are the angel's and the mother's, but I think we must also see that Blake intended them to be Christ's as well. Although the smiler is ambiguous, if one recognizes the progression from "Sweet smiles in the night" to "Sweet moans, sweeter smiles" to "Heavenly face that smiles on thee," one can see that the idea of Christ's smiles was an integral part of Blake's design throughout the poem. The early suggestion of this fact in stanzas 2 and 3 is emphasized by the subtle differentiation of smiles in stanza 3:

> Sweet smiles in the night,
> Hover over my delight.
> Sweet smiles Mothers smiles
> All the livelong night beguiles.

The first two lines suggest that the smiles are those of the angel (and ultimately the dove) which hovers over the child; the second two lines state boldly that mother's smiles are also present. The two are, in effect, joined to beguile the night away, and this juncture foreshadows the later union of child, mother, and Christ. Besides employing this ingenious verbal network Blake saturates the first three stanzas as a unit with the simple beauty of adjectives like "sweet," "lovely," "pleasant," "happy," "silent," "soft," and "mild," all of which contribute to the beguiling[3] of the terrible night of experience.

But innocence is not quite all sweetness and light: Beulah is "a place where Contrarieties are equally True." In stanzas 4, 5, and 6, consequently, Blake expands the significance of the night that must be beguiled by dreams, sleep, and smiles; and the crown of thorns implicit in the mention of the heavenly crown of stanza 2, is now analyzed in terms of its universal application to all life. Moans and sighs and weeping insinuate themselves into the happiness. But the sorrow is not lonely, for, as we have seen, no one is ever alone when a tear falls. Thus, most appropriately they are "sweet moans, dovelike sighs," like those of *On Anothers Sorrow*. By splitting these first six stanzas into two groups, however, I do not mean to imply that the train of association of the first three ceases abruptly and a new one begins. If this were the case, *A Cradle Song* would be really two poems (and this, of course, is the reason that *The Little Boy Lost* and *The Little Boy Found are* two poems). Blake was too good a poet to force such a juncture. The associations continue and become more elaborate until eventually they are crystallized in the last two stanzas.

Thus, instead of dream-sleep-angel-smiles, in the second group of three stanzas there are dovelike sighs and moans, a curious and exquisite transmutation. Whereas the hovering provided the clue to the dove earlier, now the dove appears in the form of an adjectival component with its characteristic action only implicit. The mother fears that these moans and sighs will awaken the child, and she cautions them. But then Blake explains that there is no need for caution. "Sweet moans" and "sweeter smiles" will beguile the "dovelike moans." This sounds like tautology pure and simple, but I believe it to be more than that. Blake is about to make his transition to the figure of Christ—as both child and man. The moans and sighs of the first line of the stanza, then, will not awaken the child because the sweet, sympathetic moans of

Christ will beguile them away; and further, Christ's sweet smiles, which conclude the poem by beguiling heaven and earth to peace, will beguile away *all* moans. Those smiles are sweeter than the divine moans as well as mother's moans and smiles. This is, of course, the reason why the mother can say, in stanza 5, "Sleep sleep happy child" and "Sleep sleep, happy sleep." Though the mother weeps at the thought of Christ's sacrifice (and the child's future entry into experience), the child can remain happy in innocence precisely because Christ made the sacrifice and became eternal joy. As a further tie with the first three stanzas, Blake repeats in stanza 4 the terminal line of stanza 3, with a significant variation: "All the livelong night beguiles" becomes "All the dovelike moans beguiles," once again recalling the tragic overtones of experience within the context of the Christ-child and the dove. The universalization of the child-angel-dove symbol is completed in stanza 5 with the reference to "all creation" sleeping and smiling. The line (line 18) seems abrupt at first and not a little irrelevant but it has been carefully prepared for by Blake so that stanza 6 (the last of this second triad) can reach its climax.

The climax is in the analogy drawn between the innocence of the sleeping child and the sleeping of all creation in its innocence. In the child's face is mirrored the image of the Saviour and the saved, the creator and the created. The full significance of the mother's weeping now becomes clear. Of all creation she is the only one who weeps (besides Christ, whose grief is a sympathetic projection of self); and she weeps because she knows the child's future, because she can detect the note of tragedy diffused throughout all innocence. Just so Christ wept for all creation, doomed to fall from its pristine state. The mother's sympathy is all the more poignant because the realm of experience precludes the child's protection by earthly motherhood. By her act of commiseration, however, she approximates on earth the role of Christ, who throughout eternity weeps "for me for thee for all." Christ's sympathetic grief, however, and his "sweeter smiles" continue throughout experience. He is always there for all who can see. Finally, as the mother weeps for her child, so Christ wept at one time for the mother. But since he was an infant small when he wept "for me" (the mother), it is as if her child, in whose face is Christ's image, *now* weeps for her. The mother thus sees in her child the human form divine.

In the last two stanzas, then, Blake synthesizes with his usual simple intensity the hope of mankind, the ultimate negation of self which the child must learn from Christ's example. The tears and smiles are now seen as equally true "contrarieties"; Blake emphasizes this by the striking parallelism of lines 25 and 29. For the child in innocence the divine image is ever seen smiling, even though it be there, unseen, in a fallen tear.[4] In both cases the divine image "Heaven & earth to peace beguiles."[5] The "Circle of Destiny" is now complete, having proceeded from the happy, moony beams of innocence, to the tears of the mother heralding the onset of experience, to the tears of the Christ-child in experience, to the smiles of the Christ-child which transcend all of the former in eternity. There, in Eden, the beguiling is not purgative, against the night and the moans; it is constructive, creative of peace in heaven and on earth.

The song, then, is not merely a cradle song but a prayer, the same prayer mentioned in *The Divine Image:*

> To Mercy Pity Peace and Love,
> All pray in their distress.

For all creation is an act of mercy by the babe's "maker," and pity is the weeping mother's face; peace therefore becomes the dream itself, the dream of Beulah's "happy silent moony beams"; and love, of course, is the human form divine, which

> Smiles on thee on me on all
> Who became an infant small.[6]

2

The Piper has already sung of the day and the echoing green, and the hint of night has been seen to be ever-present at the end of the day of innocence. In *A Cradle Song* the night of innocence—not without its note of tragedy—was guarded by the earthly mother, and in *The Chimney Sweeper* Blake painted a blacker night, yet with innocence preserved by means of an angelic key to the glorious world of day. In *Night* he composes another variation on the Piper's theme[7] and takes it a step further than all the others. That step leads beyond innocence and experience into "immortal day."

Night begins where *The Ecchoing Green* ended, the first two

stanzas being reminiscent of the maternal loveliness of *A Cradle Song.*
The moon smiles on the night, and joy is poured by angels bright

> On each bud and blossom,
> And each sleeping bosom.

In addition to setting the scene in Beulah or innocence, the moon reflects
the beams of love as they filter through the blackness of the night.
Those beams are less intense to be sure, but their very presence suggests
that it is partly through the night that the soul learns to bear the love of
"our immortal day." A poem in the early *Poetical Sketches,* however,
gives us the most pertinent clue to a Blakean reading of *Night.* After
describing the first appearance of the evening star as a herald of the
deep night, Blake writes in *To the Evening Star:*

> ... Soon, full soon,
> Dost thou withdraw; then the wolf rages wide,
> And the lion glares thro' the dun forest:
> The fleeces of our flocks are cover'd with
> Thy sacred dew: protect them with thine influence. (3)

By emphasizing the silent angel's feet in *Night,* then, Blake paints a
picture of a glistening, dew-covered green, where a few moments before
lambs grazed and children sported. "Unseen," the angels spread a
tutelar carpet of "sacred . . . influence"

> On each bud and blossom,
> And each sleeping bosom.

Significantly the angels do not appear as long as the children play,
the flocks delight, and the lambs nibble, because these creatures are existing and being innocent; their actions represent the rightful, or better,
the inherent qualities of innocent energy being exercised without
restraint. This is their "eternal delight."

With the cessation of this activity at nightfall, however, the angels
materialize just as the shepherd, who wanders all day, is watchful when
his flock sleeps (*The Shepherd*). The angels "look in every thoughtless
nest" and cave to keep the birds and beasts "from harm." But as we
have seen, in *The Chimney Sweeper* particularly, the only "harm" possible in the state of innocence is the act of thinking which does not

exist in these nests. Once a rationale is attempted by the soul, the dichotomy of safety and harm supersedes visionary logic, which holds energy to be the only delight. In *Night* that energy is of the prolific and the devourer, identical in essence, different in kind. On the fringe of the same associative pattern is the additional suggestion that the only "harm" the children really have to fear will be at the hands of father, priest, and king, who institute an arbitrary goodness by which to measure badness, and an even more arbitrary, self-complacent safety free of harm.

Still this connotative complex does not explain the stanza entirely, because the angels not only keep birds warm and safe but "visit caves of every beast, / To keep them all from harm." This completes the roster, so to speak, of the animal world as Blake imaginatively perceived it, a world symbolically equated with the human world in line 4 ("And I must seek for mine," that is, my nest). If we miss the significance of this skillful opening quatrain and read the poem with only "corporeal understanding," single vision, a strange kind of fairy tale unfolds with sleeping animals protected by angels and with other animals gobbling the first ones up despite the presence of "heedful" angels. With double vision the human side of the story becomes manifest, and with the triple vision characteristic of Beulah the whole story emerges.

By inference the "I" of line 4 is the Piper of the *Songs;* according to the context he is an innocent child; and by extension he is a bird like those in *The Ecchoing Green, The Blossom,* and *Spring.* Since the line concludes the thought of line 3, the corporeal understanding cannot logically read human and consequently reads bird. This is correct, but it is only a part of Blake's intention. The intellect reads both animal and human throughout the poem, from this one bird to the lamb to the beasts in the cave. The scene, then, is the peace of innocence, the peace which passeth understanding. But Blake characteristically asks more of the reader. The birds fly and sing, for that is their forte, their "immense world of delight"; the lambs (as devourers) nibble the buds and blossoms in green fields and happy groves; but the lambs (as prolifics) are eaten by the wolves and tigers (devourers), and so the circle of destiny goes. Each arc of that circle is an equally divine segment of the creation which begins and ends in the human form divine. In the first three stanzas all are blessed and protected.

But then the "wolves and tygers howl for prey," the angels "pitying stand and weep." Outside of Blake's system the angels' reaction is very curious. Should they not drive away the beasts of prey? or tell the sheep to run and hide? or call the shepherd? Blake's answer is implicit in the fact that he has them merely shed a tear. As he wrote in *On Anothers Sorrow,*

> Can I see anothers woe,
> And not be in sorrow too.

In vision the angels recognize the desire for food to be equally divine with the desire for life.[8] The beasts howl not for death but for life, which to them is devouring. To desire death is negative and even evil, for death is a denial of energy, the eternal delight of all creation. The angels, then, rightly seek to drive the bestial *thirst* away while at the same time protecting an equally divine element, the prolific sheep.

No choice is to be made between good and evil, for there is no good and evil. The limited choice open is expressible only in terms of the corporeal understanding: to protect or not to protect; and such a choice is inapplicable to these angels. As Blake wrote, again in *On Anothers Sorrow:*

> Can I see anothers grief,
> And not seek for kind relief.

The answer is "no." Thus, the apparent ineffectuality of angelic protection in the rest of the stanza is abrogated. Restraint of energy regardless of its mode of expression is satanic or Urizenic. The angels are doing their duty, and they *are* heedful of the wolves' and tigers' *right* to follow their divine instinct and the lambs' *right* to die and inherit new worlds.[9]

Blake reiterates this divinity of act many times, never more consistently and persistently than in the "Proverbs of Hell" in *The Marriage of Heaven and Hell:*

The wrath of the lion is the wisdom of God.
The roaring of lions, the howling of wolves, the raging of the stormy
   sea. and the destructive sword. are portions of eternity too great
   for the eye of man.
The fox provides for himself. but God provides for the lion.

123

And God, providing for the lion, provides also for the lamb as the prolific element; both become once again part of the divine Imagination. The lion achieves pity by giving vent to his wrath; the lion becomes *the* Lamb by devouring the lamb;

> . . . wrath by his meekness
> And by his health. sickness.
> Is driven away

from his "immortal day." The lamb becomes the Lamb (in the last two stanzas) by being devoured, and in so doing both weep, as Christ did in *A Cradle Song,*

> . . . for me for thee for all,
> When he was an infant small.

The last stanza of *Night,* then, involves a multiple identification of the lamb, the lion, the shepherd, the Christ, all now washed in the river of experience which the two contraries of prolific and devourer constitute. "To bathe in the Waters of Life," Blake wrote in *Milton,*

> to wash off the Not Human,
> I [i.e., Milton] come in Self-annihilation & the grandeur of Inspiration,
> To cast off Rational Demonstration by Faith in the Saviour. (533)

In this wise the multifold identity becomes the eternal Sun, Love, and the human form divine, which includes mercy, pity, and peace. Then, and then only, "A dead body. revenges not injuries" (*Marriage*), and the wrath of the lion and the destructive sword *are* seen as "portions of eternity."

3

For the final poem in my exposition of the state of innocence I have chosen *The Divine Image,* for it is Blake's song of the cosmos. In it are many strands of thought, many symbols and associations, that appear and reappear throughout the *Songs of Innocence.* And all of these elements add up to one, the major symbol of innocence, the child. On earth he is *The Divine Image.* In addition the divine image is also Man and the Lamb and reflects the joy of *The Ecchoing Green, Spring, Infant Joy,* and *Laughing Song;* it is the shepherd and the child on a cloud; it is the God-father of *The Chimney Sweeper, The Little Black Boy, The Little Boy Found,* and the children of *A Dream;* it is the "holy image" of *A Cradle Song,* the angels bright of *Night,* and "he who smiles on all" in *On Anothers Sorrow.* To embrace these manifold associations a complex structural frame was necessary, though the finished monument is simple, at once subtle and precise, a fitting summary of the state of innocence.

Since it should be abundantly clear by now that Blake seldom uses words loosely or indiscriminately, the "virtues of delight" listed in the first line of *The Divine Image* are not to be read as a random assortment but as a revealing departure from the traditional virtues. Moreover, the first line is not a haphazard collocation of these virtues but a precise, methodological arrangement for the purposes of the poem. *All* pray in their distress to these "virtues of delight," "all" meaning all in particular, each individual taken by himself, as well as all taken as a unit. In terms of the paradox, mercy may be considered the "virtue of delight" of those in the lower depths, Ulro. Creation, we recall, was an act of mercy. In the same way pity is the virtue of Generation ("image of regeneration") and as such provides one of the best clues to Blake's emphasis on the efficacy of tears in this world. Peace is the virtue which can be achieved only by passing through the state of experience and creating out of this world, through a special kind of "marriage," the image of the divine union. Peace is also, of course, the state of innocence, born out of the earthly marriage and destined to fall back into the depths of terror and selfhood in order to reachieve a greater union through love and imagination. These, then, are Blake's virtues of delight, each a part of, yet in this world distinct from, love, the all-inclusive virtue. Only in these terms does the cryptic fourth line of the first stanza make sense: all are initially thankful for the divine mercy and successively thankful for each additional vision in their ascent to four-foldness and the human form divine.

In each step of that ascent the relationship of the heavenly father and earthly child holds true, as Blake explains in the second stanza. Their unity and consequent division is, of course, the essential *raison d'être* of Blake's *Songs of Innocence and of Experience.* The union, which cannot be perceived by all, becomes a duality only when the soul ceases to realize that the virtues are founded on selflessness. In other words, love of self is pride (the real seed of all of Urizen's crimes in the prophetic books); it conceives of the excellence of the human form as self-induced and hence usurps for the self praise due only to the human form divine.

This fundamental idea in Blake is analyzed further in the third stanza of *The Divine Image,* a superb transition from the first part of the poem to the very significant regrouping of the virtues in the latter part of the poem:

> For Mercy has a human heart
> Pity, a human face:
> And Love, the human form divine,
> And Peace, the human dress.

To deny the human heart is to deny the human and see only the bestial; to see God in the human, however miserable and low, is to see the human heart. This, of course, might be put just as emphatically the other way around, for mercy is the first step in the ascent. He who has it not can never find pity in his heart nor show pity in his face. I think this psychosomatic relationship has been largely missed in commentary on Blake's paintings, in which the "damned," who lack the human heart, are seen only with their faces hid or so contorted that bestiality is their foremost characteristic.[10]

In the third line of stanza 3 Blake makes an apparently innocuous shift in sequence (love preceding peace), which seems to be more for the sake of meter and rhyme than anything else. But although Blake has set up his cosmos in two stanzas, he is not so careless as to forget that *The Divine Image* is a song of innocence, only a part of that cosmos. Thus "Love, the human form divine" succeeds pity, the human face, to stress once again the inclusiveness of that greatest virtue. The stanza then ends with the curious line: "And Peace, the human dress." Peace, we have already seen, is Beulah, innocence. The "human dress," then, is that which "clothes" the innocents—the chimney-sweeper's soot, the black boy's "black," the white boy's "white." The human dress is the cloud of our mortality, the human form *human.*

The greatest virtue of mortality is to be and see the human. If one does, the heart appears in the human face and they are both seen as part of the human form divine. As stanza 2 asserts, Man too is mercy, pity, peace, and love; but he is the latter only in fourfold vision, Imagination, after he has learned to bear the beams of love in the here and now. It is the here and now, innocence, that Blake writes of in the last two stanzas, in which *Man* prays to the human form divine (again the composite four virtues). All must love that human form here on earth "In heathen, turk or jew." *The Divine Image* as a whole, then, is the prayer mentioned in the second line of the poem. Love the human form, "Thine own Humanity learn to Adore" (*Everlasting Gospel,* 750), for "Where Mercy Love & Pity dwell" (that is, on earth in the human form) "There God is dwelling too" (that is, peace and the restful quiet of Beulah's moony night).

The achieving of such precision and symbolic power finally led Blake to decide that the lyric *could* carry the weight of the state of experience after all; but before he made that decision he had to experiment with other forms, other methods—in *Tiriel, The Book of Thel,* and *Visions of the Daughters of Albion.*

P·A·R·T
·IV·

CHAPTER VII

TIRIEL AND THE STATE OF EXPERIENCE

ॐ

The brook into the stream runs on;
But the deep-eyed boy is gone.
—R. W. EMERSON, *Threnody*

Tiriel

I

And Aged Tiriel. stood before the Gates of his beautiful palace
[*But dark were his once piercing eyes*]*
With Myratana. once the Queen of all the western plains
But now his eyes were darkned. & his wife fading in death
They stood before their once delightful palace. & thus the Voice
Of aged Tiriel. arose. that his sons might hear in their gates

Accursed race of Tiriel. behold your [*aged*] father
Come forth & look on her that bore you. come you accursed sons.
In my weak [*aged*] arms. I here have borne your dying mother
Come forth sons of the Curse come forth. see the death of Myratana

His sons ran from their gates. & saw their aged parents stand
And thus the eldest son of Tiriel raisd his mighty voice

* All bracketed italicized words and lines represent Blake's deletions. Question marks
indicate dubious readings.

131

Old man unworthy to be calld. the father of Tiriels race
For evry one of those thy wrinkles. each of those grey hairs
Are cruel as death. & as obdurate as the devouring pit
Why should thy sons care for thy curses thou accursed man
Were we not slaves till we rebeld. Who cares for Tiriels curse
His blessing was a cruel curse. His curse may be a blessing

He ceast the aged man raisd up his right hand to the heavens
His left supported Myratana [?*living*] [?*shriecking*] shrinking in pangs of death
The orbs of his large eyes he opend. & thus his voice went forth

Serpents not sons. wreathing around the bones of Tiriel
Ye worms of death feasting upon your aged parents flesh
Listen & hear your mothers groans. No more accursed Sons
She bears. she groans not at the birth of Heuxos or Yuva
These are the groans of death ye serpents These are the groans of death
Nourishd with milk ye serpents. nourishd with mothers tears & cares
Look at my eyes blind as the orbless scull among the stones
Look at my bald head. Hark listen ye serpents [?*all*] listen
What Myratana. What my wife. O Soul O Spirit O fire
What Myratana. art thou dead. Look here ye serpents look
The serpents sprung from her own bowels have draind her dry as this
Curse on your [letter deleted] ruthless heads. for I will bury her even here

So saying he began to dig a grave with his aged hands
But Heuxos calld a son of Zazel. to [letter deleted] dig their mother a grave

Old cruelty desist & let us dig a grave for thee
Thou hast refusd our charity thou hast refusd our food
Thou hast refusd our clothes our beds our houses for thy dwelling
Chusing to wander like a Son of Zazel in the rocks
Why dost thou curse. is not the curse now come upon your head
Was it not you enslavd the sons of Zazel. & they have cursd
And now you feel it. Dig a grave & let us bury our mother

There take the body. cursed sons. & may the heavens rain wrath
As thick as northern fogs. around your gates. to choke you up
That you may lie as now your mother lies. like dogs. cast out
The stink. of your dead carcases. annoying man & beast
Till your white bones are bleachd with age for a memorial.
No your remembrance shall perish. for when your carcases
Lie stinking on the earth. the buriers shall arise from the east
And. not a bone of all the sons of Tiriel remain
Bury your mother but you cannot bury the curse of Tiriel

He ceast & darkling oer the mountains sought his pathless way

2

He wanderd day & night to him both day & night were dark
The sun he felt but the bright moon was now a useless globe
Oer mountains & thro vales of woe. the blind & aged man
Wanderd till he that leadeth all. led him to the vales of Har

And Har & Heva like two children sat beneath the Oak
Mnetha now aged waited on them. & brought them food & clothing
But they were as the shadow of Har. & as the years forgotten
Playing with flowers. & running after birds they spent the day
And in the night like infants slept delighted with infant dreams

Soon as the blind wanderer enterd the pleasant gardens of Har
[*The aged father & mother saw him as they sat at play*]
They ran weeping like frighted infants for refuge in Mnethas arms
The blind man felt his way & cried peace to these open doors
Let no one fear for poor blind Tiriel hurts none but himself
Tell me O friends where am I now. & in what pleasant place

This is the valley of Har said Mnetha & this the tent of Har
Who art thou poor blind man. that takest the name of Tiriel on thee
Tiriel is king of all the west. who art thou I am Mnetha
And this is Har & Heva. trembling like infants by my side

I know Tiriel is king of the west & there he lives in joy
No matter who I am O Mnetha. if thou hast any food
Give it me. for I cannot stay my journey is far from hence

Then Har said O my mother Mnetha venture not so near him
For he is the king of rotten wood & of the bones of death
He wanders. without eyes. & passes thro thick walls & doors
Thou shalt not smite my mother Mnetha O thou eyeless man

[*O venerable O most piteous O most woeful day*]
A wanderer. I beg for food. you see I cannot weep
[*But I can kneel down at your door. I am a harmless man*]
I cast away my staff the kind companion of my travel
And I kneel down that you may see I am a harmless man

He kneeled down & Mnetha said Come Har & Heva rise
He is an innocent old man & hungry with his travel

133

Then Har arose & laid his hand upon old Tiriels head

God bless [letter deleted] thy poor bald pate. God bless. thy hollow winking eyes
God bless thy shriveld beard. God. bless. thy many [*?wrik*] wrinkled forehead
Thou hast no teeth old man & thus I kiss thy sleek bald head
Heva come kiss his bald head for he will not hurt us Heva

Then Heva came & took old Tiriel in her mothers arms

Bless thy poor eyes old man. & bless the old father of Tiriel
Thou art my Tiriels old father. I know thee thro thy wrinkles
Because thou smellest. like the figtree. thou smellest like ripe figs
How didst thou lose thy eyes old Tiriel. bless thy wrinkled face

[*The aged Tiriel could not speak his heart was full of grief*
He strove against his rising passions. but still he could not speak]

Mnetha said come in aged wanderer tell us of thy name
Why shouldest thou conceal thyself from those of thine own flesh

I am not of this region. said Tiriel dissemblingly
[*Fearing to tell them who he was. because of the weakness of Har*]
I am an aged wanderer once father of a race
Far in the north. but they were wicked & were all destroyd
And I their father sent an outcast. I have told you all
Ask me no more I pray for grief hath seald my precious sight

O Lord said Mnetha how I tremble are there then [letter deleted] more people
More human creatures on this earth beside the sons of Har

No more said Tiriel but I remain on all this globe
And I remain an outcast. hast thou any thing to drink

Then Mnetha gave him milk & fruits. & they sat down together

3

They sat & eat & Har & Heva smild on Tiriel

Thou art a very old old man but I am older than thou
How came thine hair to leave thy forehead how came thy face so brown
My hair is very long my beard. doth cover all my breast
God bless thy piteous face. to count the wrinkles in thy face
Would puzzle [*Har*] Mnetha. bless thy face for thou art Tiriel

TIRIEL AND THE STATE OF EXPERIENCE

[*Tiriel could scarce dissemble more & his tongue could scarce refrain*
But still he feard that Har & Heva would die of joy & grief.]

Tiriel I never saw but once I sat with him & eat
He was as chearful as a prince & gave me entertainment
But long I staid not at his palace for I am forcd to wander

What wilt thou leave us too said Heva thou shalt not leave us too
For we have many sports to shew thee & many songs to sing
And after dinner we will walk into the cage of Har
And thou shalt help us to catch birds. & gather them ripe cherries
Then let thy name be Tiriel & never leave us more

If thou dost go said Har I wish thine eyes may see thy folly
My sons have left me did thine leave thee O twas very cruel

No venerable man said Tiriel ask me not such things
For thou dost make my heart to bleed my sons were not like thine
But worse O never ask me more or I must flee away

Thou shalt not go said Heva till thou hast seen our singing birds
And [*He*] heard Har sing in the great cage & slept upon our fleeces
Go not for thou art so like Tiriel. that I love thine head
Tho it is wrinkled like the earth parchd with the summer heat

Then Tiriel rose up from the seat & said god bless these tents
[*God bless my benefactors. for I cannot tarry longer*]
My Journey is oer rocks & mountains. not in pleasant vales
I must not sleep nor rest because of madness & dismay

[*Then Mnetha led him to the door & gave to him his staff*
And Har & Heva stood & watchd him till he enterd the wood
And then they went & wept to Mnetha but they soon forgot their tears]

[*?But*] And Mnetha said Thou must not go to wander dark. alone
But dwell with us & let us be to thee instead of eyes
And I will bring thee food old man. till death shall call thee hence

Then Tiriel frownd & answerd. Did I not command you saying
Madness & deep dismay possess the heart of the blind man
The wanderer who [*?runs*] seeks the woods leaning upon his staff

Then Mnetha trembling at his frowns led him to the tent door
And gave to him his staff & blest him. he went on his way

But Har & Heva stood & watchd him till he enterd the wood
And then they went & wept to Mnetha. but they soon forgot their tears

4

Over the weary hills the blind man took his lonely way
To him the day & night alike was dark & desolate
But far he had not gone when Ijim from his woods come down
Met him at entrance of the forest in a dark & lonely way

Who art thou Eyeless wretch that thus obstructst the lions path
Ijim shall rend thy feeble joints thou tempter of dark Ijim
Thou hast the form of Tiriel but I know thee well enough
Stand from my path foul fiend is this the last of thy deceits
To be a hypocrite & stand in shape of a blind beggar

The blind man heard his brothers voice & kneeld down on his knee

O brother Ijim if it is thy voice that speaks to me
Smite not thy brother Tiriel tho weary of his life
My sons have smitten me already. and if thou smitest me
The curse that rolls over their heads will rest itself on thine
Tis now seven years Since in my palace I beheld thy face
[In margin: *Seven years of sorrow then the curse of Zazel*]

Come thou dark fiend I dare thy cunning know that Ijim scorns
To smite the in the form of helpless age & eyeless policy
Rise up for I discern thee & I dare thy eloquent tongue
Come I will lead thee on thy way & use thee as a scoff

O Brother Ijim thou beholdest wretched Tiriel
Kiss me my brother & then leave me to wander desolate

No artful fiend. but I will lead thee dost thou want to go
Reply not lest I bind thee with the green flags of the brook
Ay now thou art discoverd I will use thee like a slave

When Tiriel heard the words of Ijim he sought not to reply
He knew twas vain for Ijims words were as the voice of Fate

And they went on together over hills thro woody dales
Blind to the pleasures of the sight & deaf to warbling birds
All day they walkd & all the night beneath the pleasant Moon
Westwardly journeying till Tiriel grew weary with his travel

136

O Ijim I am faint & weary for my knees forbid
To bear me further. urge me not lest I should die with travel
A little rest I crave a little water from a brook
Or I shall soon discover that I am a mortal man
And you will lose your once lovd Tiriel alas how faint I am

Impudent fiend said Ijim hold thy glib & eloquent tongue
Tiriel is a king. & thou the tempter of dark Ijim
Drink of this running brook. & I will bear thee on my shoulders

He drank & Ijim raisd him up & bore him on his shoulders
All day he bore him & when evening drew her solemn curtain
Enterd the gates of Tiriels palace. & stood & calld aloud

Heuxos come forth I here have brought the fiend that troubles Ijim
Look knowst thou aught of this grey beard. or of these blinded eyes

Heuxos & Lotho ran forth at the sound of Ijims voice
And saw their aged father borne upon his mighty shoulders
Their eloquent tongues were dumb & sweat stood on their trembling limbs
They knew twas vain to strive with Ijim they bowd & silent stood

What Heuxos call thy father for I [?*must*] mean to sport to night
This is the hypocrite that sometimes roars a dreadful lion
Then I have [*rend*] rent his limbs & left him rotting on the forest
For birds to eat but I have scarce departed from the place
But like a tyger he would come & so I rent him too
Then like a river he would seek to drown me in his waves
But soon I buffetted the torrent anon like to a cloud
Fraught with the swords of lightning. but I bravd the vengeance too
Then he would creep like a bright serpent till around my neck
While I was Sleeping he would twine I squeezd his poisnous soul
Then like a toad or like a newt. would whisper in my ears
Or like a rock stood in my way. or like a poisnous shrub
At last I caught him in the form of Tiriel blind & old
And so Ill keep him fetch your father fetch forth Myratana

They stood confounded. and Thus Tiriel raisd his silver voice

Serpents not sons [*you see ?and ?know your father*] why do you stand fetch
    hither Tiriel
Fetch hither Myratana & delight yourselves with scoffs
For poor blind Tiriel is returnd & this much injurd head
Is ready for your bitter taunts. [letter deleted] come forth sons of the curse

Mean time the other sons of Tiriel ran around their father
Confounded at the terrible strength of Ijim they knew twas vain
Both spear & shield were useless & the coat of iron mail
When Ijim stretchd his mighty arm. the arrow from his limbs
Rebounded & the piercing sword broke on his naked [*limbs*] flesh

[*Then Ijim said Lotho. Clithyma. Makuth fetch your father*
Why do you stand confounded thus. Heuxos why art thou silent

O noble Ijim thou hast brought our father to [*the gates*] *our eyes*
That we may tremble & repent before thy mighty knees
O we are but the slaves of Fortune. & that most cruel man
Desires our deaths. O Ijim [*?tis ?one ?whose aged tongue*]
[*Decieve the noble &*] *if the eloquent voice of Tiriel*
Hath worked our ruin we submit nor strive against stern fate

He spoke & kneeld upon his knee. Then Ijim on the pavement
Set aged Tiriel. in deep thought whether these things were so]

Then is it true Heuxos that thou hast turnd thy aged parent
To be the sport of wintry winds. (said Ijim) is this true
It is a lie & I am [*?torn ?like*] like the tree torn by the wind
Thou eyeless fiend. & you dissemblers. Is this Tiriels house
It is as false & [*matha*] Matha. & as dark as vacant Orcus
Escape ye fiends for Ijim will not lift his hand against ye

So saying. Ijim gloomy turnd his back & silent sought
The [*gloom*] secret forests & all night wanderd in desolate ways

5

And aged Tiriel stood & said where does the thunder sleep
Where doth he hide his terrible head & his swift & fiery daughters
Where do they shroud their fiery wings & the terrors of their hair
Earth thus I stamp thy bosom rouse the earthquake from his den
[*Display thy*] To raise his dark & burning visage thro the cleaving [*?world*]
   ground
To thrust these towers with his shoulders. let his fiery dogs
Rise from the center belching flames & roarings. dark smoke
Where art thou Pestilence that bathest in fogs & standing lakes
Rise up thy sluggish limbs. & let the loathsomest of poisons
Drop from thy garments as thou walkest. wrapt in yellow clouds
Here take thy seat. in this wide court. let it be strown with dead
And sit & smile upon these cursed sons of Tiriel
Thunder & fire & pestilence. here you not Tiriels curse

He ceast the heavy clouds confusd rolld round the lofty towers
Discharging their enormous voices. at the fathers curse
The earth trembled fires belched from the yawning clefts
And when the shaking ceast a fog possest the accursed clime

The cry was great in Tiriels palace his five daughters ran
And caught him by the garments weeping with cries of bitter woe

Aye now you feel the curse you cry. but may all ears be deaf
As Tiriels & all eyes as blind as Tiriels to your woes
May never stars shine on your roofs may never [?slee] sun nor moon
Visit you but eternal fogs hover around your walls
[?Hili]* Hela my youngest daughter you shall lead me from this place
And let the curse fall on the rest & wrap them up together

He ceast & [?Hili] Hela led her father from the noisom place
In haste they fled while all the sons & daughters of Tiriel
Chaind in thick darkness utterd cries of mourning all the night
And in the morning Lo an hundred men in ghastly death
The four daughters [& all the children in their silent beds] [deletion] stretchd
    on the marble pavement silent all
[And] falln by the pestilence the rest moped round in [ghastly fea] guilty fears
And all the children in their beds were cut off in one night
Thirty of Tiriels sons remaind. to wither in the palace
Desolate. Loathed. Dumb [Con] Astonishd waiting for black death

6

And [?Hili] Hela led her father thro the silent of the night
Astonishd silent. till the morning beams began to spring

Now [?Hili] Hela I can go with pleasure & dwell with Har & Heva
Now that the curse shall clean devour all those guilty sons
This is the right & ready way I know it by the sound
That our feet make. Remember [?Hili] Hela I have savd thee from death
Then be obedient to thy father for the curse is taken off thee
I dwelt with Myratana five years in the desolate rock
And all that time we waited for the fire to fall from heaven
Or for the torrents of the sea to overwhelm you all
But now my wife is dead & all the time of grace is past
You see the parents curse. Now lead me where I have commanded

O Leagued with evil spirits thou accursed man of sin
True I was born thy [child] slave who askd thee to save me from death—
Twas for thy self thou cruel man because thou wantest eyes

* Both vowels of this name are written over to produce "Hela." "Hili" is conjectural,
but in all cases a dot is visible over the second vowel.

True Hela this is the desert of all those cruel ones
Is Tiriel cruel look. his daughter & his youngest daughter
Laughs at affection glories in rebellion. scoffs at Love:—
I have not eat these two days lead me to Har & Hevas tent
Or I will wrap the up in such a terrible fathers curse
That thou shalt feel worms in thy marrow creeping thro thy bones
Yet thou shalt lead me. Lead me I command to Har & Heva

O cruel O destroyer O consumer. O avenger
To Har & Heva I will lead thee then would that they would curse
Then would they curse as thou hast cursed but they are not like thee
O they are holy. & forgiving filld with loving mercy
Forgetting the offences of their most rebellious children
Or else thou wouldest not have livd to curse thy helpless children

Look on my eyes Hela & see for thou hast eyes to see
The tears swell from my stony fountains. wherefore do I weep
Wherefore from my blind orbs art thou not siezd with poisnous stings
Laugh serpent youngest venomous reptile of the flesh of Tiriel
Laugh. for thy father Tiriel shall give the cause to laugh
Unless thou lead me to the tent of Har child of the curse

Silence thy evil tongue thou murderer of thy helpless children
I lead thee to the tent of Har not that I mind thy curse
But that I feel they will curse thee & hang upon thy bones
Fell shaking agonies. & in each wrinkle of that face
Plant worms of death to feast upon the tongue of terrible curses

Hela my daughter listen. thou [word deleted] art the daughter of Tiriel
Thy father calls. Thy father lifts his hand unto the [air] heavens
For thou hast laughed at my tears. & curst thy aged father
Let snakes rise from thy bedded locks & laugh among thy curls

He ceast her dark hair upright stood while snakes infolded round
Her madding brows. her shrieks apalld the soul of Tiriel

What have I done Hela my daughter fearst thou now the curse
Or wherefore dost thou cry Ah wretch to curse thy aged father
Lead me to Har & Heva & the curse of Tiriel
Shall [fall] fail. If thou refuse howl in the desolate mountains

7

She howling led him over mountains & thro frighted vales
Till to the caves of Zazel they approachd at even tide

Forth from their caves [*the sons of Zazel*] old Zazel & his sons ran. [&] when they saw
Their tyrant prince blind & his daughter howling & leading him

They laughd & mocked some threw dirt & stones as they passd by
But when Tiriel turnd around & raisd his awful voice
[*They*] Some fled away [& *hid themselves*] but [*some*] [?*Za*] Zazel stood still & thus [?*scoffing*] begun

Bald tyrant. wrinkled cunning [*wretch*] listen to Zazels chains
Twas thou that chaind thy brother Zazel where are now thine eyes
Shout beautiful daughter of Tiriel. thou singest a sweet song
Where are you going. come & eat some roots & drink some water
Thy crown is bald old man. the sun will dry thy brains away
And thou wilt be as foolish as thy foolish brother Zazel

The blind man heard. & smote his breast & trembling passed on
They threw dirt after them. till to the covert of a wood
[*They*] The howling maiden led her father where wild beasts resort
Hoping to end her [*life*] woes. but from her cries the tygers fled
All night they wanderd thro the wood & when the sun arose
They enterd on the mountains of Har at [*n*] Noon the happy tents
Were frighted by the dismal cries of Hela on the mountains

But Har & Heva slept fearless as babes. on loving breasts
Mnetha awoke she ran & stood at the tent door [*in*] & saw
The aged wanderer led towards the tents she took her bow
And chose her arrows then advancd to meet the terrible pair

8

And Mnetha hasted & met them at the gate of the lower garden

Stand still or from my bow recieve a sharp & winged death

Then Tiriel stood. saying what soft voice threatens such bitter things
Lead me to Har & Heva I am Tiriel King of the west

[The rest of the MS. is written in the same hand, but with a different pen]
And Mnetha led them to the tent of Har. and Har & Heva
Ran to the door. when Tiriel felt the ankles of aged Har
He said. O weak mistaken father of a lawless race
Thy laws O Har & Tiriels wisdom end together in a curse
[*Thy God of love thy heaven of joy*]
Why is one law given to the lion & the [*Pa*] patient Ox

[*Dost thou not see that men cannot be formed all alike*
Some nostrild wide breathing out blood. Some close shut up
In silent deceit. poisons inhaling from the morning rose
With daggers hid beneath their lips & poison in their tongue
Or eyed with little sparks of Hell or with infernal brands
Flinging flames of discontent & plagues of dark despair
Or those whose mouths are graves whose teeth the gates of eternal death
Can wisdom be put in a silver rod or love in a golden bowl
Is the son of a king warmed without wool or does he cry with a voice
Of thunder does he look upon the sun & laugh or stretch
His little hands into the depths of the sea, to bring forth
The deadly cunning of the [*scaly tribe*] *flatterer & spread it to the morning*]
And why men bound beneath the heavens in a reptile form
A worm of sixty winters creeping on the dusky ground
The child springs from the womb. the father ready stands to form
The infant head while the mother idle plays with her dog on her couch
The young bosom is cold for lack of mothers nourishment & milk
Is cut off from the weeping mouth with difficulty & pain
The little lids are lifted & the little nostrils opend
The father forms a whip to rouze the sluggish senses to act
And scourges off all youthful fancies from the new-born man
Then walks the weak infant in sorrow compelld to number footsteps
Upon the sand. &c
And when the [*foolish ?crawling*] drone has reachd his crawling length
Black berries appear that poison all around him. Such [*is*] was Tiriel
[*Hypocrisy the idiots wisdom & the wise mans folly*]
Compelld to pray repugnant & to humble the immortal spirit
Till I am subtil as a serpent in a paradise
Consuming all both flowers & fruits insects & warbling birds
And now my paradise is falln & a drear sandy plain
Returns my thirsty hissings in a curse on thee O Har
Mistaken father of a lawless race my voice is past

He ceast outstretchd at Har & Hevas feet in awful death

I

The *Songs of Innocence* and *Songs of Experience* are so commonly
referred to as a unit that we seldom think, today, of the four or five
years which elapsed between the etching of the two books. In that
interval, among other things Blake wrote *Tiriel*. It is a difficult poem
and a poor one, but an understanding of it seems to me essential to an
understanding of Blake's concept of the state of experience—and of

the *Songs of Experience.* Though it is true that vague notions of a non-innocence had constantly insinuated themselves into Blake's thought and poetry, from the *Poetical Sketches* on, nowhere had he systematized those notions before 1789, when *Tiriel* was probably written. There are villains in the early poems, in *To Winter, Fair Elenor, Gwin, King of Norway,* and others, but most of them are conventional tyrants, only distantly related to the father-priest-king of the state and songs of experience, or to Urizen of the prophetic books. After etching the *Songs of Innocence,* however, Blake was able to turn his full attention to the problem of what form this non-innocence was to take. Though it is probable that some of the songs of experience were composed before 1793, when they were advertised for sale, it is far from certain that before or during his writing of *Songs of Innocence* another song series occurred to Blake as the best way to dramatize non-innocence. With help from the Elizabethans and the eighteenth century he had molded the lyric into an ideal vehicle for the Piper: the songs could make one dance and laugh and sometimes weep for a lost moment. But could they strike terror into the human heart? Could the lyric form register the imprint of mind-forged manacles and the tyrant's whip? It is unlikely that such questions occurred to Blake at this time; there were too many others that had to be answered first: What is the earthly father? Where does he come from and where does he go? What happens to the child after innocence? Does he merely grow up, grow old, and die? What happens to the mother of innocence? Why is the night so terrible that the mother shields her child from it even while he sleeps? What happens to innocence when the innocent children leave it? Or suppose they stay, what then? These questions and others like them taxed Blake's brain from 1789, probably even before, until sometime in 1793. And he wrote of them all.

Even so, for Blake, a furious worker when inspired, the year 1789-90 probably held few fears, few ominous complications, except that Swedenborg's influence was reaching its height and Lavater made him uneasy as well as pleased with himself.[1] Avidly reading, strenuously thinking and annotating, and diligently writing, Blake produced a body of work for the year that reveals the inevitable confusion of false starts and hesitancies as well as the remarkable resolution of his mind. Groping for the form that eluded him until about 1793, Blake nevertheless created a framework within which that form could be born. He also produced a stumbling but no doubt air-clearing experiment (*Tiriel²*), a beautifully conceived dramatic poem (*Thel*), a fascinating diatribe (*The Marriage of Heaven and Hell*), a lusty but premature attempt at regeneration before experience fully wreaked its havoc on his pages (*Visions of the Daughters of Albion*), a taunting fragment (*The French Revolution*), and a confused revolutionary document (*America*). Of these the most important for our purposes are *Tiriel* and *The Marriage,* the former providing the first real expository key to Blake's evolving concept of experience, the second an essay of rebellion against the adulteration of this concept as well as a paradoxically sound basis for its justification.

To include *Tiriel* among the prophetic books, as most critics do, is to ignore the significance of its contemporaneousness with the *Songs of Innocence* and its suggestion of experience as a contrary state. In the *Songs of Innocence* Blake avoided the person of the earthly father; reigning was the earthly mother, at once protectress and teacher of the thoughtless child. On the basis of the *Songs of Innocence* alone, however, it is difficult to attach any particular importance to the father's absence. It is unusual, perhaps, but not significant. Yet when one reads *Tiriel,* realizing that it was composed at about the same time as *Songs of Innocence,* Blake's curiously vehement insistence on the hypocrisy and villainy of the father-king does seem strange in view of his absence from the state of innocence. A look at Blake's annotations to Lavater's *Aphorisms* can help us here. Written about 1789, they corroborate much of Blake's concept of the state of innocence, but they also indicate unequivocally that the hypocrite was fast becoming the Lucifer of his cosmos. For example, Lavater wrote: "I know not which of these two I should wish to avoid most; the scoffer at virtue and religion, who, with heartless villainy, butchers innocence and truth; *or the pietist, who crawls, groans, blubbers, and secretly says to gold, thou art* my hope! and to his belly, thou art my god!" (Lavater's italics.) Blake's comment is, "I hate crawlers" (67). In another marginal note he calls them "mimickers of humility & love" (68). He cries "Bravo!" to Lavater's admonition to "fear the boisterous savage of passion less than the sedate grin of villainy" (68); and he substitutes "hypocrite" for "fanatic" in Lavater's sentence: "If you see one cold and vehement at the same

time, set him down for a fanatic" (73). Finally Blake applauds Lavater's warning: "The frigid smiler, crawling, indiscreet, obtrusive, brazen-
faced, is a scorpion whip of destiny—avoid him!" (79) The general
tenor of all of Blake's comments on Lavater reveals his serious concern
over such universal antipodes as true and false wisdom, honesty and
knavery, openness and cunning, energy and restraint, order and dis-
order; and the first terms of these pairs he illustrated clearly in *Songs
of Innocence*. What, then, would be more logical than to organize the
second terms into the opposite of innocence, or at least to explore on
paper the ramifications and complexities of Lavater's fanatical dis-
sembler? "Without contraries is no progression," Blake wrote; and
with the child, the Piper, and the mother in mind as the major symbols
of innocence, Blake's poetic instinct led him quickly toward an anthro-
pomorphic concept of non-innocence, Tiriel, the earthly father whose
hypocrisy is "the idiots wisdom & the wise mans folly" (deleted line in
Tiriel).

The opening lines of *Tiriel*, though inept poetry,[3] are an admirable
introduction to the doctrinal complexities of the poem. Myratana
is a queen, of course, but more important she is also a mother. And
unlike the mothers in *Innocence* she is dying. By thus eliminating this
great source of comfort and protection, Blake seems to suggest that
once the end of innocence is reached the mother has no further hold
over the child. In effect her function expires.[4] On the other hand,
the earthly father (Tiriel), who has no function in innocence, is here
dominant. The tremendous difference in their treatment of the child
is partly due to the nature of the change in the child himself. In
innocence he is selfish (without knowing it), instinctive, uninhibited,
and free; a mother's love and protection insures this freedom as long
as possible. But when the child begins to think, to reason, to identify
himself as an individual separate from others and from the divine, and
with a will of his own (that is, when unconscious selfhood becomes
conscious), protection and love are discarded and the father exerts his
power to control the child, to bind him with the man-made laws,
restrictions, duties, and morals of this world. And the state of experience
is begun. This distinction can be made most clear by recalling the child
of *Infant Joy* and comparing him to the miniature adult created by
Blake in *Infant Sorrow*, a song of experience. The most important part

of the distinction is that the child of *Infant Sorrow* can think, can come to a decision, and can act upon that decision:

> Bound and weary I thought best
> To sulk upon my mothers breast.

In the same way Tiriel's sons have rebelled (from both mother and father) and he curses them for their disobedience. Significantly Tiriel is well aware of the mother's earlier role ("Nourishd with milk ye serpents. nourishd with mothers tears & cares"), and, demonstrating his hypocrisy, he attempts to use the mother-child relationship to pressure his rebelling sons into subservience to him (lines 6-23). He concludes this tirade with a line that admirably sums up the relative positions of father, mother, and children as I have suggested them: "Bury your mother but you cannot bury the curse of Tiriel."

There is another important difference between this passage and the *Songs of Innocence*: in the latter the children are very young, occasionally infants, while in *Tiriel* the sons and daughters are young adults who have sloughed off the care of their mother and achieved their own identities. This is as it should be, as I pointed out above, but at this point Blake was not fully convinced that the small children of innocence, as symbols of that state, had any place in the poetry of non-innocence. Perhaps he believed that their coexistence with the father-hypocrite would be anomalous in view of their earlier roles: certainly he did not foresee clearly that inherent in that anomaly was the terrible power of *London, Holy Thursday, Nurses Song, Infant Sorrow, A Little Boy Lost,* and other songs of experience.

Finally, in addition to presenting the essence of the state of experience in these opening lines, Blake also suggests in a speech by one of Tiriel's sons the manner of the king-father-hypocrite's ultimate destruction:

> Why dost thou curse. is not the curse now come upon your head
> Was it not you enslavd the sons of Zazel. & they have cursd
> And now you feel it. . . .[5]

To oppose this law and curse, the growing child who enters the state of experience brings with him the legacy of innocence—unbridled action and energy—which can break the bonds created by man's mind, society, and institutionalized religion. "Damn. braces: Bless relaxes," wrote Blake in *The Marriage;* "Sooner murder an infant in its cradle than nurse unacted desires." But along with the desires and energy of innocence comes the self, a product of the same thought processes necessary to intellectual, moral, and spiritual growth; incognito in innocence, unrecognized and unthought of by the child, this self assumes a body, so to speak, with the first dawning of thought and becomes Blake's greatest evil. And though it can be destroyed by "an improvement of sensual enjoyment," self plus energy shackled by the moral law produces the tyrant, the libertine, the devourer. In *Tiriel* he is the king and father. To achieve the innocence of wisdom, Tiriel's children *must* rebel against their father or, to change the image, they must find their way through the terrible night of experience against which their mother had protected them. To do this, they must see at the heart of the father-hypocrite the same error that exists in their own souls—selfhood; they must free themselves from it and acknowledge once again brotherhood with the human form divine; they must temper their newly acquired thought with the affection of innocence; and they must become "prolific" as well as "devourer." Then an Eden finer than all of the ignorant innocence of childhood will open up to them.

In 1789, however, Blake probably had not yet developed fully his concept of Eden; his mind was too full of experience. Partly because of this, Tiriel is one of Blake's most complex characters, a combination of Lear, Oedipus, and Tamburlaine with few of their finer qualities.[6] His initial appeal to his rebellious sons bristles with the authority they have flouted, but it is followed by the more eloquent appeal to pity for their dying mother. Her blood, Tiriel feels, is on their hands because of their rebellion; his curse he will not retract, for with it he hopes to win back the "once delightful palace" and the domination of his sons. But Blake's irony must not be lost. It is Tiriel's tyranny that has prompted the rebellion; the blood drips from his fingers, but his eyes are blinded to all save his crown and sceptre, which have never been thrown down. Under the impression that he has given his sons everything, Tiriel has in fact woven a net of worldly values and, under the guise of love, snared in it the hapless human race (his sons and daughters).[7] When the net is sundered, his self-conceived, self-built, self-mastered universe begins to crumble, and he curses the dimly enlightened agents of that destruction.[8]

Despite Tiriel's curses his sons offer him sanctuary, but since his pride cannot allow him to accept it he is "forced" to wander along a "pathless way":

> He wanderd day & night to him both day & night were dark
> The sun he felt but the bright moon was now a useless globe.

"Wandering is essentially mortal; it corresponds to error," wrote Ellis and Yeats,[9] and Beulah, the moony protectress of the innocent child, cannot help Tiriel find the way out of the night of error and selfhood. He is warmed and comforted by the heat of the sun but blinded by his own selfhood to its light. Then a curious thing occurs: Tiriel "Wanderd till he that leadeth all. led him to the vales of Har." Just as the little boy in *Songs of Innocence* was lost momentarily and then found by his *spiritual* father, so here Tiriel, the *earthly* father, is lost and found. Again Blake's irony should be made clear. Shorn of authority (at least for all practical purposes), Tiriel cannot remain in experience; on the other hand he cannot return to innocence either (having once left one can never return). Blake's apparent confusion here is, in reality, his way of introducing the heart of his concept of experience.

Har and Heva, as we learn later in the poem, are the parents of Tiriel. They have molded him in their own image; they have imbued him with a law (the final curse) that he visits upon his sons in turn, and that will come full circle at the end of the poem. The final tragedy, then, lies with the parents, the authors of the law and curse. All error is created, said Blake, and Tiriel, once created, accepted his own creation as good. He knew no other way, for in effect he was born blind. Har and Heva are the eternal parents who, according to Blake's system, were originally androgynous in the state of Eden, but separated in experience into "spectre" and "emanation." To reachieve the primal unity both must participate in an act in which both give, both receive, both devour and yet both are prolific. The result of such a union is creation, the child of innocence. However, when Har (the rational self) predominates, the act becomes a rape and a bastard is produced—like Blake's "infant sorrow," like Tiriel. In *Tiriel,* then, Har and Heva, terrified by their progeny, have fled back in search of the innocence they have lost. Blake described that flight and its result in *The Song of Los:*

... that dread day when Har and Heva fled
Because their brethren & sisters liv'd in War & Lust;
And as they fled they shrunk
Into two narrow doleful forms
Creeping in reptile flesh upon
The bosom of the ground;
And all the vast of Nature shrunk
Before their shrunken eyes.

Thus the terrible race of Los & Enitharmon gave
Laws & Religions to the sons of Har, binding them more
And more to Earth, closing and restraining,
Till a Philosophy of Five Senses was complete. (246)

Thus Har's and Heva's loss is irrevocable. Only the mother of
memory remains, Mnetha (who may be related to mother earth, the
prototype of the earthly mother of innocence, as *The Song of Los*
suggests). Mnetha waits on Har and Heva, brings them food and
clothing, and like all children they live off her prolific abundance. This
is precisely the existence that Tiriel's sons and daughters escape by their
revolt. In contrast to Har's and Heva's weak acceptance of borrowed
life, Tiriel's children offer him such life. And Tiriel's refusal of the
offer is as wrong as Har's and Heva's acceptance of it. Acceptance
by Tiriel would be a surrender of his authority, a step toward realizing
the error in his own make-up; refusal by Har and Heva would constitute a step toward self-assertion and ultimate wisdom. Since one cannot
escape the existence one has created, Har and Heva live in fear in the
sham, infantile pleasantness of their valley, where the law they have
turned their backs upon is not abrogated but thrives in withering,
self-consuming fear of its own creation, Tiriel.

Tiriel's return to "innocence," then, is doubly damnable. Just as
Har and Heva cling to Mnetha for protection, Tiriel has, in effect, never
broken out of the mold of his father. Yet, "He that leadeth all" leads
him back to the architect of that mold with the opportunity now
to deny the mold: it is never too late according to Blake. But Tiriel,
of course, cannot apprehend the divine guidance because of his blindness to all save his mundane existence and the failure of his god,

power. Hence his "pathless" search in the forests of night, seeking to grasp the infinite (godhood) by means of the finite (sense alone).

But let us examine this "innocence" which Blake has conceived in such detail and with such terrible meaning. The first few lines are admirably rich in allusion:

> And Har & Heva like two children sat beneath the Oak
> Mnetha now aged waited on them. & brought them food & clothing
> But they were as the shadow of Har. & as the years forgotten
> Playing with flowers. & running after birds they spent the day
> And in the night like infants slept delighted with infant dreams.

The picture is a duplicate of *The Ecchoing Green* with significant modifications. Har and Heva grotesquely ape the innocents who sported on the green, but when the heat of the sun becomes too hot to bear, they seek the oak tree's shade like Old John or the mother of the black boy. Not having learned, like the black boy did, "to bear the beams of love," they are "as the shadow of Har." They may play with flowers, but they vainly chase the elusive bird with whom the innocents are identified. Their dreams are infant dreams, but in them is no angel with a bright key to free them from their soot-covered bodies (as in *The Chimney Sweeper*). Rooted to the earth, confined by its morality, and circumscribed by its fear, their pretense of peace is shattered by the realization that fear lives in their hearts. It is a deeply symbolic act on their part, seeking the mother's lap with the approach of blind Tiriel, for experience reveals itself to them anew despite the fact that they have "escaped" it. As Har says,

> O my mother Mnetha venture not so near him
> For he is the king of rotten wood & of the bones of death
> He wanders. without eyes. & passes thro thick walls & doors.

Har, the not-so-innocent "child," recognizes Tiriel as the earthly tyrant, the error incarnate which will be the agent of its own destruction, the king of rotten wood which will be consumed because of his total physicality. It is significant, then, that Tiriel asks for relief not for his eyes, his spiritual blindness, but for his gluttonous senses. Beaten and cast out, his essential self reveals itself throughout the poem as the eternal devourer.

Night saw the devourer not only tolerated but welcomed by the guardian angels; the devourer and the devoured both inherit "new worlds." Tiriel, however, reduced now to what would be a pitiable state if he had any of the nobility, the compassion, and the wisdom that comes to Lear in the storm, dissembles and begs and feigns helplessness:

> ... you see I cannot weep
> I cast away my staff the kind companion of my travel
> And I kneel down that you may see I am a harmless man.

To Har and Heva (and to Tiriel himself) Tiriel's inability to weep means little; to the reader it should recall the associative meaning of the intellectual tear of innocence, the all-powerful pity of *The Little Boy Lost,* the human face of *The Divine Image.* Tiriel's plea, however, is not for the divine guidance given the weeping lost boy of innocence; but he will go so far as to give up his staff to "prove" that he is "harmless." With no conception of the divine good of selflessness, the three inhabitants of the vales of Har quickly accept in its place harmlessness as the greatest good. In this way Blake makes it clear that the present condition of Tiriel and the pseudo-peace of the vales are identical: both are governed only by the conventional laws of good and evil which recognize physical harm as the greatest evil. All of the subsequent actions of Har and Heva must be considered in the light of this all-important concept. Heva immediately assumes her role as the comforting mother because now, as Har says with almost imbecilic simplicity, "He will not hurt us Heva." Both "innocents" pity him in turn, but it is the pity of ignorance, bred of circumspection, mistrust, and relief, lacking the spontaneity of love which perceives divinity in the human form. They offer him only the sports of the darkened green which sharply parody the carefree play in innocence.

Tiriel dissembles continually throughout his visit because his hauteur instinctively refuses to acknowledge the failure of the law which puffs it up. Har and Heva, blind to their own error-creation, blandly bless him as someone else. And if for a moment it seems as if they will discover Tiriel's true identity ("bless thy face for thou art Tiriel"), they would pity him only because he has returned as a kind of prodigal who saw the error of his "desertion." Thus Heva says:

Then let thy name be Tiriel & never leave us more

If thou dost go said Har I wish thine eyes may see thy folly
My sons have left me did thine leave thee O twas very cruel.

Tiriel agrees—and paradoxically condemns himself unawares:

No venerable man said Tiriel ask me not such things
For thou dost make my heart to bleed my sons were not like thine
But worse O never ask me more or I must flee away.

Mnetha, as ignorant as Har and Heva but well within her province as
the earthly mother, softly entreats Tiriel as if he were a lost boy of
innocence:

Thou must not go to wander dark. alone
But dwell with us & let us be to thee instead of eyes
And I will bring thee food old man. till death shall call thee hence.

Naturally King Tiriel is not attracted by the idea of a motherly protectress, but, more important, he cannot sleep or rest "because of madness
& dismay." Seeking benightedly for the infinite with only the withered
tools of sensuality can be his only destiny, and his spectrous self punctu-
ates his repulsion from Mnetha's suggestion with an instinctive assertion
of authority:

Did I not command you saying
Madness & deep dismay possess the heart of the blind man
The wanderer who seeks the woods leaning upon his staff.

Mnetha returns his staff; Har and Heva weep—but only momentarily
as, no doubt with a sigh of relief, they return to their puerile existence.

2

The Ijim and Zazel episodes of the poem should be considered together despite the fact that they are not precisely consecutive. Their
significance can be made clearer by referring again to Blake's annotations to Lavater. In several places Blake remarks upon the moralist's
"mistake" in writing "superstition" where he should have written
"hypocrisy." To dramatize this idea and thus to scrutinize more closely

the essentials of experience, Blake poses the meeting of hypocrisy and superstition in the Ijim section.[10] In the Lavater book Blake briefly distinguished between the two, employing superstition, as the world calls it, as the foil: "No man was ever truly superstitious who was not truly religious as far as he knew. True superstition is ignorant honesty & this is beloved of god and man. I do not allow that there is such a thing as superstition taken in the strict sense of the word. A man must first deceive himself before he is thus Superstitious and so he is a hypocrite. Hipocrisy is as distant from superstition as the wolf from the lamb" (75). And in one other annotation Blake wrote: "Superstition has been long a bugbear by reason of its being united with hypocrisy; but let them be fairly seperated & then superstition will be honest feeling, & God, who loves all honest men, will lead the poor enthusiast in the paths of holiness" (85). Ijim obviously is not being led in the paths of holiness; on the contrary, he inhabits the woods of error and experience. Because of his low intellectual state, he has been duped by the manmade god, Tiriel, until he has become bestial, the brute man. This, however, does not deny his honesty, only his mental capacity. Now his chance has come: he is face to face with the very error that plagues his existence and denies him his place in the sun. He realizes his good fortune and moves to act accordingly:

> Stand from my path foul fiend is this the last of thy deceits
> To be a hypocrite & stand in shape of a blind beggar.

But Ijim fails to capitalize on the circumstances. Caught in the web of rational religion—Tiriel's, with Tiriel as god—Ijim tries to seize the "fiend" bodily and expose it before the altar of his true master, who is also Tiriel. No argument can convince him, for to his honest ear the explanations of Tiriel are cunning, deceitful, glib, and eloquent, just as to his honest but corporeal eye Tiriel is a fraud:

> . . . I discern thee & I dare thy eloquent tongue
> Come I will lead thee on thy way & use thee as a scoff.

Thus honesty, helpless in the face of superior wisdom, whether true or false, and not spiritually strong enough to venture forth from the woods of error, resorts to physical force to subdue what can be destroyed only by intellectual effort. In vengeance Ijim makes of Tiriel a scoff, leads him against his will, uses him like "a slave," and then stubbornly refuses to believe his mistake when Tiriel's identity is revealed.

Having chased the false light like the little boy lost and, unlike the boy, caught it, Ijim merely becomes further disillusioned. With his icon smashed, there is nothing left, as he sees it, except to seek "The secret forests & all night . . . [wander] in desolate ways." The ironic parallel to Tiriel's situation is now clear. Ijim, ignorant, experiences the downfall of his god and sees only desolate wandering as his destiny; Tiriel, worldly wise but without divine wisdom, experiences the downfall of his god, self, and must wander in an eternal but vain search for lost authority.

The Zazel episode completes Blake's picture. Zazel is the broken intellect without the physical power to cope, however vainly, with the author of its destruction. With his mind enchained by the manacles of reason, he has in weakness sought the caves of despair; he can throw dirt and stones and mock the law which has produced the fool, but he cannot share in the act of Ijim. Zazel's vengeance is thus more subtle than Ijim's. He sees in Tiriel the image of his former self, slowly being blinded by the too-brilliant sun and suffocating under the pall of rational religion until the mind is destroyed completely:

> Thy crown is bald old man. the sun will dry thy brains away
> And thou wilt be as foolish as thy foolish brother Zazel.

Thus, in a sense the "curses" of Zazel and Ijim join with that of Tiriel himself ultimately to destroy the created error.

After his withering curse upon his sons and daughters, Tiriel feels that he can return to the false innocence of Har and Heva, having regained enough authority to live in peace and in majesty as king of the vales of Har. His intention becomes clearer if we compare his earlier words to Har and Heva and those uttered on his return. Previously, with nothing to guide him in place of his spiritually and physically sightless eyes, Tiriel

> felt his way & cried peace to these open doors
> Let no one fear for poor blind Tiriel hurts none but himself.

Now rejuvenated by his triumph over Ijim and the destruction of his rebellious progeny, and guided by his youngest daughter, Hela,[11] Tiriel enters the scene with customary pomp and circumstance: "Lead me to

Har & Heva I am Tiriel king of the west."[12] But it is not to immediate peace and pleasantness that Tiriel returns. The curse is now coming full circle; error is closing in upon itself.

In perhaps the best poetry of the poem Tiriel blames everything on his father, Har, the "weak mistaken father of a lawless race." Stamped with the die of his father's law, Tiriel's wisdom is as that of a fool: "Hypocrisy the idiots wisdom & the wise mans folly. The sexual union of Har and Heva, which could have been the selfless wedding of thought and affection, was instead lustful, selfish, and all-consuming. The mother, in whose lap the child finds refuge and whose breast provides him nourishment, "idle plays with her dog on her couch," indifferent to the greatness of creation. The father, bound by his own mind-forged manacles, extends them to the child's brain and drags him down to be branded with the iron image of self. "Youthful fancies," the free, unbounded joy of innocence, are purged away from him with the whip, and the senses take over unopposed. "Compelld to pray repugnant & to humble the immortal spirit," Tiriel, the devourer, recognizes that he has become

> . . . subtil as a serpent in a paradise
> Consuming all both flowers & fruits insects & warbling birds
> And now my paradise is falln & a drear sandy plain
> Returns my thirsty hissings in a curse on thee O Har.

The created error, the self, seeing the father as the author of that error, brings the curse down on himself and expires. As Blake wrote in *The Four Zoas,* "Attempting to be more than Man We become less" (376).

Tiriel approaches wisdom in this last passage, the very wisdom that must destroy him, for it consists of recognizing and thus annihilating the created error.[13] As Blake wrote later, again in *The Four Zoas:*

> What is the price of Experience? do men buy it for a song?
> Or wisdom for a dance in the street? No, it is bought with the
>   price
> Of all that a man hath, [his house,] his wife, his children.
> Wisdom is sold in the desolate market where none come
>   to buy
> And in the wither'd field where the farmer plows for bread
>   in vain. (290)

Experience cannot be bought by the Piper of innocence and his "songs that all may joy to hear"; contrary to innocence, where existing and being is all, experience demands everything man has. When he has learned this, he will have made the step toward Eden that involves the reciprocal coexistence of devourer and prolific.

Tiriel and Har would give up nothing. They wanted all. The former's insistence on revenge for the existence of an error which he himself constituted leads inevitably to his own destruction. In contrast, Har is content to live with the error of his creation and pretend it is the greatest good. In Blake's eyes both ways are wrong, both self-destructive. Similarly each of the methods of escaping from or annihilating error and authority is ineffective, simply because each is vengeful. The sons and daughters of Tiriel revolt, it is true, and this is good; but their assumption of the very authority, material wealth, and power they deny to Tiriel constitutes an assumption of his error as well. Ijim tries to seize the error bodily and Zazel merely scoffs and scourges in revenge. Har and Heva run from it in terror to a land of make-believe. There is something wrong with the vision of all of them. None sees that Tiriel is merely the outward manifestation of the error in themselves. A candle is merely a momentary expedient to dispel the darkness; if one never raises the window-blinds, the candle soon dies and the sun seems never to rise. Tiriel's children live in the darkened palace, Ijim in the woods, Zazel in a cave, Har and Heva in a valley beneath an oak tree. Till they lift the iron lids of their sluggard intellects, to paraphrase Emerson, they will remain in a darkness impervious to the beams of the sun, self-revelation, and love. In this sense Tiriel's self-destruction, though unintentional, is a far greater act than any performed by the other characters.

3

As an experiment in the ways of the state of experience, then, *Tiriel* is poetically ineffective, crude, even turgid, yet a valuable aid in understanding the working out in Blake's mind of the contrary of innocence. With relief one comes to the finer poetry of *Songs of Experience,* in which the hypocrite-father image is so central—and controlled. But one wonders whether the *Songs* would have been so fine without the fumbling, yet powerful attempt to develop their central image in *Tiriel.*

CHAPTER VIII

A SPIRITUAL FAILURE

ॐ

> I wish that I might be a thinking stone.
> —WALLACE STEVENS, *Le Monocle de Mon Oncle*

THEL'S Motto,

Does the Eagle know what is in the pit?
Or wilt thou go ask the Mole:
Can Wisdom be put in a silver rod?
Or Love in a golden bowl?

THE BOOK of THEL

The daughters of Mne Seraphim led round their sunny flocks,
All but the youngest. she in paleness sought the secret air.
To fade away like morning beauty from her mortal day:
Down by the river of Adona her soft voice is heard:
And thus her gentle lamentation falls like morning dew.

O life of this our spring! why fades the lotus of the water?
Why fade these children of the spring? born but to smile & fall.
Ah! Thel is like a watry bow, and like a parting cloud,
Like a reflection in a glass. like shadows in the water.
Like dreams of infants. like a smile upon an infants face.
Like the doves voice. like transient day, like music in the air;
Ah! gentle may I lay me down and gentle rest my head.
And gentle sleep the sleep of death. and gentle hear the voice
Of him that walketh in the garden in the evening time.

The Lilly of the valley breathing in the humble grass
Answerd the lovely maid and said; I am a watry weed,
And I am very small, and love to dwell in lowly vales;
So weak the gilded butterfly scarce perches on my head
Yet I am visited from heaven and he that smiles on all.
Walks in the valley, and each morn over me spreads his hand
Saying, rejoice thou humble grass, thou new born lilly flower,
Thou gentle maid of silent valleys. and of modest brooks:
For thou shalt be clothed in light, and fed with morning manna:
Till summers heat melts thee beside the fountains and the springs
To flourish in eternal vales: then why should Thel complain,
Why should the mistress of the vales of Har, utter a sigh.

She ceasd & smild in tears, then sat down in her silver shrine.

Thel answerd. O thou little virgin of the peaceful valley.
Giving to those that cannot crave, the voiceless, the o'ertired
Thy breath doth nourish the innocent lamb. he smells thy milky garments.
He crops thy flowers. while thou sittest smiling in his face,
Wiping his mild and meekin mouth from all contagious taints.
Thy wine doth purify the golden honey, thy perfume,
Which thou dost scatter on every little blade of grass that springs
Revives the milked cow, & tames the fire-breathing steed.
But Thel is like a faint cloud kindled at the rising sun;
I vanish from my pearly throne, and who shall find my place.

Queen of the vales the Lilly answerd, ask the tender cloud,
And it shall tell thee why it glitters in the morning sky,
And why it scatters its bright beauty thro' the humid air.
Descend O little cloud & hover before the eyes of Thel.
The Cloud descended, and the Lilly bowd her modest head:
And went to mind her numerous charge among the verdant grass.

II

O little Cloud the virgin said. I charge thee tell to me
Why thou complainest not when in one hour thou fade away,
Then we shall seek thee but not find; ah Thel is like to Thee.
I pass away. yet I complain, and no one hears my voice.

The Cloud then shewd his golden head & his bright form emerg'd,
Hovering and glittering on the air before the face of Thel.

O virgin knowst thou not. our steeds drink of the golden springs
Where Luvah doth renew his horses; look'st thou on my youth,

And fearest thou because I vanish and am seen no more.
Nothing remains; O maid I tell thee. when I pass away,
It is to tenfold life, to love, to peace, and raptures holy:
Unseen descending, weigh my light wings upon balmy flowers;
And court the fair eyed dew. to take me to her shining tent;
The weeping virgin, trembling kneels before the risen sun,
Till we arise link'd in a golden band, and never part;
But walk united, bearing food to all our tender flowers

Dost thou O little Cloud? I fear that I am not like thee;
For I walk through the vales of Har. and smell the sweetest flowers;
But I feed not the little flowers: I hear the warbling birds,
But I feed not the warbling birds. they fly and seek their food:
But Thel delights in these no more because I fade away,
And all shall say, without a use this shining woman liv'd.
Or did she only live. to be at death the food of worms.

The cloud reclind upon his airy throne and answer'd thus.

Then if thou art the food of worms. O virgin of the skies,
How great thy use. how great thy blessing; every thing that lives,
Lives not alone. nor for itself: fear not and I will call
The weak worm from its lowly bed. and thou shalt hear its voice.
Come forth worm of the silent valley, to thy pensive queen.

The helpless worm arose, and sat upon the Lillys leaf,
And the bright Cloud saild on, to find his partner in the vale.

III

Then Thel astonish'd view'd the Worm upon its dewy bed.

Art thou a Worm? image of weakness. art thou but a Worm?
I see thee like an infant wrapped in the Lillys leaf:
Ah weep not little voice, thou can'st not speak, but thou can'st weep;
Is this a Worm? I see thee lay helpless & naked: weeping.
And none to answer, none to cherish thee with mothers smiles.

The Clod of Clay heard the Worms voice, & raisd her pitying head;
She bowd over the weeping infant, and her life exhal'd
In milky fondness, then on Thel she fix'd her humble eyes.

O beauty of the vales of Har, we live not for ourselves.
Thou seest me the meanest thing, and so I am indeed;
My bosom of itself is cold and of itself is dark,

THE PIPER AND THE BARD

But he that loves the lowly, pours his oil upon my head.
And kisses me, and binds his nuptial bands around my breast,
And says: Thou mother of my children, I have loved thee.
And I have given thee a crown that none can take away
But how this is sweet maid, I know not, and I cannot know,
I ponder, and I cannot ponder; yet I live and love.

The daughter of beauty wip'd her pitying tears with her white veil,
And said. Alas! I knew not this, and therefore did I weep;
That God would love a Worm I knew, and punish the evil foot
That wilful, bruis'd its helpless form: but that he cherish'd it
With milk and oil, I never knew; and therefore did I weep.
And I complain in the mild air, because I fade away,
And lay me down in thy cold bed, and leave my shining lot.

Queen of the vales, the matron Clay answerd; I heard thy sighs,
And all thy moans flew o'er my roof. but I have call'd them down:
Wilt thou O Queen enter my house. 'tis given thee to enter,
And to return; fear nothing. enter with thy virgin feet.

IV

The eternal gates terrific porter lifted the northern bare
Thel enter'd in & saw the secrets of the land unknown:
She saw the couches of the dead, & where the fibrous roots
Of every heart on earth infixes deep its restless twists:
A land of sorrows & of tears where never smile was seen.

She wanderd in the land of clouds thro' valleys dark, listning
Dolours & lamentations: waiting oft beside a dewy grave
She stood in silence. listning to the voices of the ground,
Till to her own grave plot she came, & there she sat down.
And heard this voice of sorrow breathed from the hollow pit.

Why cannot the Ear be closed to its own destruction?
Or the glistning Eye to the poison of a smile!
Why are Eyelids stord with arrows ready drawn,
Where a thousand fighting men in ambush lie?
Or an Eye of gifts & graces. show'ring fruits & coined gold!
Why a Tongue impress'd with honey from every wind?
Why an Ear, a whirlpool fierce to draw creations in?
Why a Nostril wide inhaling terror trembling & affright
Why a tender curb upon the youthful burning boy!
Why a little curtain of flesh on the bed of our desire?

> The Virgin started from her seat, & with a shriek:
> Fled back unhindered till she came into the vales of Har

One of the most important elements in Blake's system is the concept of a higher innocence to which all creatures aspire but which not all have the necessary qualities to attain. Though Blake referred to such a state in the *Songs of Innocence,* as of 1789 he had not delineated its exact nature. In *Tiriel* he dramatized the result of a failure to attain that higher innocence, and yet, though the reasons for that failure and its pitiful consequences could be inferred, they were not completely apparent. Nor was the higher innocence in that poem more than an ephemeral goal from which the grasp of earthly man easily slipped. *The Book of Thel* fills many of these gaps in the gradually evolving picture of experience and what is beyond.

Though *Thel* is essentially uncomplicated, it begins with the cryptic "Motto" from which most misinterpretations of the entire poem stem:

> Does the Eagle know what is in the pit?
> Or wilt thou go ask the Mole:
> Can Wisdom be put in a silver rod?
> Or Love in a golden bowl?

On the literal level the first two questions make fairly good sense: certainly one does not ask a denizen of the air about the characteristics of the nether world; one asks the mole. Blake's point, however, is that one does not ask about experience at all; one must experience experience. "Understanding or Heaven . . . is acquir'd by means of Suffering & Distress & Experience," he wrote (Annotations to Swedenborg, 89). Thel's great tragedy is that she feels she can learn by merely asking, and then, satisfied in her new-found knowledge,

> . . . gentle sleep the sleep of death. and gentle hear the voice
> Of him that walketh in the garden in the evening time.

Blake thought this folly, not wisdom, and if *Thel* is read carefully, an embryonic hypocrite, like Tiriel, can be seen here succumbing to the curse that is the product of his own false wisdom.

If the act of asking were Thel's ultimate goal and Blake's true intention in the poem, the second two lines of the motto would be superfluous. The silver rod and golden bowl have little to do with the eagle and mole. Indeed, Blake believed that "When thou seest an Eagle. thou seest a portion of Genius" (*Marriage*). If this is true, the answer to the first question in the motto is "yes," for genius is synonymous in Blake's works with the higher innocence based on wisdom.[1] "The eagle never lost so much time. as when he submitted to learn of the crow"; "The tygers of wrath are wiser than the horses of instruction"; "The apple tree never asks the beech how he shall grow, nor the lion, the horse. how he shall take his prey" (*Marriage*). Given the inefficacy of depending upon other creatures for the knowledge attainable only by acting, the remaining two lines of the motto make very good sense in presenting the opposite extreme, the overemphasis on self which in *Tiriel* proved to be self-destructive. Wisdom can be got neither by asking, nor by asserting one's own standards—that is, reducing all knowledge to one standard, the self, which is always right *because* it is the only standard. Similarly love cannot be bought with earthly riches nor can it be given in coin of mundane value. It is as unmeasurable as it is uncontainable whether the container be a royal chalice or a cistern.[2] Love, as we have seen in *The Divine Image,* is the human form divine, not a man-made creation outwardly brilliant, inwardly empty and dead. "The cistern contains: the fountain overflows," Blake wrote in *The Marriage;* just so, true love is an outpouring of heart and soul and all of self, while earthly love merely stores up the fruits of its outward benevolence. The symbolic rod and bowl do have sexual overtones, of course, but the sexual theme usually insisted upon is subverted beneath the over-all Blakean emphasis on the concept of self. Such a concept inevitably involves sexual relationships, which play their part in *Thel,* but they are only a *modus operandi* for Blake's theme, not the *modus vivendi.*

The Book of Thel is not another song of innocence, then, and Thel herself assumes a gloomier aspect than her many admirers have seen fit to allow.[3] The fact is that Thel is proud, is indeed a prototypical Tiriel, or the early Heva (before her retreat to the vales of Har). But Blake has also made her one of the "daughters of Mne Seraphim" and thus given no end of trouble to all of his admirers.[4] On the surface seraphic paternity seems to prescribe for Thel a place in the angelic realm, perhaps as an unborn spirit as has been suggested; examined in the light of the rest of the poem, however, this assumption will not stand (even the third line refers to her "mortal" day). Thel's identity can be made clear only when we see the older daughters of Mne Seraphim as higher innocents, who have gone through the state of experience to achieve eternal delight among the "sunny flocks." In contrast Thel has remained below, because she has turned her back upon experience without ever really having seen it; and she has accepted in its stead the shadows of eternal delight in a mundane "paradise." That paradise is Har, where joy is neither eternal nor real. The fact that Thel knows of some other state besides her own but shrinks from its unknown qualities with trepidation is revealed immediately in her "paleness" at seeking the secret air. While she is conscious of the mutability of all life, that mutability is impressed upon her forcefully by her dawning realization that she is useless. The idea of "use" and its extension, the uselessness of love without wisdom, Blake may have got from Swedenborg, who was still in Blake's favor at this time, and who maintained that "love is nothing without wisdom; for only by means of wisdom does it become really of use; therefore, when love by means of wisdom is expressed in use, it is manifested as something real."[5] Thel exists, as did Har and Heva in *Tiriel,* in a synthetic, unreal paradise which, however pleasant to outward show, reveals its lack of foundation in the prevalent fear of anything outside itself. That "outside-itself" must be broached, Blake said, and this poem is the record of Thel's fumbling attempt to overcome her lack of wisdom and her self-destructive doubt. Her first step is a heroic one. The air is "secret" to Thel because it is, in terms of her present existence, what Blake calls a "Thou shalt not." Her initial act, however, is all but nullified by what follows.

Thel's opening complaint (lines 6-14) sets the mood of all her subsequent speeches. It is, in effect, a masterful self-analysis. The youthful, vibrant, almost ephemeral quality of the lotus, the children, the rainbow, the cloud, etc. is explicit evidence of Thel's view of herself and of her inability to comprehend the facts of earthly existence. The subtle overtones of vanity in "Like a reflection in a glass" become the dominant note a few lines later when Blake heavily accents the fervor of Thel's plea by the fourfold repetition of the word "gentle." Rather than submit to the fading of her beauty, the loss of her youth, indeed the annihilation of her very identity, she craves "gentle sleep"[6] to shield her eyes from the tragedy, so that she may glide gently from innocence into a communion with God.

The effectiveness of the passage, however, can be fully realized only when read in the light of the final section of the poem, the violent shattering of Thel's dream. There she lays herself in the grave of existence, but instead of flowers there are "fibrous roots / Of every heart"; instead of the infant smile there is "a land of sorrows & of tears where never smile was seen"; instead of a rainbow and pleasant daylight there is a "land of clouds thro' valleys dark"; instead of "music in the air" there are "Dolours & lamentations" and "voices of the ground"; and, finally, instead of gently hearing "the voice of him that walketh in the garden in the evening time," she hears the "voice of sorrow breathed from the hollow pit."

But the final tragedy of the poem springs from Thel's vanity, a tragic flaw which can lead only to failure, though Blake's craftsmanship transforms that inevitability into a suspenseful character drama. Even if the revelations of vanity in Thel's opening lament escape the reader, her comment upon the lily's existence can leave no doubt. After exclaiming over the remarkable beneficence of the tiny flower, Thel cries:

But Thel is like a faint cloud kindled at the rising sun;
I vanish from my pearly throne, and who shall find my place.

Though also kindled at the rising sun ("visited from heaven" is her phrase), the lily vanishes in the heat of noon, but only to be rejuvenated with "morning manna" and returned to her "silver shrine." Her humility and faith admit of no vanity or doubt. On the other hand, Thel immediately fears that no one will find her when once she leaves her high estate ("pearly throne").

In greeting the cloud, Thel reiterates the same self-pity:

. . . ah Thel is like to Thee.
I pass away. yet I complain, and no one hears my voice.

Fearing the loss of her corporeal identity, Thel craves the sympathy of another. But after the cloud reveals his lofty purpose, Thel again complains, in words which unintentionally confess her selfish pleasure in the vales of Har:

I fear that I am not like thee;
For I walk through the vales of Har. and smell the sweetest flowers;
But I feed not the little flowers: I hear the warbling birds,
But I feed not the warbling birds. they fly and seek their food:
But Thel delights in these no more because I fade away,
And all shall say, without a use this shining woman liv'd.
Or did she only live. to be at death the food of worms.

Finally, Blake rounds out his development of this aspect of Thel's character in a skillfully wrought passage in which Thel responds to the matron clay's explanation that "we live not for ourselves":

Alas! I knew not this, and therefore did I weep;
That God would love a Worm I knew, and punish the evil foot
That wilful, bruis'd its helpless form: but that he cherish'd it
With milk and oil, I never knew; and therefore did I weep.
And I complain in the mild air, because I fade away,
And lay me down in thy cold bed, and leave my shining lot.

Thel has in fact heard the three voices of lily, cloud, and clay without ever really understanding. She can comprehend only their superficial goodness, which to her is the ultimate criterion on earth. She is, then, the soul in experience who refuses to face the *actus* of that experience and hence languishes in the stasis of pseudo-innocence. Though the three voices have shown her the way to the higher innocence she presumably seeks, she has successively assumed and then denied the similarity between her existence and theirs. She senses a bond between her mutation and that of the lotus or lily (significantly it is the first simile to enter her head), but after the lily's recital of her eternal reincarnation through the visitation of him "that smiles on all," Thel immediately reconsiders the analogy and alters the image pattern: "But Thel is like a faint cloud kindled at the rising sun." Unable to grasp the essential sameness of the lily and herself, Thel chooses the cloud to commiserate with. He too propounds the idea of altruistic existence, and again Thel misses the point. She cannot conceive of transferring the cloud-dew-flower relationship to her own plane of existence but rather perversely bewails the fact that she cannot feed flowers *or* birds. This brings her to the point where she suffers the

165

final blow to her vanity: though she is shining and beautiful and a queen regnant, people will say she is good for nothing, except perhaps "to be at death the food of worms."

The prospect of dust to dust, of course, is repulsive to her in all respects, and it is not without some bitterness that the thought crosses her mind. Thus she is astonished to see the helpless worm caressed and pitied by the apparently cold, lifeless, and benighted clay. The scene calls forth Thel's tears, and with them the notion that in the clay's speech and action is the solution to her problem. Ignoring the all-important last line of the clay's speech ("I ponder, and I cannot ponder; yet I live and love"), Thel clutches to her breast the image of ugliness cherished by God. She knew, she says, that God loved the worm, but that he cherished it she knew not; and therefore she wept. She complained because she fades away and has to trade her "shining lot" for the earth's "cold bed." In other words, Thel's opening wish to gently lay her down and sleep the sleep of death is here come true, despite the fact that her beauty fades, and her shining lot shall cease. She complained not because of her uselessness, but because of her personal loss.[7] She is not an innocent at all, but rather a fallen soul in experience trying desperately to escape the rigors of that experience. And to her the worm's situation "proves" that this can be done. The clay can only teach Thel; the decision to act and enter the house of the grave must be her own, and it is given her to enter and return. When the dream of the voice of him that walketh in the garden in evening is smashed by the reality of the sorrowful voice of the hollow pit, Thel must inevitably flee. The way of the lily, cloud, and matron clay was opened to her, but in the ignorance and pride of her human form human she cannot take advantage of it.

Indeed Thel's flight from the grave constitutes a denial of act; she cannot bring herself to act in terms of the self-immolation upon which the realm of higher innocence is based. Experience "is bought with the price / Of all that a man hath," said Blake, "[his house,] his wife, his children" (Zoas, 290). Thel has the vales of Har: she is the queen; she need give up nothing, for her silver sceptre and golden bowl command ease, beauty, pleasantness, longevity, love. Like Tiriel, she cannot see that her power to command is a curse. That these attributes would be hers instantaneously if she could but surrender herself is exemplified by the three other speakers in the poem. Within his own realm of existence each has his own grave, through which he has passed to attain the higher innocence; each exemplifies a slightly different aspect of that higher realm in direct contrast to Thel herself.

The lily, long associated with reincarnation and both spiritual and physical productive powers, is

> . . . visited from heaven and he that smiles on all.
> Walks in the valley, and each morn over me spreads his hand
> Saying, rejoice thou humble grass, thou new born lilly flower,
> Thou gentle maid of silent valleys. and of modest brooks.

Drawing sustenance from the very waters that keep her earthbound, the lily nevertheless loves to live. Clothed in light and fed with manna, she blooms only to be devoured by the innocent lamb. She gives herself willingly, "smiling in his face," and, as if to prove the universality of this altruism, she "Revives the milked cow, & tames the fire-breathing steed." Hers is a life-giving function, and by means of her "death" she lives "to flourish in eternal vales." There is no questioning, no analysis upon which to base a complaint of transiency or lack of recognition. The world of experience, as well as the world of higher innocence, is a sensual one; the one is a debasement of the other, or better, the latter is a refinement of the former. As Blake wrote in *The Marriage,* "For the cherub with his flaming sword is hereby commanded to leave his guard at tree of life, and when he does, the whole creation will be consumed, and appear infinite. and holy whereas now it appears finite & corrupt. This will come to pass by an improvement of sensual enjoyment." The finite world is the grave; the infinite is that of the lily, and her existence in it is dependent upon her capacity for "sensual enjoyment." Thel sees the lily's self-abnegation but rationalizes it as inapplicable to herself; she turns to what she hopes is the more sympathetic cloud, brilliant as she, who also vanishes from human eyes.

As the lily scatters perfume on every blade of grass, the cloud "scatters its bright beauty thro' the humid air" and explains to Thel that when he passes away "It is to tenfold life, to love, to peace, and raptures holy." To reinforce the contrast between the cloud's higher innocence and Thel's earthly vanity, Blake employs the simple natural phenomena of dew evaporating in the sun and the formation of cloud as images of sexual-spiritual union. Thel at first thinks she is like this faint cloud merely because it fades away, whereas in fact each evening the moisture "unseen" descends to unite with the morning dew in her "shining tent" whence they fade away "link'd in a golden band" to feed their flowers. Thus whereas Thel worries only about "who shall find . . . [her] place," the cloud, unthinking, acts according to the dictates of his "senses."

The circle is now complete. Just as the lily is visited by God each morn, clothed in light, and fed with morning manna so that she may nourish the beasts of the field, so the cloud appears like a sun to the morning dew and joins with her to provide morning manna for all their tender flowers. Thel once again misses the full import of the cloud's—and the dew's—act. She cannot feed the flowers. Indeed, like the true Blakean devourer she can only take from them their perfume and from the birds their song.[8] She has successively craved the sympathy of others for her plight and then realized that their apparent similarity to her is only superficial.

She is astonished, then, at the apparent analogy between her situation and that of the worm:

Is this a Worm? I see thee lay helpless & naked: weeping.
And none to answer, none to cherish thee with mothers smiles.

But there is a mother for all *innocents*. The clod of clay raises her "pitying head" at the worm's voice and "her life exhal'd / In milky fondness." Blake's point here is crucial. By identifying herself with the worm, Thel reveals her basic dilemma: she conceives of herself as an innocent to whom should accrue all due comfort and protection (like that afforded the worm by the clay). And thinking in these terms she will inevitably flee the inconceivable horror of the grave where, as always in experience, self must be annihilated. Accordingly, as the poem nears its climax, the image pattern swiftly changes from that which reflected Thel's superficial beauty to that which reflects her real self, ugly, cold, mean, dark. In contrast to Thel, the clay lives and loves despite her lowliness, coldness, and darkness, and her speech summarizes the central idea of the whole poem:

O beauty of the vales of Har, we live not for ourselves.
Thou seest me the meanest thing, and so I am indeed;
My bosom of itself is cold and of itself is dark,
But he that loves the lowly, pours his oil upon my head.
And kisses me, and binds his nuptial bands around my breast,
And says: Thou mother of my children, I have loved thee.
And I have given thee a crown that none can take away
But how this is sweet maid, I know not, and I cannot know,
I ponder, and I cannot ponder; yet I live and love.[9]

The reference to self in the third line is implicitly directed at Thel, the warm, bright queen of the vales of Har. Trampled beneath the feet of such a ruler in this earthly existence, the clay, like the lily, is visited from heaven and, like the cloud, is bound in nuptial bands. For the clay gives to all; she is the great earth mother. Thus she receives the "crown that none can take away," not the elegant but temporary crown that adorns the proud head of Thel. But what is most important, the clay does not analyze, rationalize, or dogmatize her reign; she cannot ponder and cannot know—that is, consciously. By merely living and loving, acting and being, she has attained the higher innocence, and this is all you know and all you need to know.

In a sense, then, the lily is the womb within which is formed the child of the cloud and the dew (the worm, it will be remembered, arises upon the lily's leaf); that child, lowly or great, is a portion of eternity to be cherished in the bosom of the matron clay. But Thel has not seen. Blinded by her own brilliance, to her the grave is a chamber of horror within whose walls the thought of giving herself cannot possibly be born. It is the secret air she sought at the beginning of the poem, but it remains secret, unknown, because of her complete insensibility to the holiness of all life around her. The lily's grave is described in terms of the consuming beasts of the field, the cloud's in terms of the consuming flowers, the clay's in terms of all creation. Each annihilates the selfhood, which to Thel is corporeal existence, through acts which foreshadow the supreme act of the human, the act which Thel must perform on the bed of her desire. But the bed is cloaked with a curtain of flesh within which thrive the all-consuming senses. It is those very senses which must be purified, not purged, in the act of giving sensually. "Men are admitted into Heaven," Blake wrote in *A Vision of the Last Judgment,* "not because they have curbed & govern'd their Passions or have No Passions, but because they have Cultivated their Understandings. The Treasures of Heaven are not Negations of Passion, but Realities of Intellect, from which all the Passions Emanate Uncurbed in their Eternal Glory" (615). The "Realities of Intellect" can be achieved only by throwing down the silver sceptre and breaking the mind-forged manacles which "protect" us from our sensual selves. The ear, eye, nose, tongue, and fingers are all windows to eternity if they can but be cleansed of the cobwebs of religion, hypocrisy, and selfishness.[10]

With her "windows" closed, Thel can only be terrified at the prospect of their destruction in experience, as the dread voice of the grave warns. The grave's terrifying speech is, in effect, the true meaning of Thel's opening words. The soft, sorrowful tone of Thel's lament at the fading of the corporeal body is here changed to the tortured cry at the "evil" that that body can encompass before it completely fades Her desire is still for the easy way out, to skip experience and listen to the Word in the cool gardens at evening-time. But Blake insists that before that garden can be reached, one must stumble through the forest of experience. And before the silver shrine of the lily can be the resting place of the soul, the bed of our desire must witness untrammeled senses in infinite creation, for "the soul of sweet delight can never be defil'd."[11]

The essence of the grave's lament recurs again and again in Blake's poetry, because in a sense it is the vortex into which are swept all of the complaints of earthly man. For example, Urizen, bloated with ignorant pride, blind to the simple road to higher innocence, revelling in unhealthy lust for egocentric sensual enjoyment, and smugly chastising the iconoclast of self-instituted moral codes, loudly cries in *The First Book of Urizen:*

> "From the depths of dark solitude, From
> The eternal abode in my holiness,
> Hidden, set apart, in my stern counsels,
> Reserv'd for the days of futurity,
> I have sought for a joy without pain,
> For a solid without fluctuation.

Why will you die, O Eternals?
Why live in unquenchable burnings?" (224)

And again Urizen (to whom Thel bears no distant resemblance) laments, in a passage whose dominant imagery bespeaks the basic similarity of his situation and Thel's, and perhaps also Tiriel's:

"Ah! how shall Urizen the King submit to this dark mansion?
Ah! how is this? Once in the heights I stretch'd my throne sublime;
The mountains of Urizen, once of silver, where the sons of wisdom dwelt,
And on whose tops the Virgins sang, are rocks of desolation.
.   .   .   .
"Once how I walked from my palace in gardens of delight,
The sons of wisdom stood around, the harpers follow'd with harps,
Nine virgins cloth'd in light compos'd the song to their immortal voices,
And at my banquets of new wine my head was crown'd with joy.

"Then in my ivory pavilions I slumber'd in the noon
And walked in the silent night among sweet smelling flowers,
Till on my silver bed I slept & sweet dreams round me hover'd,
But now my land is darken'd & my wise men are departed.
.   .   .   .
"O Fool! to think that I could hide from his all piercing eyes
The gold & silver & costly stones, his holy workmanship!
O Fool! could I forget the light that filled my bright spheres
Was a reflection of his face who call'd me from the deep!

"I well remember, for I heard the mild & holy voice
Saying, 'O light, spring up & shine,' & I sprang up from the deep.
He gave to me a silver scepter, & crown'd me with a golden crown,
& said, 'Go forth & guide my Son who wanders on the ocean.'

"I went not forth: I hid myself in black clouds of my wrath;
I call'd the stars around my feet in the night of councils dark;
The stars threw down their spears & fled naked away.
We fell."[12]

To join the voice of Thel with that of the grave in one image cluster Blake has employed a fine network of sub-themes and echoes, which not only make the poem work but make it one of Blake's rare artistic triumphs in this verse form. In addition to the systematic progression of the three interviews toward Thel's climactic final speech, and the obvious progression from morning-spring to the clouded "valleys dark" of the grave, there is the fear motif. In *Tiriel* Har and Heva, self-convinced of their own pleasure and ease, *consciously* distract themselves from the everpresent fear of the state they have escaped. And when that state appears incarnate in Tiriel, they cannot accept him until he is rendered "harmless," a condition without validity in both childhood innocence and the higher innocence. Such a fear is inherent in Thel's sorrowful recognition of her evanescence ("I vanish from my pearly throne, and who shall find my place"); but it is intensified when, in direct contrast to the lily's humility, Thel, the fallen innocent, commands the cloud to tell her his secret of overcoming transience: "I charge thee tell to me / Why thou complainest not when in one hour thou fade away." When the cloud explains, Thel immediately answers with: "I fear that I am not like thee." Recognizing her fear, and its cause, the cloud introduces the worm in the same terms: "fear not, and I will call / The weak worm from its lowly bed. and thou shall hear its voice." Upon seeing the worm Thel misses the whole point of the clay's crucial speech and gives voice to her own limited vision in terms of earth-bound morality, good and evil, rewards and punishments:

> That God would love a Worm I knew, and punish the evil foot
> That wilful, bruis'd its helpless form: but that he cherish'd it
> With milk and oil, I never knew; and therefore did I weep.
> And I complain in the mild air, because I fade away,
> And lay me down in thy cold bed, and leave my shining lot.

To Thel, God's punishment of the foot that bruises the worm is right; the foot is evil. What she does not know is that for the worm, clod, lily, cloud—and Blake—"The cut worm forgives the plow" and "the soul of sweet delight can never be defil'd" (*Marriage*). The solution to fear, which Thel cannot find because of her self-delusion, is simply to have no fear, to act, to descend into the grave of experience

(" 'tis given thee to enter, / And to return; fear nothing," says the clay), and annihilate the self on which that fear subsists.

Another verbal pattern, most of it ironic, revolves around the fact that each speaker is, at least figuratively, the wearer of a crown; each is an important personage, if not the ruler, in his own special realm. In contrast to Thel's sovereignty and power, theirs is God-given, not self-appropriated. The lily has her silver shrine and is comparable to "the mistress of the vales of Har" by being called "thou gentle maid of silent valleys"; the cloud shows his golden head and reclines "upon his airy throne"; and the clay is "given . . . a crown that none can take away." Their realms are the realms of love, freedom, selflessness, and wisdom; Thel's is the realm of fear, vassalage, selfishness, and ignorance. Their values are spiritual, their reward eternal unity. Her values are material, her reward spiritual exile in the vales of Har and Heva. Thel's silver rod gleams with hypocritical purity; it can beat on the slave's back, but it cannot elicit wisdom therefrom. Thel's golden bowl radiates richness and luxury, but it tarnishes in the secret air and holds only love of self.

Finally, the word "virgin" (or "maid") is used throughout the poem with pregnant irony. Thel is so addressed constantly—and with apparent approval; yet when the poem is ended the term has become one of opprobrium. It is the lily and the dew and the clay, who everlastingly copulate, that symbolize to Blake true virginity; Thel will later develop in Blake's poems into the greatest whore of all, Babylon.

All of these strains lead unerringly back to the motto which has been so variously interpreted. Thel has asked the eagle and the mole, and they have told her; but their teachings are worthless as long as the sceptre of self-appointed authority and the golden bowl of self-love and material possessions are retained. Thel claims immortality but denies the efficacy of mortality as a step in that direction. As Vala later laments in a similar situation in *The Four Zoas*:

"Alas! am I but as a flower? then will I sit me down,
Then will I weep, then I'll complain & sigh for immortality,
And chide my maker, thee O Sun, that raisedst me to fall." (368)

Thel's existence is clouded by the encroachment of the "secret air," which will reveal her "innocence" to be empty and meaningless, gnawed by a desire for the infinite. "If any could desire what he is incapable of possessing," wrote Blake in *There Is No Natural Religion,* "despair must be his eternal lot" (97). Thel is incapable because irretrievably finite as long as she is blind to the spiritual meaning of the lily-cloud-clay. "He who sees the Infinite in all things, sees God. He who sees the Ratio only, sees himself only" (*No Natural Religion,* 98).

CHAPTER IX

BLAKE'S QUARREL WITH SWEDENBORG

I am as steadfast in my religion as he is in his.
—G. B. SHAW, *The Devil's Disciple*

THE MARRIAGE of HEAVEN and HELL

The Argument.

Rintrah roars & shakes his fires in the burdend air;
Hungry clouds swag on the deep

Once meek, and in a perilous path,
The just man kept his course along
The vale of death.
Roses are planted where thorns grow.
And on the barren heath
Sing the honey bees.

Then the perilous path was planted:
And a river, and a spring
On every cliff and tomb;
And on the bleached bones
Red clay brought forth.

Till the villain left the paths of ease,
To walk in perilous paths, and drive
The just man into barren climes.

Now the sneaking serpent walks
In mild humility.
And the just man rages in the wilds
Where lions roam.
Rintrah roars & shakes his fires in the burdend air;
Hungry clouds swag on the deep.

As a new heaven is begun, and it is now thirty-three years since its advent: the Eternal Hell revives. And lo! Swedenborg is the Angel sitting at the tomb; his writings are the linen clothes folded up. Now is the dominion of Edom, & the return of Adam into Paradise; see Isaiah XXXIV & XXXV Chap:

Without Contraries is no progression. Attraction and Repulsion, Reason and Energy, Love and Hate, are necessary to Human existence.

From these contraries spring what the religious call Good & Evil. Good is the passive that obeys Reason Evil is the active springing from Energy.

Good is Heaven. Evil is Hell.

The voice of the Devil

All Bibles or sacred codes. have been the causes of the following Errors.

1. That Man has two real existing principles Viz: a Body & a Soul.

2. That Energy. calld Evil. is alone from the Body. & that Reason. calld Good. is alone from the Soul.

3. That God will torment Man in Eternity for following his Energies.

But the following Contraries to these are True.

1 Man has no Body distinct from his Soul for that calld Body is a portion of Soul discernd by the five Senses, the chief inlets of Soul in this age

2 Energy is the only life and is from the Body and Reason is the bound or outward circumference of Energy.

3 Energy is Eternal Delight

Those who restrain desire, do so because theirs is weak enough to be restrained; and the restrainer or reason usurps its place & governs the unwilling.

And being restraind it by degrees becomes passive till it is only the shadow of desire.

The history of this is written in Paradise Lost. & the Governor or Reason is call'd Messiah.

And the original Archangel or possessor of the command of the heavenly host, is calld the Devil or Satan and his children are call'd Sin & Death

But in the Book of Job Miltons Messiah is call'd Satan.

For this history has been adopted by both parties

It indeed appear'd to Reason as if Desire was cast out. but the Devils account is, that the Messiah fell. & formed a heaven of what he stole from the Abyss

This is shown in the Gospel, where he prays to the Father to send the comforter or Desire that Reason may have Ideas to build on, the Jehovah of the

Bible being no other than he who dwells in flaming fire. Know that after Christs death, he became Jehovah.

But in Milton; the Father is Destiny, the Son, a Ratio of the five senses. & the Holy-ghost, Vacuum!

Note. The reason Milton wrote in fetters when he wrote of Angels & God, and at liberty when of Devils & Hell, is because he was a true Poet and of the Devils party without knowing it

A Memorable Fancy.

As I was walking among the fires of hell, delighted with the enjoyments of Genius; which to Angels look like torment and insanity. I collected some of their Proverbs; thinking that as the sayings used in a nation, mark its character, so the Proverbs of Hell, shew the nature of Infernal wisdom better than any description of buildings or garments.

When I came home; on the abyss of the five senses. where a flat sided steep frowns over the present world. I saw a mighty Devil folded in black clouds. hovering on the sides of the rock, with corroding fires he wrote the following sentence now percieved by the minds of men, & read by them on earth.

> How do you know but ev'ry Bird that cuts the airy way,
> Is an immense world of delight, clos'd by your senses five?

Proverbs of Hell.

In seed time learn, in harvest teach, in winter enjoy.
Drive your cart and your plow over the bones of the dead.
The road of excess leads to the palace of wisdom.
Prudence is a rich ugly old maid courted by Incapacity.
He who desires but acts not, breeds pestilence.
The cut worm forgives the plow.
Dip him in the river who loves water.
A fool sees not the same tree that a wise man sees.
He whose face gives no light, shall never become a star.
Eternity is in love with the productions of time.
The busy bee has no time for sorrow.
The hours of folly are measur'd by the clock, but of wisdom: no clock can
measure.
All wholsom food is caught without a net or a trap.
Bring out number weight & measure in a year of dearth
No bird soars too high. if he soars with his own wings.
A dead body. revenges not injuries.
The most sublime act is to set another before you.
If the fool would persist in his folly he would become wise
Folly is the cloke of knavery.

Shame is Prides cloke.

Prisons are built with stones of Law, Brothels with bricks of Religion.

The pride of the peacock is the glory of God

The lust of the goat is the bounty of God.

The wrath of the lion is the wisdom of God.

The nakedness of woman is the work of God.

Excess of sorrow laughs. Excess of joy weeps.

The roaring of lions, the howling of wolves, the raging of the stormy sea. and
  the destructive sword. are portions of eternity too great for the eye of man.

The fox condemns the trap. not himself.

Joys impregnate. Sorrows bring forth.

Let man wear the fell of the lion. woman the fleece of the sheep.

The bird a nest, the spider a web, man friendship.

The selfish smiling fool. & the sullen frowning fool, shall be both thought wise.
  that they may be a rod.

What is now proved was once, only imagin'd.

The rat, the mouse, the fox, the rabbet; watch the roots, the lion, the tyger. the
  horse. the elephant, watch the fruits.

The cistern contains: the fountain overflows

One thought, fills immensity.

Always be ready to speak your mind, and a base man will avoid you.

Every thing possible to be believ'd is an image of truth.

The eagle never lost so much time. as when he submitted to learn of the crow.

The fox provides for himself. but God provides for the lion.

Think in the morning. Act in the noon, Eat in the evening, Sleep in the night.

He who has sufferd you to impose on him knows you.

As the plow follows words, so God rewards prayers.

The tygers of wrath are wiser than the horses of instruction

Expect poison from the standing water.

You never know what is enough unless you know what is more than enough.

Listen to the fools reproach! it is a kingly title!

The eyes of fire, the nostrils of air, the mouth of war the beard of earth.

The weak in courage is strong in cunning.

The apple tree never asks the beech how he shall grow, nor the lion, the horse.
  how he shall take his prey.

The thankful reciever bears a plentiful harvest.

If others had not been foolish, we should be so.

The soul of sweet delight. can never be defil'd,

When thou seest an Eagle. thou seest a portion of Genius. lift up thy head!

As the catterpiller chooses the fairest leaves to lay her eggs on, so the priest lays
  his curse on the fairest joys.

To create a little flower is the labour of ages.

Damn. braces: Bless relaxes.

The best wine is the oldest. the best water the newest.

Prayers plow not! Praises reap not!

Joys laugh not! Sorrows weep not!

The head Sublime, the heart Pathos, the genitals Beauty, the hands & feet Proportion.

As the air to a bird or the sea to a fish, so is contempt to the contemptible.

The crow wish'd every thing was black, the owl, that every thing was white.

Exuberance is Beauty.

If the lion was advised by the fox. he would be cunning

Improvent makes strait roads, but the crooked roads without Improvement, are roads of Genius.

Sooner murder an infant in its cradle than nurse unacted desires

Where man is not nature is barren.

Truth can never be told so as to be understood, and not be believ'd.

Enough! or Too much

The ancient Poets animated all sensible objects with Gods or Geniuses, calling them by the names and adorning them with the properties of woods, rivers, mountains, lakes, cities, nations, and whatever their enlarged & numerous senses could percieve.

And particularly they studied the genius of each city & country. placing it under its mental deity.

Till a system was formed, which some took advantage of & enslav'd the vulgar by attempting to realize or abstract the mental deities from their objects; thus began Priesthood.

Choosing forms of worship from poetic tales.

And at length they pronouncd that the Gods had orderd such things.

Thus men forgot that All deities reside in the human breast.

A Memorable Fancy.

The Prophets Isaiah and Ezekiel dined with me, and I asked them how they dared so roundly to assert. that God spake to them; and whether they did not think at the time, that they would be misunderstood, & so be the cause of imposition.

Isaiah answer'd. I saw no God, nor heard any, in a finite organical perception; but my senses discover'd the infinite in every thing, and as I was then perswaded, & remain confirm'd; that the voice of honest indignation is the voice of God, I cared not for consequences but wrote.

Then I asked: does a firm perswasion that a thing is so, make it so?

He replied. All poets believe that it does. & in ages of imagination this firm perswasion removed mountains: but many are not capable of a firm perswasion of any thing.

Then Ezekiel said. The philosophy of the east taught the first principles of human perception some nations held one principle for the origin & some another we of Israel taught that the Poetic Genius (as you now call it) was the first principle and all the others merely derivative, which was the cause of our despising the Priests & Philosophers of other countries. and prophecying that all Gods would at last be proved to originate in ours & to be the tributaries of the Poetic Genius, it was this. that our great poet King David desired so fervently & invokes so patheticly, saying by this he conquers enemies governs kingdoms; and we so loved our God. that we cursed in his name all the deities of surrounding nations, and asserted that they had rebelled; from these opinions the vulgar came to think that all nations would at last be subject to the jews.

This said he, like all firm perswasions. is come to pass, for all nations believe the jews code and worship the jews god. and what greater subjection can be

I heard this with some wonder, & must confess my own conviction. After dinner I ask'd Isaiah to favour the world with his lost works, he said none of equal value was lost. Ezekiel said the same of his.

I also asked Isaiah what made him go naked and barefoot three years? he answerd, the same that made our friend Diogenes the Grecian.

I then asked Ezekiel. why he eat dung. & lay so long on his right & left side? he answerd, the desire of raising other men into a perception of the infinite this the North American tribes practise. & is he honest who resists his genius or conscience. only for the sake of present ease or gratification?

The ancient tradition that the world will be consumed in fire at the end of six thousand years is true. as I have heard from Hell.

For the cherub with his flaming sword is hereby commanded to leave his guard at tree of life, and when he does, the whole creation will be consumed and appear infinite. and holy whereas it now appears finite & corrupt.

This will come to pass by an improvement of sensual enjoyment.

But first the notion that man has a body distinct from his soul, is to be expunged; this I shall do, by printing in the infernal method, by corrosives, which in Hell are salutary and medicinal, melting apparent surfaces away, and displaying the infinite which was hid.

If the doors of perception were cleansed every thing would appear to man as it is. infinite.

For man has closed himself up, till he sees all things thro' narrow chinks of his cavern.

A Memorable Fancy

I was in a Printing house in Hell & saw the method in which knowledge is transmitted from generation to generation.

In the first chamber was a Dragon-Man, clearing away the rubbish from a caves mouth; within, a number of Dragons were hollowing the cave,

In the second chamber was a Viper folding round the rock & the cave, and others adorning it with gold silver and precious stones

In the third chamber was an Eagle with wings and feathers of air, he caused the inside of the cave to be infinite, around were numbers of Eagle like men, who built palaces in the immense cliffs.

In the fourth chamber were Lions of flaming fire raging around & melting the metals into living fluids.

In the fifth chamber were Unnam'd forms, which cast the metals into the expanse.

There they were reciev'd by Men who occupied the sixth chamber, and took the forms of books & were arranged in libraries.

The Giants who formed this world into its sensual existence and now seem to live in it in chains are in truth. the causes of its life & the sources of all activity, but the chains are, the cunning of weak and tame minds. which have power to resist energy. according to the proverb, the weak in courage is strong in cunning.

Thus one portion of being, is the Prolific. the other, the Devouring; to the devourer it seems as if the producer was in his chains, but it is not so, he only takes portions of existence and fancies that the whole.

But the Prolific would cease to be Prolific unless the Devourer as a sea reciev'd the excess of his delights.

Some will say. Is not God alone the Prolific? I answer, God only Acts & Is, in existing beings or Men.

These two classes of men are always upon earth. & they should be enemies; whoever tries to reconcile them seeks to destroy existence.

Religion is an endeavour to reconcile the two.

Note. Jesus Christ did not wish to unite but to separate them, as in the Parable of sheep and goats! & he says I came not to send Peace but a Sword.

Messiah or Satan or Tempter was formerly thought to be one of the Antediluvians who are our Energies.

A Memorable Fancy

An Angel came to me and said O pitiable foolish young man! O horrible! O dreadful state! consider the hot burning dungeon thou art preparing for thyself to all eternity, to which thou art going in such career.

I said. perhaps you will be willing to shew me my eternal lot & we will contemplate together upon it and see whether your lot or mine is most desirable

So he took me thro' a stable & thro' a church & down into the church vault at the end of which was a mill; thro' the mill we went, and came to a cave. down the winding cavern we groped our tedious way till a void boundless as a nether sky appeard beneath us, & we held by the roots of trees and hung over this immensity, but I said, if you please we will commit ourselves to this void and see whether providence is here also, if you will not I will? but he answerd, do not presume O young-man but as we here remain behold thy lot which will soon appear when the darkness passes away

So I remaind with him sitting in the twisted root of an oak. he was suspended in a fungus which hung with the head downward into the deep;

By degrees we beheld the infinite Abyss, fiery as the smoke of a burning city; beneath us at an immense distance was the sun, black but shining round it were fiery tracks on which revolv'd vast spiders, crawling after their prey; which flew or rather swum in the infinite deep, in the most terrific shapes of animals sprung from corruption. & the air was full of them, & seemd composed of them; these are Devils. and are called Powers of the air, I now asked my companion which was my eternal lot? he said, between the black & white spiders

But now, from between the black & white spiders a cloud and fire burst and rolled thro the deep blackning all beneath. so that the nether deep grew black as a sea & rolled with a terrible noise: beneath us was nothing now to be seen but a black tempest, till looking east between the clouds & the waves. we saw a cataract of blood mixed with fire and not many stones throw from us appeard and sunk again the scaly fold of a monstrous serpent at last to the east, distant about three degrees appeard a fiery crest above the waves slowly it reared like a ridge of golden rocks till we discoverd two globes of crimson fire. from which the sea fled away in clouds of smoke, and now we saw, it was the head of Leviathan, his forehead was divided into streaks of green & purple like those on a tygers forehead: soon we saw his mouth & red gills hang just above the raging foam tinging the black deep with beams of blood. advancing toward us with all the fury of a spiritual existence.

My friend the Angel climb'd up from his station into the mill; I remain'd alone, & then thier appearance was no more, but I found myself sitting on a pleasant bank beside a river by moonlight hearing a harper who sung to the harp, his theme was, The man who never alters his opinion is like standing water, & breeds reptiles of the mind.

But I arose, and sought for the mill & there I found my Angel, who surprised asked me, how I escaped?

I answerd. All that we saw was owing to your metaphysics: for when you ran away, I found myself on a bank by moonlight hearing a harper, But now we have seen my eternal lot, shall I shew you yours? he laughd at my proposal; but I by force suddenly caught him in my arms, & flew westerly thro' the night, till we were elevated above the earths shadow: then I flung myself with him directly into the body of the sun, here I clothed myself in white, & taking in my hand Swedenborgs volumes sunk from the glorious clime, and passed all the planets till we came to saturn, here I staid to rest & then leap'd into the void. between saturn & the fixed stars.

Here said I! is your lot, in this space, if space it may be calld. Soon we saw the stable and the church, & I took him to the altar and open'd the Bible, and lo! it was a deep pit, into which I descended driving the Angel before me, soon we saw seven houses of brick, one we enterd; in it were a number of monkeys, baboons, & all of that species chaind by the middle, grinning and snatching at one another. but withheld by the shortness of their chains: however I saw that they sometimes grew numerous, and then the weak were caught by the strong and with a grinning aspect first coupled with & then devourd, by plucking off first one limb and then another till the body was left a helpless trunk. this after grinning & kissing it with seeming fondness they devourd too; and here & there I saw one savourily picking the flesh off of his own tail; as the stench terribly annoyd us both we went into the mill, & I in my hand brought the skeleton of a body, which in the mill was Aristotles Analytics.

So the Angel said: thy phantasy has imposed upon me & thou oughtest to be ashamed.

I answerd: we impose on one another. & it is but lost time to converse with you whose works are only Analytics

I have always found that Angels have the vanity to speak of themselves as the only wise; this they do with a confident insolence sprouting from systematic reasoning:

Thus Swedenborg boasts that what he writes is new: tho' it is only the Contents or Index of already publish'd books

A man carried a monkey about for a shew, & because he was a little wiser than the monkey, grew vain, and conciev'd himself as much wiser than seven men. It is so with Swedenborg; he shews the folly of churches & exposes hypocrites, till he imagines that all are religious. & himself the single one on earth that ever broke a net.

Now hear a plain fact: Swedenborg has not written one new truth: Now hear another: he has written all the old falshoods.

And now hear the reason. He conversed with Angels who are all religious. & conversed not with Devils who all hate religion, for he was incapable thro' his conceited notions.

Thus Swedenborgs writings are a recapitulation of all superficial opinions, and an analysis of the more sublime. but no further.

Have now another plain fact: Any man of mechanical talents may from the writings of Paracelsus or Jacob Behmen, produce ten thousand volumes of equal value with Swedenborg's. and from those of Dante or Shakespear, an infinite number.

But when he has done this, let him not say that he knows better than his master, for he only holds a candle in sunshine.

A Memorable Fancy

Once I saw a Devil in a flame of fire, who arose before an Angel that sat on a cloud. and the Devil utterd these words,

The worship of God is. Honouring his gifts in other men each according to his genius. and loving the greatest men best, those who envy or calumniate great men hate God, for there is no other God.

The Angel hearing this became almost blue but mastering himself he grew yellow, & at last white pink & smiling. and then replied,

Thou Idolater, is not God One? & is not he visible in Jesus Christ? and has not Jesus Christ given his sanction to the law of ten commandments and are not all other men fools sinners & nothings.

The Devil answer'd; bray a fool in a morter with wheat. yet shall not his folly be beaten out of him: if Jesus Christ is the greatest man, you ought to love him in the greatest degree; now hear how he has given his sanction to the law of ten commandments: did he not mock at the sabbath, and so mock the sabbaths God? murder those who were murderd because of him? turn away the law from the woman taken in adultery? steal the labor of others to support him? bear false witness when he omitted making a defence before Pilate? covet when he pray'd for his disciples, and when he bid them shake off the dust of their feet against such as refused to lodge them? I tell you, no virtue can exist without breaking these ten commandments: Jesus was all virtue, and acted from impulse. not from rules.

When he had so spoken: I beheld the Angel who stretched out his arms embracing the flame of fire & he was consumed and arose as Elijah.

Note. This Angel, who is now become a Devil, is my particular friend: we often read the Bible together in its infernal or diabolical sense which the world shall have if they behave well

I have also: The Bible of Hell: which the world shall have whether they will or no.

One Law for the Lion & Ox is Oppression

A Song of Liberty

1. The Eternal Female groand! it was heard over all the Earth:
2. Albions coast is sick silent; the American meadows faint!
3. Shadows of Prophecy shiver along by the lakes and the rivers and mutter across the ocean? France rend down thy dungeon;
4. Golden Spain burst the barriers of old Rome;
5. Cast thy keys O Rome into the deep down falling, even to eternity down falling,
6. And weep
7. In her trembling hands she took the new born terror howling:
8. On those infinite mountains of light now barr'd out by the atlantic sea, the new born fire stood before the starry king!
9. Flag'd with grey brow'd snows and thunderous visages the jealous wings

wav'd over the deep.

10. The speary hand burned aloft, unbuckled was the shield, forth went the hand of jealousy among the flaming hair. and hurl'd the new born wonder thro' the starry night.

11. The fire, the fire, is falling!

12. Look up! look up! O citizen of London enlarge thy countenance; O Jew, leave counting gold! return to thy oil and wine; O African! black African! (go. winged thoughts widen his forehead.)

13. The fiery limbs, the flaming hair. shot like the sinking sun into the western sea.

14. Wak'd from his eternal sleep, the hoary element roaring fled away:

15. Down rushd beating his wings in vain the jealous king; his grey brow'd councellors, thunderous warriors, curl'd veterans. among helms, and shields, and chariots horses, elephants: banners, castles. slings and rocks.

16. Falling, rushing, ruining! buried in the ruins, on Urthona's dens.

17. All night beneath the ruins, then their sullen flames faded emerge round the gloomy king,

18. With thunder and fire: leading his starry hosts thro' the waste wilderness he promulgates his ten commands, glancing his beamy eyelids over the deep in dark dismay,

19. Where the son of fire in his eastern cloud, while the morning plumes her golden breast.

20. Spurning the clouds written with curses. stamps the stony law to dust, loosing the eternal horses from the dens of night. crying. Empire is no more! and now the lion & wolf shall cease.

Chorus

Let the Priests of the Raven of dawn, no longer in deadly black, with hoarse note curse the sons of joy. Nor his accepted brethren whom. tyrant. he calls free: lay the bound or build the roof. Nor pale religious letchery call that virginity. that wishes but acts not!

For every thing that lives is Holy

Though *The Marriage of Heaven and Hell* is hardly poetic, seldom even good rhetoric, it occupies a peculiarly pivotal place in the Blake canon, especially in relation to the more or less contemporary *Tiriel, Thel,* and *Visions of the Daughters of Albion.* However, the very nature of the work, its title, and its content, militate against comparing it on common terms with the poetry of the period. Despite the fact that in the near future Blake would begin *Songs of Experience,* the year 1790, when *The Marriage* was written, was filled for Blake with Swedenborg. His influence on the poet reaches its zenith and its nadir, and *The Marriage* is its death knell. In these terms it is almost true, as H. N. Morris has said, that Blake had two states, pro-Swedenborg and anti-Swedenborg.[1]

The Marriage, however, is not a conventional eulogy of the departed, but rather an angry rebuttal to a man who, Blake suddenly realized, was leading him along the wrong path. The change in Blake's attitude was abrupt. Though particulars are lacking, his reading and annotating of *The Wisdom of Angels Concerning Divine Providence* and his knowledge of *Heaven and Hell*[2] probably constituted sufficient motivation in themselves, the more so when the annotations are compared with those Blake made in the *Divine Love and Divine Wisdom* only a year or so earlier.[3] Since any personal reasons for Blake's "conversion" are outside the limits of this study, it need only be remarked that *The Marriage* seems to reflect the rage of one who felt himself deliberately cheated by a conniving hypocrite. Blake calls Swedenborg an "Angel," and in that imprecation lies the seed of meaning out of which he generated *The Marriage*. With passion as its basis, the artistic subtlety characteristic of Blake's other works is understandably lacking.[4] What form the work has derives from the vague pattern Blake saw in the works of Swedenborg, and in a sense *The Marriage* fails for much the same reason that the prolifically redundant seer is not read today: too much damning, too much praising, too little art.

Still an understanding of *The Marriage* is prerequisite to a complete appreciation of Blake's philosophical-poetic intentions, particularly those leading toward the *Songs of Experience*. Martin K. Nurmi has written a fine explicatory essay on the entire *Marriage,* in which he elucidates most fully Blake's anti-Swedenborgian intentions. But he dismisses "The Argument" in a few lines. My emphasis is precisely reversed, for I believe "The Argument" to be at once more complex and more significant than Professor Nurmi suggests. While taking into account Blake's anti-Swedenborgian diatribe, then, I shall concentrate especially on "The Argument" and "A Song of Liberty" and their relationship to that diatribe.

"The Argument" begins and ends with an uneven but powerful couplet in which Blake manages to sublimate some of his fury. Rintrah may be taken as that fury personified (and thus as Blake himself), or

perhaps more accurately as a "Devil" or "Genius" identifiable with
the roaming lions of the last stanza, and several other characters who
appear later to amplify and clarify his significance. In the first "Memorable Fancy," for example, Blake, on the way home from "the fires of
hell," meets "a mighty Devil folded in black clouds, hovering on the
sides" of a "flat sided steep [which] frowns over the present world."
Just as Rintrah "shakes his fires in the burdend air," this devil (energy,
genius, imagination) burns through the swagging clouds of the enclosed senses "with corroding fires" and writes a "sentence now percieved by the minds of men, & read by them on earth":

> How do you know but ev'ry Bird that cuts the airy way,
> Is an immense world of delight, clos'd by your senses five?

The sentence is double-edged. On the surface the answer is "we don't":
with "hungry clouds" obscuring the sun of imagination, "Man cannot
naturally Perceive but through his natural or bodily organs" (*No
Natural Religion,* 97). The air is "burdend" with bibles and sacred
codes that teach the dissociation of body and soul, the false dichotomy
of good and evil, and the doctrine of rewards and punishments. The
senses, being "evil," deny infinity and close man up in a cavern with
but "narrow chinks" to see through.

Similarly in "The Argument" the just man, too, is an "immense
world of delight," but encumbered by a rational theos and a conventional ethos, he is meek and keeps "his course along / The vale of
death," devoid of the energy which is "Eternal Delight." The devil
is that energy incarnate and can burn the sentences into man's man-
acled brain. But he can do no more than this. Just as Thel can listen
to the lily, cloud, and clay but cannot substitute the listening for the
real thing, so the just man can be given the Word to read but he
must act by himself. As Blake wrote, "First the notion that man has
a body distinct from his soul, is to be expunged; this I shall do, by
printing in the infernal method, by corrosives, which in Hell are
salutary and medicinal, melting apparent surfaces away, and displaying
the infinite which was hid" (*Marriage*).[5] Thus in the third "Memorable Fancy" the "Lions of flaming fire" rage around and melt the
brilliant but dead "gold silver and precious stones" into "living fluids."[6]
This is the fluid used by the "mighty Devil," this is the fire with

which the devil of the fifth "Memorable Fancy" consumes the angel who "arose as Elijah," the prophet-initiate. To the Swedenborgian angel this is all torment and insanity: his hell is cloud-covered, bituminous, and putrescent. To his eyes (in the fourth "Memorable Fancy") the "fury of a spiritual existence," Leviathan, is terrifying and he flees. Owing to his "metaphysics," the true reality is blanketed with fear and loathing, and all that remains on earth is the straight and narrow path, bounded by the enslaving gods of the priesthood and the sacred code which leads but to the "vale of death."

In other words, the just man of "The Argument" in his weakness has allowed his divine desire to be restrained; "and the restrainer or reason usurps its place & governs the unwilling. And being restraind it by degrees becomes passive till it is only the shadow of desire." This is perhaps what Boehme meant when he wrote: "Desire [that is, desire restrained], like heat, leads to self-destruction; and freedom [of desire], like light, is self-projection."[7] In this state of restraint the just man is a hypocrite to Blake because he is ignorant of any other existence upon which to base his self-assumption of righteousness. He has "forgot that All deities reside in the human breast." In reality,

> Roses are planted where thorns grow.
> And on the barren heath
> Sing the honey bees.

The Blakean devil knows this, and the human form divine knows this. Thus, whereas the angel of the fourth "Memorable Fancy" reveals his own "reptiles of the mind" in his attempt to show Blake the poet's destiny, Blake sees "a spiritual existence" and is transported instantaneously (with the angel's precipitous exit) to "a pleasant bank beside a river by moonlight." So also the just man: owing to his spiritual weakness and imprisoned sense, the straight narrow path is all there is; everything else is "thorns," "barren heath," "tombs," and "bleached bones"—that is, the Swedenborgian hell.[8]

Like the framing couplet, however, the entire first stanza of "The Argument" is pregnant with association and irony, the latter stemming from Blake's thorough knowledge of both Swedenborg and the Bible. Swedenborg proclaimed a new heaven as of 1757, and he himself sat as an angel at the tomb of the old, "his writings . . . the linen clothes folded up." The pre-Adamite kings of Edom once again reigned and Adam existed unfallen in Paradise. For Blake the date signified a more important event, the rebirth of the "Eternal Hell" (perhaps identified in his mind with his own birth). Blake's perverseness is not merely supercilious, for he insisted that "Without Contraries is no progression. Attraction and Repulsion, Reason and Energy, Love and Hate, are necessary to Human Existence." Swedenborg's "religious" version of this is: "All things must be balanced in equilibrium, in order that any thing may be capable of existing."[9] With Swedenborg in mind, Blake then goes on to point out that "from these contraries spring what the religious call Good & Evil. Good is the passive that obeys Reason Evil is the active springing from Energy. Good is Heaven. Evil is Hell." The last two sentences are a precis of Swedenborg's *Heaven and Hell,* in which we find: "It is known in the church that all good is from God, and . . . evil is from the devil"; and "whether you say evil or hell, it amounts to the same thing."[10] Blake's cosmos embraces both worlds, heaven and hell, and the asininity of the former must be consumed in an everlasting marriage with the energy of the latter. This does not mean, however, that they should be reconciled. The two realms are but extensions of Blake's concept of the prolific (hell) and devourer (heaven).

Like the meek, just man, the devourer lives a self-satisfied existence, for it appears to him "as if the producer was in his chains." That is, it seems as if hell is fenced out from the straight, narrow, "perilous path." The senses seem under control. "But it is not so," shouts Blake; the devourer "only takes portions of existence and fancies that the whole." The barren heath has no honey bees, and there are no roses between the thorns. The "Bird that cuts the airy way" is only a bird after all. And yet, despite these strictures, the devourer is "one portion of being." Indeed, "the Prolific would cease to be Prolific unless the Devourer as a sea recieved the excess of his delights. . . . These two classes of men are always upon earth. & they should be enemies; who-ever tries to reconcile them seeks to destroy existence." Religion is an endeavor to reconcile the two, and for Blake in 1790, Swedenborg was religion.

Swedenborg's doctrine of the separation of spirit and body, and the purgation and restraint of the latter to forward the career of the former, is diametrically opposed to the one Blake had been formulating so assiduously in the poems discussed in this study. It is the very disjunction of spectre and emanation that occasions the Blakean fall; a last judgment can be effected only by their marriage. Far from constituting a quibble, Blake's distinction between a marriage and a reconciliation is most precise. The former unites reason and energy— or, better, wisdom and affection—in such a way that neither loses its basic quality but dovetails that quality into its opposite. This process constitutes the imaginative re-creation of the androgynous human form divine from which the warring contraries are torn.[11] If the devourer ceases to devour and the prolific ceases to produce, there is reconciliation but there is also non-existence. Hence Blake's postulate that contraries are "necessary to Human existence." Without them, heaven is reduced to the status of a protectorate governed by laws to prevent experience. Blake believed there could be no heaven *without* experience; it is the only state in which the marriage can be accomplished—"by an improvement of sensual enjoyment."[12]

Thus *The Marriage* extirpates Swedenborg's rationale, which leads to predestination, and out of the ashes of that rationale rises the phoenix of Blake's wisdom: reason combined with the fires of the senses. The prolific is not inhibited but encouraged; the devourer is not chastised but impelled; and they both actively conform to their essential characteristics while sublimating them in a higher creative act in which *both* give. The result is Eden, not Swedenborg's heaven; the product is Orc, not Tiriel.

Though we have already wandered far from the first stanza of "The Argument" in an attempt to make clear the two roads delineated there by Blake, there is still a further allusion which must be remarked upon. It illustrates Blake's characteristic use of scriptural allusion, in this case to show the irony of the just man's single vision. He dutifully walks the perilous path in meek reverence, for he hears "a word behind" him, "saying, This is the way, walk ye in it, when ye turn to the right hand, and when ye turn to the left" (Isaiah xxx.21). Yet that road leads along the vale of death, the very destruction and evil against which Isaiah's God here admonishes and with which he threatens his rebellious people:

For it is the day of the Lord's vengeance, and the year of recompenses for the controversy of Zion.

And the streams thereof shall be turned into pitch, and the dust thereof into brimstone, and the land thereof shall become burning pitch.

.   .   .   .

And thorns shall come up in her palaces, nettles and brambles in the fortresses thereof: and it shall be a habitation of dragons, and a court for owls. (Isaiah xxiv.8-13)

But Blake says in "The Argument" that roses are planted with the thorns, and the honey bees sing on the heath. God's curse is thus transformed into Blake's experience, where there is no road, only human existence. This is all very well until:

> Then the perilous path was planted:
> And a river, and a spring
> On every cliff and tomb;
> And on the bleached bones
> Red clay brought forth.

This is not only Swedenborg's new heaven of 1757 but the biblical god's New Jerusalem: "The wilderness and the solitary place shall be glad for them; and the desert shall rejoice, and blossom as the rose. It shall blossom abundantly, and rejoice even with joy and singing . . ." (Isaiah xxxv.1-2). To Blake, however, it is the rebirth of the biblical-Swedenborgian hell, the one of restraint, not energy, for

> . . . the villain left the paths of ease,
> To walk in perilous paths, and drive
> The just man into barren climes.

The just man, now totally confused as to the right path, approaches insanity (in the context of Blake's dialectic) and flees into the wilds. There he will find the right path with the release of energy and the expansion of his five senses. The villain, however, hypocritically assumes the just man's place and basks in the superficial sunshine of God's new paradise. "No lion shall be there, nor any ravenous beast shall go up thereon, it shall not be found there; but the redeemed shall walk there" (Isaiah xxxv.9). The parallel with Isaiah is even more remarkable if one more passage from the prophet is considered. Believing as he did in the improvement of sensual enjoyment as the way to the higher innocence, Blake selected his text well, the vengeful God's description of the result of his destruction: "Then the eyes of the blind shall be opened, and the ears of the deaf shall be unstopped. Then shall the lame man leap as a hart, and the tongue of the dumb sing" (Isaiah xxxv.5-6). To this point Blake concurs, but the significance of the whole picture is vitiated in his eyes when God subsequently returns man to the same perilous path: "And a highway shall be there, and a way, and it shall be called the way of holiness; the unclean shall not pass over it; but it shall be for those: the wayfaring men, though fools, shall not err therein" (Isaiah xxxv.8). Thus the marriage of Swedenborg's heaven and Blake's hell takes place in Blake's experience, through which the just man must pass to achieve the higher innocence.

The actual "marriage" does not take place until the fifth "Memorable Fancy" and "A Song of Liberty." As Max Plowman writes, " 'The Marriage' is, among other things, an historical study of spiritual enslavement."[13] That enslavement has been at the hands of Swedenborg's angels. Thus, whereas the latter presented his heaven as a glowing paradise and gave only occasional glimpses of hell, Blake has overloaded *The Marriage* with the Blakean heaven (which in *The Marriage* he calls "hell") and relegated the angels to a mere bystander's role. Every facet of life has been touched upon insofar as it is a part of Blake's concept and Swedenborg's error: the essence of all life, the contraries; bibles and sacred codes; the body and soul; the after-life; the fall of the "original Archangel" and Milton's error; moral codes and modes of conduct; birth, life, and death; sublimity, pathos, beauty, and proportion; the priesthood and poetry; prophetic wisdom and the efficacy of infinite sense perception; religion and "sensual enjoyment"; the transmission of knowledge from generation to generation; man's destiny according to his career; analytics, metaphysics, and vision or imagination.

With the contraries so set up, Blake consummates the marriage in a "flame of fire." Perception and religion are united in Blake's basic tenet, the identity of God and man, which reflects the irrefrangible unity of soul and body. The devil (Blake) announces to the angel (Swedenborg), who is sitting complacently on a cloud: "The worship of God is. Honouring his gifts in other men each according to his genius. and loving the greatest men best, those who envy or calumniate great men hate God, for there is no other God." To the angel, of course, this is heresy and it provokes a reaction typical of Swedenborgian devils when a Swedenborgian angel propounds "divine" wisdom. Blake's angel "hearing this became almost blue but mastering himself he grew yellow, & at last white pink & smiling. and then replied, Thou Idolator, is not God One?"[14] He then goes on to explain Christ's sanction of the "law of ten commandments" and to point out that other men are "fools sinners & nothings." To this the devil retorts with a systematic disavowal of Christ's adherence to the commandments and ends with the pronouncement Blake will dramatize more fully in *The Everlasting Gospel:* "I tell you, no virtue can exist without breaking these ten commandments: Jesus was all virtue, and acted from impulse. not from rules." The angel reacts to this much as Blake reacted to the conversation of Isaiah and Ezekiel, with a "firm perswasion," and "stretched out his arms embracing the flame of fire & he was consumed and arose as Elijah," the spirit of prophecy.

This, then, is the consummation into which Blake has woven many threads both from *The Marriage* itself and from his other works. In one sense it represents the somewhat ludicrous thought of Blake merging with Swedenborg. This is not without some basis in fact. Blake did absorb, though in greatly different context, much of Swedenborg's divine wisdom, and even some of his "infernal" wisdom. More closely integrated with the present context, however, is the marriage of Swedenborg's hell with Blake's hell, an act that involves a very complicated shuffling of terminology. Blake reversed the Swedenborgian appelations so that heaven, as a place of restriction, actually represented hell in the Blakean cosmos. In turn, Blake's hell, as delineated in *The Marriage,* is obviously his conception of the highest imaginative realm, and accordingly he posits no heaven to balance it, except insofar as he wishes by so doing to destroy the Swedenborgian heaven. This is extremely significant in terms of Blake's over-all intention, for the juggling of terms results in Blake's hell being equated with Blake's heaven; that is, they are married. Even more important, the juncture is made by means of a devil and his consuming fire: heaven and hell are consumed together and rise as one, the prophet Elijah, or, more accurately in terms of the conclusion of *The Marriage,* as Orc, the "new born terror."

By personalizing the conflict, Blake has thus amalgamated it into his concept of perception. Heaven and hell do not exist per se except, like all deities, within the human breast. They are states through which individuals pass in order to attain a higher state as soon as the doors of perception are completely cleansed. Blake's innocence has in it much of Swedenborg's heaven; but, as we have seen, that state is not self-sufficient because it is based on ignorance. To learn, however, one does not turn to angels who think themselves the only wise, but to the devils of hell whose wisdom burns with corrosive fire. By uniting heaven-innocence and hell-experience, the higher innocence can be attained. Blake presumably resides there at the end of *The Marriage* proper. Rintrah has roared and shaken his fires in the burdened air; now the air has been cleared, though hungry clouds still swag on the deep. All they need is a Blakean devil, not the meek man or the angel, to disperse them. Then the flaming prophet, the revived "Eternal Hell," arises as the divine imagination to smash the Mosaic law and the iron-clad oppression of lion and ox.

In a sense this is the Bible "in its infernal or diabolical sense," which Blake and his new devil-friend read together; it is the "Bible of Hell" which Blake promises the world "whether they will or no"; it is Christ the law-breaker falling from on high to form "a heaven of what he stole from the Abyss" in defiance of the law-giving Jehovah-Urizen. As Blake put it in "A Song of Liberty":

> On those infinite mountains of light now barr'd out by the at-lantic sea, the new born fire stood before the starry king!
>
> Flag'd with grey brow'd snows and thunderous visages the jealous wings wav'd over the deep.
>
> The speary hand burned aloft, unbuckled was the shield, forth went the hand of jealousy among the flaming hair. and hurl'd the new born wonder thro' the starry night.

The new-born infant is of course Christ, but he is also everyman, born of woman and exposed to this world. Blake's "Eternal Female" is at once mother earth, the mother in Beulah, and the mother of Christ. Apropos the last of these, Blake insisted throughout his whole life that Mary was not a virgin but an earthly mother like all others in the *Songs of Innocence.* For example, in *The Everlasting Gospel,* we find:

> The morning blush'd fiery red:
> Mary was found in Adulterous bed;
> Earth groan'd beneath, & Heaven above
> Trembled at discovery of Love (753);

and

> Was Jesus Born of a Virgin Pure
> With narrow Soul & looks demure?
> If he intended to take on Sin
> The Mother should an Harlot been,
> Just such a one as Magdalen
> With seven devils in her Pen. (756)

That is, Christ—and all mankind—was born of generation so that he could be regenerated by means of the divine imagination. But Blake goes even further and, in so doing, gives a sample of his "Bible of Hell." The passage quoted above from "A Song of Liberty" closely parallels Herod's attempt to destroy the new-born Christ. The starry king is the law, the official god of mankind, the ancient idols foisted upon ignorant and meek mankind. He is described in terms which ally him to Tiriel, Urizen, and all of Blake's great tyrants, and his immediate jealousy reflects the fear inherent in his own precarious dictatorial position. His attempt to destroy the imaginative rebirth of hell takes the form characteristic of Blake's realm of experience, rationalization[15] ("grey brow'd councellors") and violent war ("thunderous warriors, curl'd veterans. among helms, and shields, and chariots horses, elephants: banners, castles. slings and rocks"). "War is energy Enslav'd," as Blake wrote in *The Four Zoas* (361). When the ocean of materialism, the clever reasoning of counsellors, and direct violence cannot smother the flame, the "gloomy king . . . With thunder and fire" turns to his most powerful weapon, which is also his last resort, the law: "leading his starry hosts thro' the waste wilderness," into which they have been catapulted from their complacent but false autonomy, "he promulgates his ten commands, glancing his beamy

eyelids over the deep in dark dismay." But the son of fire, the roaring
Rintrah, the omnipotent imagination spurns the clouds which swag
on the deep, "written with curses" like Tiriel's, and "stamps the stony
law to dust, loosing the eternal horses from the dens of night."
"EMPIRE IS NO MORE"; the just man no longer rages like a lion
in "barren climes" but lies down with the lamb in the heaven of the
higher innocence.

The energetic final chorus of *The Marriage* presents the millennium
in idiom most significant for Blake's later purposes: the priest in
black contrasted to the sons of joy; the religious tyrant to his enslaved
brethren "whom . . . he calls free"; the finite, metaphysical creator to
the infinite, imaginative creation; and "pale religious letchery" (virginity) to the real virginity of improved sensual enjoyment.[16] Blake
used this idea of the millennium as well as the same images over and
over again, but perhaps nowhere but in *America* did he so concisely
blend the images and ideas of *The Marriage*.[17] Orc, the new-born terror
of "A Song of Liberty," speaks:

"I am Orc, wreath'd round the accursed tree:
The times are ended; shadows pass, the morning 'gins to break;
The fiery joy, that Urizen perverted to ten commands,
What night he led the starry hosts thro' the wide wilderness,
That stony law I stamp to dust; and scatter religion abroad
To the four winds as a torn book, & none shall gather the leaves;
But they shall rot on desart sands, & consume in bottomless deeps,
To make the desarts blossom, & the deeps shrink to their fountains,
And to renew the fiery joy, and burst the stony roof;
That pale religious lechery, seeking Virginity,
May find it in a harlot, and in coarse-clad honesty
The undefil'd, tho' ravished in her cradle night and morn;
For everything that lives is holy, life delights in life.
Because the soul of sweet delight can never be defil'd.
Fires inwrap the earthly globe, yet man is not consum'd;
Amidst the lustful fires he walks; his feet become like brass,
His knees and thighs like silver, & his breast and head like gold."

(198-199)

The Marriage of Heaven and Hell, then, though it may only
loosely be termed a work of art, is an essential step in the formulation

of Blake's basic system. In the *Songs of Innocence, Tiriel,* and *Thel* that system took form in terms of a progression from innocence to experience to higher innocence. In the first of these states there was definite evidence of Swedenborgian dogma, though for the most part it was adapted by Blake for his own special poetic purposes. With the gradual evolution of experience, Swedenborg began to sound to Blake a little off-key. The final smashing of whatever chord of sympathy existed between the two men occurred when Blake was shocked into the realization that Swedenborg, despite his protests of man's freedom and "equilibrium," was a thoroughgoing predestinarian. A review of the mystic's other writings then unfolded for Blake the fact that he had been taken in: Swedenborg's good life depended upon law, order, and conventional morality; Swedenborg's man was twofold, and only the spirit could be saved by expunging the evils of the body. Blake felt, though certainly in more violent and less specialized terms, the same as W. H. Auden did in "A New Year Letter":

> O foolishness of man to seek
> Salvation in an ordre logique!

Auden's poem ends with "no order anywhere." Swedenborg was a Miltonic angel, and there was no order. Unlike Milton, Swedenborg was not of the devil's party, and he knew it. *The Marriage,* then, became Blake's *Messiah,* and the Miltonic angel was vanquished in his true form, Tiriel-Urizen-Jehovah, the law-giver "Religion." The Satan of *Paradise Lost* becomes Blake's God. Though this furious battle is an integral part of Blake's intellectual history, the most important aspect of *The Marriage* seems to me to be the terminology. Because Blake makes the popular, Miltonic, Swedenborgian conception of hell his highest realm (his heaven), heaven and hell are virtually denied any efficacious existence as far as man goes; action, energy, sensual enjoyment are the desiderata. Only through these qualities can wisdom and eternal joy exist. Without them the road of life leads but to the vale of death, no matter how just the just man is. He must deny the popular God, the priest, as well as the father and king. The religion of imagination is now a fact in Blake's cosmos, and it is in that idiom, or within that mythos, that the *Songs of Experience* find their fullest significance.

CHAPTER X

A TRAGIC VISION

ह~

It was at length the same to me,
Fettered or fetterless to be.
—LORD BYRON, *The Prisoner of Chillon*

VISIONS of the Daughters of Albion
        The Eye sees more than the Heart knows.

The Argument

I loved Theotormon
And I was not ashamed
I trembled in my virgin fears
And I hid in Leutha's vale!

I plucked Leutha's flower,
And I rose up from the vale;
But the terrible thunders tore
My virgin mantle in twain.

Visions

Enslav'd, the Daughters of Albion weep: a trembling lamentation
Upon their mountains; in their valleys. sighs toward America.

A TRAGIC VISION

For the soft soul of America, Oothoon wanderd in woe,
Along the vales of Leutha seeking flowers to comfort her;
And thus she spoke to the bright Marygold of Leutha's vale

Art thou a flower! art thou a nymph! I see thee now a flower;
Now a nymph! I dare not pluck thee from thy dewy bed!

The Golden nymph replied pluck thou my flower Oothoon the mild
Another flower shall spring, because the soul of sweet delight
Can never pass away. she ceas'd & closd her golden shrine.

Then Oothoon pluck'd the flower saying. I pluck thee from thy bed
Sweet flower. and put thee here to glow between my breasts
And thus I turn my face to where my whole soul seeks.

Over the waves she went in wing'd exulting swift delight;
And over Theotormons reign, took her impetuous course.

Bromion rent her with his thunders. on his stormy bed
Lay the faint maid, and soon her woes appalld his thunders hoarse

Bromion spoke. behold this harlot here on Bromions bed,
And let the jealous dolphins sport around the lovely maid;
Thy soft American plains are mine, and mine thy north & south:
Stampt with my signet are the swarthy children of the sun:
They are obedient, they resist not, they obey the scourge:
Their daughters worship terrors and obey the violent:
Now thou maist marry Bromions harlot, and protect the child
Of Bromions rage, that Oothoon shall put forth in nine moons time

Then storms rent Theotormons limbs; he rolld his waves around.
And folded his black jealous waters round the adulterate pair
Bound back to back in Bromions caves terror & meekness dwell

At entrance Theotormon sits wearing the threshold hard
With secret tears; beneath him sound like waves on a desart shore
The voice of slaves beneath the sun, and children bought with money.
That shiver in religious caves beneath the burning fires
Of lust, that belch incessant from the summits of the earth

Oothoon weeps not: she cannot weep! her tears are locked up;
But she can howl incessant writhing her soft snowy limbs.
And calling Theotormons Eagles to prey upon her flesh.

199

I call with holy voice! kings of the sounding air,
Rend away this defiled bosom that I may reflect.
The image of Theotormon on my pure transparent breast.

The Eagles at her call descend & rend their bleeding prey;
Theotormon severely smiles. her soul reflects the smile;
As the clear spring mudded with feet of beasts grows pure & smiles.

The Daughters of Albion hear her woes. & eccho back her sighs.

Why does my Theotormon sit weeping upon the threshold;
And Oothoon hovers by his side, perswading him in vain:
I cry arise O Theotormon for the village dog
Barks at the breaking day, the nightingale has done lamenting.
The lark does rustle in the ripe corn, and the Eagle returns
From nightly prey, and lifts his golden beak to the pure east;
Shaking the dust from his immortal pinions to awake
The sun that sleeps too long. Arise my Theotormon I am pure.
Because the night is gone that clos'd me in its deadly black.
They told me that the night & day were all that I could see;
They told me that I had five senses to inclose me up.
And they inclos'd my infinite brain into a narrow circle
And sunk my heart into the Abyss, a red round globe hot burning
Till all from life I was obliterated and erased.
Instead of morn arises a bright shadow, like an eye
In the eastern cloud: instead of night a sickly charnel house:
That Theotormon hears me not! to him the night and morn
Are both alike: a night of sighs, a morning of fresh tears;
And none but Bromion can hear my lamentations.

With what sense is it that the chicken shuns the ravenous hawk?
With what sense does the tame pigeon measure out the expanse?
With what sense does the bee form cells? have not the mouse & frog
Eyes and ears and sense of touch? yet are their habitations.
And their pursuits, as different as their forms and as their joys:
Ask the wild ass why he refuses burdens: and the meek camel
Why he loves man: is it because of eye ear mouth or skin
Or breathing nostrils? No. for these the wolf and tyger have.
Ask the blind worm the secrets of the grave, and why her spires
Love to curl round the bones of death; and ask the rav'nous snake
Where she gets poison: & the wing'd eagle why he loves the sun
And then tell me the thoughts of man, that have been hid of old.

200

A TRAGIC VISION

Silent I hover all the night, and all day could be silent.
If Theotormon once would turn his loved eyes upon me;
How can I be defild when I reflect thy image pure?
Sweetest the fruit that the worm feeds on. & the soul prey'd on by woe
The new wash'd lamb ting'd with the village smoke & the bright swan
By the red earth of our immortal river: I bathe my wings.
And I am white and pure to hover round Theotormons breast.

Then Theotormon broke his silence. and he answered.

Tell me what is the night or day to one o'erflowd with woe?
Tell me what is a thought? & of what substance is it made?
Tell me what is a joy? & in what gardens do joys grow?
And in what rivers swim the sorrows? and upon what mountains
Wave shadows of discontent? and in what houses dwell the wretched
Drunken with woe forgotten. and shut up from cold despair.

Tell me where dwell the thoughts forgotten till thou call them forth
Tell me where dwell the joys of old! & where the ancient loves?
And when will they renew again & the night of oblivion past?
That I might traverse times & spaces far remote and bring
Comforts into a present sorrow and a night of pain
Where goest thou O thought! to what remote land is thy flight?
If thou returnest to the present moment of affliction
Wilt thou bring comforts on thy wings and dews and honey and balm;
Or poison from the desart wilds, from the eyes of the envier.

Then Bromion said: and shook the cavern with his lamentation

Thou knowest that the ancient trees seen by thine eyes have fruit;
But knowest thou that trees and fruits flourish upon the earth
To gratify senses unknown? trees beasts and birds unknown:
Unknown, not impercievd, spread in the infinite microscope,
In places yet unvisited by the voyager. and in worlds
Over another kind of seas, and in atmospheres unknown.
Ah! are there other wars, beside the wars of sword and fire!
And are there other sorrows, beside the sorrows of poverty!
And are there other joys, beside the joys of riches and ease?
And is there not one law for both the lion and the ox?
And is there not eternal fire, and eternal chains?
To bind the phantoms of existence from eternal life?

Then Oothoon waited silent all the day. and all the night,
But when the morn arose, her lamentation renewd,
The Daughters of Albion hear her woes, & eccho back her sighs.

O Urizen: Creator of men! mistaken Demon of heaven:
Thy joys are tears! thy labour vain, to form men to thine image.
How can one joy absorb another? are not different joys
Holy, eternal, infinite! and each joy is a Love.

Does not the great mouth laugh at a gift? & the narrow eyelids mock
At the labour that is above payment, and wilt thou take the ape
For thy councellor? or the dog, for a schoolmaster to thy children?
Does he who contemns poverty, and he who turns with abhorrence
From usury: feel the same passion or are they moved alike?
How can the giver of gifts experience the delights of the merchant?
How the industrious citizen the pains of the husbandman.
How different for the fat fed hireling with hollow drum,
Who bays whole corn fields into wastes, and sings upon the heath:
How different their eye and ear! how different the world to them!
With what sense does the parson claim the labour of the farmer?
What are his nets & gins & traps. & how does he surround him
With cold floods of abstraction, and with forests of solitude,
To build him castles and high spires. where kings & priests may dwell.
Till she who burns with youth. and knows no fixed lot; is bound
In spells of law to one she loaths: and must she drag the chain
Of life, in weary lust; must chilling murderous thoughts. obscure
The clear heaven of her eternal spring? to bear the wintry rage
Of a harsh terror driv'n to madness, bound to hold a rod
Over her shrinking shoulders all the day: & all the night
To turn the wheel of false desire; and longings that wake her womb
To the abhorred birth of cherubs in the human form
That live a pestilence & die a meteor & are no more,
Till the child dwell with one he hates. and do the deed he loaths
And the impure scourge force his seed into its unripe birth
E'er yet his eyelids can behold the arrows of the day.

Does the whale worship at thy footsteps as the hungry dog?
Or does he scent the mountain prey because his nostrils wide
Draw in the ocean? does his eye discern the flying cloud
As the ravens eye? or does he measure the expanse like the vulture?
Does the still spider view the cliffs where eagles hide their young?
Or does the fly rejoice. because the harvest is brought in?
Does not the eagle scorn the earth & despise the treasures beneath?
But the mole knoweth what is there, & the worm shall tell it thee.
Does not the worm erect a pillar in the mouldering church yard?
And a palace of eternity in the jaws of the hungry grave
Over his porch these words are written. Take thy bliss O Man!
And sweet shall be thy taste & sweet thy infant joys renew!

Infancy, fearless, lustful, happy! nestling for delight
In laps of pleasure; Innocence! honest, open, seeking
The vigorous joys of morning light: open to virgin bliss.
Who taught thee modesty, subtil modesty! child of night & sleep
When thou awakest. wilt thou dissemble all thy secret joys
Or wert thou not, awake when all this mystery was disclos'd!
Then com'st thou forth a modest virgin knowing to dissemble
With nets found under thy night pillow, to catch virgin joy
And brand it with the name of whore; & sell it in the night,
In silence. ev'n without a whisper, and in seeming sleep:
Religious dreams and holy vespers, light thy smoky fires:
Once were thy fires lighted by the eyes of honest morn
And does my Theotormon seek this hypocrite modesty!
This knowing, artful, secret, fearful, cautious, trembling hypocrite.
Then is Oothoon a whore indeed! and all the virgin joys
Of life are harlots: and Theotormon is a sick mans dream
And Oothoon is the crafty slave of selfish holiness.

But Oothoon is not so, a virgin fill'd with virgin fancies
Open to joy and to delight where ever beauty appears
If in the morning sun I find it; there my eyes are fix'd
In happy copulation; if in evening mild. wearied with work:
Sit on a bank and draw the pleasures of this free born joy.

The moment of desire! the moment of desire! The virgin
That pines for man; shall awaken her womb to enormous joys
In the secret shadows of her chamber; the youth shut up from
The lustful joy. shall forget to generate. & create an amorous image
In the shadows of his curtains and in the folds of his silent pillow.
Are not these the places of religion? the rewards of continence?
The self enjoyings of self denial? Why dost thou seek religion?
Is it because acts are not lovely, that thou seekest solitude,
Where the horrible darkness is impressed with reflections of desire.

Father of Jealousy. be thou accursed from the earth!
Why hast thou taught my Theotormon this accursed thing?
Till beauty fades from off my shoulders darken'd and cast out,
A solitary shadow wailing on the margin of non-entity.

I cry. Love! Love! Love! happy happy Love! free as the mountain wind!
Can that be Love, that drinks another as a sponge drinks water?
That clouds with jealousy his nights, with weepings all the day:
To spin a web of age around him. grey and hoary! dark!
Till his eyes sicken at the fruit that hangs before his sight.

Such is self-love that envies all! a creeping skeleton
With lamplike eyes watching around the frozen marriage bed.

But silken nets and traps of adamant will Oothoon spread,
And catch for thee girls of mild silver, or of furious gold;
I'll lie beside thee on a bank & view their wanton play
In lovely copulation bliss on bliss with Theotormon:
Red as the rosy morning, lustful as the first born beam,
Oothoon shall view his dear delight, nor e'er with jealous cloud
Come in the heaven of generous love; nor selfish blightings bring.

Does the sun walk in glorious raiment. on the secret floor
Where the cold miser spreads his gold? or does the bright cloud drop
On his stone threshold? does his eye behold the beam that brings
Expansion to the eye of pity? or will he bind himself
Beside the ox to thy hard furrow? does not that mild beam blot
The bat, the owl, the glowing tyger, and the king of night.
The sea fowl takes the wintry blast. for a cov'ring to her limbs:
And the wild snake, the pestilence to adorn him with gems & gold.
And trees & birds & beasts, & men. behold their eternal joy.
Arise you little glancing wings, and sing your infant joy!
Arise and drink your bliss, for every thing that lives is holy!

Thus every morning wails Oothoon. but Theotormon sits
Upon the margind ocean conversing with shadows dire.

The Daughters of Albion hear her woes, & eccho back her sighs.

I

Visions of the Daughters of Albion is at once Blake's first prophetic book and the first song of experience. The quasi-generic term "prophecy" has often been used rather loosely to mean a poem in which there are strange names and confused action. It warrants more precise definition. After the *Songs of Innocence,* Blake searched for a vehicle for experience while not yet having formulated completely the particulars of that state. *Tiriel* gave form to the earthly father, and *Thel* to the failure of man to come to grips with the harsh reality of this world. Even *The Marriage* has its place in this series of experiments although its prosaic hodgepodge of many strands of Blake's thought makes it difficult to integrate it in a discussion of poetical experiments. Most critics claim for *Tiriel* the dubious distinction of being the first prophetic book. I doubt this seriously. Although it contains elements which might forcibly be construed as similar to elements in *The Four Zoas, Milton,* and *Jerusalem,* the prevailing humanity of the characters, the incisive analysis of Tiriel's mind and existence, and the general orderliness of the over-all structure belie such an intention by Blake. *Thel* is the same. Neither *Tiriel* nor *Thel* is prophetic, and they are certainly not lyric; rather, they are transitions from the one form to the other, as Blake's vision gradually expanded beyond his experience. This would seem to pose an immediate problem when we come to consider the *Songs of Experience,* but I hope to show in my discussion of that book that it is a logical outgrowth of the interim experiments as well as a necessary (to Blake) terminus to part of his poetical career.

As noted above, *The Marriage* cleared the air for Blake; the rage which I think blinded his poetical ability was consumed in the new-born infant's fire. His next poem, then, is quite properly a vision. It seems a tremendous leap from the aesthetic ugliness of *The Marriage* to the dramatic and beautiful *Visions,* but if *The Marriage* is considered somewhat outside the main line of Blake's poetic development, the leap largely disappears. *The Book of Thel* bridges the gap. Indeed, the *Visions* is reminiscent of *Thel* in many ways, but like the earlier poem it has been criticized and analyzed a little off the mark. The key is to be found, perhaps somewhat ironically, not in *Thel* but in *The Marriage,* and, in view of this, the exact relationship between the poetry of the *Visions* and the dogma of *The Marriage* must be examined in some detail. In this relationship lies the justification for calling the *Visions* Blake's first prophetic book.

The plane on which *The Marriage* was conceived may be called either supramundane or submundane depending upon whether one is Blake or the Pope. At any rate, the level of action is hardly that of *The Ecchoing Green* or even *Thel* or *Tiriel.* Somewhat paradoxically the huge figures of Satan, Christ, Isaiah, the prolific, the devils, and the angels are actors in a basically personal, comparatively petty quarrel between Blake and Swedenborg. Yet Blake was able to apply the elements of that quarrel and its epic heroes to the formulation of a necessary adjunct to his concepts of innocence and experience: by establishing the two fundamental contraries as states instead of identities, and thus denying the applicability of goodness and evil in the conventional sense, the road to the higher innocence was opened. Heretofore, as in *Thel*, Blake prescribed only what not to do and gave but a vague notion of what the ordeal of Tirielism led to. Almost goaded into a statement of his principles by the defection of Swedenborg to the angels' camp, Blake announced in no uncertain terms the contents of his "Bible of Hell: which the world shall have whether they will or no." Even the "Proverbs of Hell" were not enough. With almost Swedenborgian prolixity he reiterates the way many times in *The Marriage:* "Energy is Eternal Delight"; ". . . is he honest who resists his genius or conscience. only for the sake of present ease or gratification?" "The whole creation will be consumed, and appear infinite. and holy . . . by an improvement of sensual enjoyment"; "If the doors of perception were cleansed every thing would appear to man as it is. infinite. For man has closed himself up, till he sees all things thro' narrow chinks of his cavern." And, especially, "No virtue can exist without breaking these ten commandments: Jesus was all virtue, and acted from impulse. not from rules."

Hoarse from his declaiming, Blake almost revived his muse in "A Song of Liberty," and it is there, especially in the final chorus, that the other half of the transition (with *Thel*) to the *Visions* is to be found. What is more important, however, is the fact that *The Marriage* approaches in prose a method which Blake was to try in poetry— prophecy. *The Marriage,* combined with the poetry of *Thel* (which suffers in its consequent adulteration), gives birth to the prosody and form of the *Visions*. But at least it must be recognized that the *Visions* is Blake's initial attempt to exploit the road to the higher innocence insofar as that road is visible in the depths of experience. This, of course, is the essence of the *Songs of Experience,* but as yet the lyric form for Blake exuded only innocence. The *Visions* serves, in a negative way, to discredit that restrictive view of the lyric's capabilities, as well as to provide the visionary-eternal world pattern for the exclusively human conflict that constitutes Blake's state of experience.

2

In *The Book of Thel* the white-robed virgin balked at "the abyss of the five senses" and fled back into non-entity, eternal death in the vales of Har. Her virginity was revealed to be, in effect, harlotry, the "virginity that wishes but acts not!" *Visions of the Daughters of Albion* are visions of the act. "Pale religious letchery" finds a habitation and a name in Theotormon, and "the Priests of the Raven of dawn" who "with hoarse note curse the sons of joy" are concentrated in the terrific Bromion. Oothoon, like Thel, is not, as she is so often interpreted, the innocent who finally musters enough courage to enter the fearsome grave of experience, but rather the timorous and proud queen of Har (here the "soft soul of America") whose main concerns are personal immortality and the sorrowful fear of human mortality. In the interim between *Thel* and the *Visions, The Marriage* provided Blake the spur for the needed step forward, desire and love on the human level, as they are reflected in eternity. Oothoon loves Theotormon, and whereas Thel's desire was only for the finite (immortality of the body), Oothoon's is for the infinite (the human form divine) inherent in the finite (the human form human). Her tragedy, if it can actually be called one in the final analysis, is not a fear neurosis but the spiritual frustration caused by the defection of the object of bodily desire. In vision—the vision of the poet, not of the daughters of Albion—the real tragedy centers about Theotormon, whose enslavement is the one most fundamental to an understanding of the poem. This is not to say, however, that Oothoon achieves anything like the higher innocence— even in Blake's eyes. Nevertheless she does occupy a position which serves to define the motto and illuminate the basic irony of the titular characters' weeping.

"The Argument" contains the entire love story of Oothoon and Theotormon; in the rest of the poem Blake himself outlines several different perspectives from which to view the rape. "The Argument" also provides the first clue to Oothoon's identity or state of existence, a more advanced state than Thel's:

> I loved Theotormon
> And I was not ashamed.

Thel loved no one or no thing other than her own existence, the reason being that she could not suffer her selfhood to be destroyed or even threatened. The grave could do both; so she fled. Oothoon's first step toward the breaking of her enslavement is seen in the fact that she loves unashamed in the light of day. The significance of such an act becomes clearer later in the poem, but an antithesis is immediately apparent between openly-confessed love before the eyes of the world, and the guilty love which seeks the cover of night in its fear of moralistic scrutiny.[1]

Oothoon is not an innocent, just as Thel was not: both tremble in their virgin fears, and both flee the terrifying prospect of their own grave plots, Thel to the vales of Har, Oothoon to Leutha's vale. The two places are identical, except for one important point. Wrapped in selfhood, Thel ignored the spiritual implications of the lily, cloud, and clay, entered the grave and fled in terror back to where she came from. Oothoon has experienced the awakening of desire, and though not ashamed (as Thel would be), she nevertheless fears the consequences of love in this world. Thus, she too flees, but not back to where she came from. With great care Blake has transformed the vales of Har of *Thel* into the secret air of the higher innocence, through which Thel wandered but failed to recognize or comprehend. In Leutha's vale Oothoon finds not solace but the same teaching Thel ignored. Oothoon receives the wisdom of the marigold eagerly and returns to consummate her love regardless of the terrors of the grave. Whereas she started out, in her fear, as the virginity "that wishes but acts not," she now assumes the character of Blake's true virgin, called by "pale religious letchery" the harlot.

If the first stanza of "The Argument" identifies Oothoon with Thel, the second identifies her with the maiden dew of *The Book of Thel*. In that poem the cloud descended unseen to court the fair-eyed dew to take him to her shining tent, and

> The weeping virgin, trembling kneels before the risen sun,
> Till we arise link'd in a golden band, and never part.

In the *Visions,* however, something is lacking. After Oothoon plucks the flower of sexual experience and is spiritually fortified by the marigold's wisdom, she rises from the vale only to have "terrible thunders" tear her "virgin mantle in twain." In terms of Blake's evolving system, the contrast is obvious. The dew and the cloud unite in the realm of the higher innocence, where copulation is continuous so that the flowers may be nourished. Oothoon's act is in experience, where the monster of religion lives, and this being so, her rise from the vales cannot possibly be instantaneous. Besides this, Theotormon is not there, and it is he who must consummate the act symbolized by Oothoon's plucking of the flower.

The poem proper opens with the daughters of Albion:

Enslav'd, the Daughters of Albion weep: a trembling lamentation
Upon their mountains; in their valleys. sighs toward America.

These lines are trebly important to an understanding of the *Visions*. Since the daughters are enslaved, any comment they may make on the action must be considered in that light. Had Blake not based the poem on enslaved vision, the story element would have been a rather hackneyed closet drama of the eternal triangle, which for some reason or other is not resolved. The tragic element, which is there in either case, would be identified with Oothoon and would thus invalidate completely the role of the titular characters. At best they would be superfluous.

The daughters of Albion weep for the "soft soul of America, Oothoon," who wanders in woe because her love for Theotormon faces the abysmal fear of experience. They weep because they see Oothoon as an image of themselves before their enslavement; they know the terrors of the grave because they are still in it. Bromion's first speech makes this perfectly clear:

Stampt with my signet are the swarthy children of the sun:
They are obedient, they resist not, they obey the scourge:
Their daughters worship terrors and obey the violent.

In other words their desire has been enslaved because it "is weak enough to be restrained; and the restrainer or reason usurps its place & governs the unwilling" (*Marriage*). Oothoon, however, the soft virgin soul recently fugitive from her own grave plot, wanders until she comes to the "bright Marygold of Leutha's vale," the vale, as we have seen, akin to the realm of higher innocence. There in the familiar parlance of the lily, cloud, and clay, the marigold expounds the wisdom which can be gained only in experience:

... pluck thou my flower Oothoon the mild
Another flower shall spring, because the soul of sweet delight
Can never pass away.

Unlike the daughters of Albion, Oothoon accepts the teaching of the marigold and turns her face to where her "whole soul seeks," the realm of Theotormon.

The initial contrast between the daughters and Oothoon can be clarified even further by looking ahead to the use Blake makes of the characterizations in his later works. In *Jerusalem*, for example, Albion laments because righteousness and justice (in the worldly sense) have been visited upon him as a result of his own self-righteousness. "O thou ingratitude!" he cries,

"Give me my Emanations back, food for my dying soul.
My daughters are harlots: my sons are accursed before me.
Enitharmon is my daughter, accursed with a father's curse.
O! I have utterly been wasted. I have given my daughters to devils."
(669-670)

And again in *Jerusalem* the daughters' enslavement is described co-incident with the furious vengeance of Los, who

Drave the Sons & Daughters of Albion from their ancient mountains.
They became the Twelve Gods of Asia Opposing the Divine Vision.
(714)

And perhaps most pointed of all is Albion's lament over his defeat at the hands of America:

And like the voices of religious dead heard in the mountains
When holy zeal scents the sweet valleys of ripe virgin bliss,
Such was the hollow voice that o'er America lamented.
(Cancelled plate for *America,* 205)

Oothoon's "ripe virgin bliss" is short-lived. Bromion immediately ravishes her upon his stormy bed and then labels her his harlot:

. . . behold this harlot here on Bromions bed,
And let the jealous dolphins sport around the lovely maid;
Thy soft American plains are mine, and mine thy north & south.

Bromion is, of course, restraint of energy and desire, and as such can be expected to produce religious associations in Blake's mind. After describing the unnatural union of Bromion and Oothoon ("Bound back to back in Bromions caves"), Blake characteristically catches up one of the significant words, "caves," to expand Bromion's characterization:

At entrance Theotormon sits wearing the threshold hard
With secret tears; beneath him sound like waves on a desart shore
The voice of slaves beneath the sun, and children bought with money.
That shiver in religious caves beneath the burning fires
Of lust, that belch incessant from the summits of the earth.

This whole section is richly associative, as well as being, perhaps, the structural keystone of the entire poem. It recalls the weeping daughters of Albion, it establishes Bromion's character, it defines Oothoon's predicament, and it introduces Theotormon.

The first of these elements is reflected mainly in the part of Bromion's speech quoted earlier in connection with the first word of the poem. Less direct, but with perhaps more meaning, is the reference in the third line of the speech: "Thy soft American plains are mine, and mine thy north & south." In the context of rape, of course, Bromion means he possesses Oothoon's whole body; in the context of Blake's system the north (the breast) is the realm of spirit, soul, wisdom, and the south the loins, the body, the senses. Thus in the important first two lines of the *Visions* the enslaved daughters of Albion weep, "a trembling lamentation / Upon their mountains" (the north) and "in their valleys. sighs toward America."[2] Just as the daughters "worship terrors and obey the violent" in their ignorance, so they "are obedient, they resist not, they obey the scourge" of their senses. They are indeed "slaves beneath the sun," imprisoned in "religious caves." The caves are, of course, Bromion's, constructed upon the premises Blake outlined in *There Is No Natural Religion:*

I. Man cannot naturally Percieve but through his natural or bodily organs.
II. Man by his reasoning power can only compare & judge of what he has already perciev'd. (97)

In his final platitudinous speech, Bromion reveals his source of knowledge to be these very senses; he "visualizes" new things on the basis of the rational analysis of, and comparison with, like things already known (*Visions,* 192). He then goes on to demonstrate his essential ignorance and lack of vision, the same qualities by which he justified his union with and authority over Oothoon:

> Ah! are there other wars, beside the wars of sword and fire!
> And are there other sorrows, beside the sorrows of poverty!
> And are there other joys, beside the joys of riches and ease?
> And is there not one law for both the lion and the ox?
> And is there not eternal fire, and eternal chains?
> To bind the phantoms of existence from eternal life?

Bromion, therefore, is self-created from the very elements which his terror and violence purpose to scourge. He is essentially lust, the same burning fire that belches "incessant from the summits of the earth" while at the same time being chilled by the religious caves built to control them. Employing force to subdue Oothoon, Bromion calls her harlot (for this is what she is according to his law); her bastard offspring must be legitimized by the blessing of the marriage tie.

Blake has posed two contraries between which Theotormon must choose, the "good" proceeding from reason and the "evil" proceeding from the senses.[3] Unfortunately for Oothoon, Theotormon is "holy," his choice the "good." As Tharmas' spectre says to Enion in *The Four Zoas,* so might Theotormon have spoken here:

> "If thou hast sinn'd & art polluted, know that I am pure
> And unpolluted, & will bring to rigid strict account
> All thy past deeds. . . ." (268)

Oothoon's sin, of course, is her ravishment at the hands of her accuser, and despite the fact that "the soul of sweet delight can never be defil'd,"

> . . . should the Watch Fiends find it, they would call it Sin
> And lay its Heavens & their inhabitants in blood of punishment.
>
> *(Jerusalem, 668)*

Accordingly Theotormon allows his eagles to prey upon the flesh of Oothoon in a lurid Promethean scene used again and again by Blake.[4]

Almost all the rest of the *Visions* is taken up with Oothoon's various arguments to make Theotormon understand her position and his in relation to hers. Theotormon smiles at the eagles ripping Oothoon's flesh because he sees in it the righteous punishment for her "crime," the devilification of her body. What he should have sent, of course, is his love, but with his affections and thoughts nullified by the moralistic dichotomy of black-evil and white-good, he weeps on for Oothoon's blackness. Thus her first plea to him concerns the idea of eternal re-birth, but, unlike the marigold she carefully couches the idea in language that will appeal to Theotormon's jealousy. "Arise my Theo-tormon," she cries; "I am pure. / Because the night is gone that clos'd me in its deadly black." But Theotormon cannot hear this argument, for the night and day are to him the same, drowned in tears of jealousy which reflect the basic selfishness of his grief. Oothoon then goes on to assert the divine individuality of all creatures and the fact that, though the eye sees many strange phenomena, the heart truly knows but little. The analogy she draws is clear: just as we know not "with what sense . . . the bee forms cells," although we see it forming cells, so Theo-tormon's vindictive heart knows not that the soul of sweet delight is undefiled even though it is plain to the eyes of the wise:

How can I be defild when I reflect thy image pure?
Sweetest the fruit that the worm feeds on. & the soul prey'd on by woe
The new wash'd lamb ting'd with the village smoke & the bright swan
By the red earth of our immortal river: I bathe my wings.
And I am white and pure to hover round Theotormons breast.[5]

Yet, Theotormon remains blind to the patent fact of Oothoon's vir-ginity, for under the law she is as black as the little black boy of *Songs of Innocence*. Though reflecting Theotormon's image after the eagles have torn her flesh, Oothoon's soul remains tinged with red earth from the rivers of life.

With typical ignorance Theotormon resorts only to vague question ings, to speculation on the world's eternal truths, and to an analytical attempt at dissecting his situation. Just so Jerusalem cries out to Albion in the poem *Jerusalem*:

"Why wilt thou number every little fibre of my Soul,
Spreading them out before the Sun like stalks of flax to dry?
The Infant Joy is beautiful, but its anatomy
Horrible, ghast & deadly! nought shalt thou find in it
But dark despair & everlasting brooding melancholy." (645)

With Theotormon thus irremediably imprisoned in the caves of thought-provoked jealousy and despair, Oothoon attacks the law that created those caves, in the same dialectic and image pattern as Tiriel's curse on Har. The cruel kneading of the infant joy by the father constitutes the tragedy of Theotormon, who, seeing, sees not. Oothoon's vision is clear; in the light of self-knowledge and a contemptuous denial of the law's validity in matters of the soul, she sees that "different joys [are] Holy, eternal, infinite! and each joy is a Love." Theotormon, the victim of pale religious lechery, surrounds himself

With cold floods of abstraction, and with forests of solitude,
To build him castles and high spires. where kings & priests may dwell.
Till she who burns with youth. and knows no fixed lot; is bound
In spells of law to one she loaths: and must she drag the chain
Of life, in weary lust; must chilling murderous thoughts. obscure
The clear heaven of her eternal spring? to bear the wintry rage
Of a harsh terror driv'n to madness, bound to hold a rod
Over her shrinking shoulders all the day: & all the night
To turn the wheel of false desire. . . .

Instead of dissecting the infant joy, Theotormon should take his "bliss" and sweet would be his taste, and sweet his infant joys renew.

The dangers of the situation are apparent. With the woman shamed and mocked by the law for improving sensual enjoyment, her openness will gradually be transformed into secret pleasure, the clandestine amour, the hypocrisy of the faithless wife, the modesty of the coy mistress. As Oothoon cries,

And does my Theotormon seek this hypocrite modesty!
This knowing, artful, secret, fearful, cautious, trembling hypocrite.
Then is Oothoon a whore indeed! and all the virgin joys
Of life are harlots: and Theotormon is a sick mans dream
And Oothoon is the crafty slave of selfish holiness.

In the divinity of desire the day and night are the same, but not so to Theotormon, whose heart and mind are glutted with selfish grief and despair. Although the joys of day and night are forever "free born" joys, the law forces those of the day out of existence and changes those of the night into secret longings, perversion, "the self enjoyings of self denial," when "the horrible darkness is impressed with reflections of desire." "One Law for the Lion & Ox is Oppression," wrote Blake in *The Marriage,* but the "generous" lover makes his own laws, laws of delight that disperse the jealous clouds. "Why trembles honesty," cries Boston's Angel in *America,*

>   "and like a murderer
> Why seeks he refuge from the frowns of his immortal station?
> Must the generous tremble & leave his joy to the idle, to the
>   pestilence,
> That mock him? who commanded this? what God? what
>   Angel?
> To keep the gen'rous from experience till the ungenerous
> Are unrestrain'd performers of the energies of nature;
> Till pity is become a trade, and generosity a science
> That men get rich by. . . ?" (200)

Thus Oothoon makes her final plea to rescue Theotormon from the "self-love that envies all! a creeping skeleton / With lamplike eyes watching around the frozen marriage bed." She will even spread nets and traps to provide Theotormon with virgin lovers and

>   view his dear delight, nor e'er with jealous cloud
> Come in the heaven of generous love; nor selfish blightings bring.

But still "Theotormon sits / Upon the margind ocean conversing with shadows dire." He cannot understand this kind of generosity. To him it is harlotry; and Oothoon becomes both whore and pimp. In a sense, then, Theotormon's crime is worse than Bromion's, for it is at once the crime of inaction and of ignorance. (The comparison is perhaps not legitimate since Bromion's act is but the doctrinal backdrop against which the tragedy of Theotormon is projected.) The daughters of Albion weep for Oothoon just as Theotormon does, and they too are ignorant. Though ravished, Oothoon is not enslaved, and her ravishment is the blessing inherent in the curse of the law. Just as Tiriel's curse on his sons and daughters foments their rebellion, upon which they tragically fail to capitalize, so Oothoon is actually free in the knowledge of her own virginity. The daughters of Albion and Theo- ·

tormon see but the defilement of her flesh; Blake and Oothoon know the purity of her soul.

But the *Visions* is not only the vindication of divine vision. Although Oothoon's triumph is a fact, viewed in terms of the cosmos and all human life, the vision is a tragic one. Improvement of sensual enjoyment does indeed reveal the infinite in the finite, but to attain the higher innocence personally requires more. It requires a Theotormon who is wise, whose thought is unrestrained. Sensuality unaided by wisdom degenerates into clandestine love, which is lust; thought by itself leads to the palace of the fool.

In the *Visions* Blake has caught up the many strands of *Thel, Tiriel,* and *The Marriage* and woven them into the context of personalized experience. That personalized experience itself will now become the *Songs of Experience,* and Oothoon will reappear, under different names, in *Earth's Answer, The Sick Rose, The Angel, A Little Girl Lost,* and *To Tirzah;* Theotormon and Bromion, along with Tiriel, will become fathers, priests, and kings.

PART
V

CHAPTER XI

A PASSAGE TO EXPERIENCE

[He] Forsook the courts of everlasting day,
And chose with us a darksom house of mortal clay.
—JOHN MILTON, *On the Morning of Christ's Nativity*

I

We have seen how experience encroaches upon innocence in the *Songs of Innocence,* and we have seen Blake's wrestling with the problem of what experience is in *Tiriel, Thel,* and the *Visions.* The two poems to be considered in this chapter are additional evidence of that struggle, but more important they form together a passage song between innocence and experience. Both poems, *The Little Girl Lost* and *The Little Girl Found,* are difficult, even confusing, partly because of Blake's as yet inadequate control of ambiguity, partly because they are always consecutive in the various arrangements of the *Songs,* and partly because Blake himself was apparently uncertain as to which state of the soul they best described. Until the *Songs of Experience* was engraved, Blake included these two songs in *Innocence,* where they were not a little anachronistic. The speaker of the opening lines of *The Little Girl Lost* is clearly not the Piper but the prophetic Bard of the *Introduction* to *Experience;* the earth's awakening is similar to *Earth's Answer;* and the "desart wild" and "garden mild" echo the prophetic section of *Night.* On the other hand, there *are* elements of innocence in the poem: the never-fading summer's day; a possible echo of *The Little Black Boy* in the line, "In the southern clime"; the aimless wandering of Lyca, reminiscent of the Piper's wandering in the *Introduction* to *Innocence;* and most of all, the presence of the weeping mother who seeks to protect her child. It is almost as if Blake tried to put innocence, experience, and the higher innocence all into one poem.[1]

More than likely Blake wrote the two poems to balance the two poems on the lost boy in *Innocence,* the link between them being the search for a father or maker. Both girl and boy fail to find him. More important than their failure, however, are the methods by which the children seek to find him. The boy actively sought to grasp the father, and hence the higher life, bodily, while the girl approaches him in complete passivity, in surrender, in "sleep." Herein is the key to the basic difference between the two pairs of poems and between the children. The boy was completely an innocent, while Lyca is on the brink of experience, a kind of younger Thel. Thus Lyca *never* wakes as the introduction prophesies, and though she is "found" by her parents, they do not rescue her at all. She is not carried off to the realms of "immortal day" mentioned in *Night,* but to the caves of wild beasts. And finally God does not appear like the father in white but, if at all, as the lions and tigers which sport around the sleeping maid.

The Bard opens the poem by foreseeing the future, the higher innocence, conceiving of it in terms of Lyca's past life and present condition. After this prophetic introduction he flashes back to innocence (the present) and merges it with a dream or vision of the higher innocence. In that present Lyca is described as seven summers old: she has wandered for seven years and now lies awaiting sleep. Blake's point, supported by the traditional symbolism of the number seven,[2] is that a phase of life, of existence, of the soul is coming to an end. The creation as such has been completed, but life itself has yet to begin. Life as we know it, however, begins only in the "grave," in experience; consequently Lyca calls for sleep:

> Sweet sleep come to me
> Underneath this tree.

The tree, like the one in *The Little Black Boy,* is the shelter from which the innocent child must emerge to learn to bear the beams of love. During her sleep, which is the equivalent of "death" in the grave (*The Book of Thel*), the protective shade of innocence will become the caves of beasts of experience, where there is no mother. Lyca's final awakening (which Blake rightly did not include in either of these two poems) will be her birth into the higher innocence heralded by the Bard in the first two stanzas. Before she can awaken, she must sleep; before innocence can become a higher innocence, it must descend to experience. Thus contrary to the situation in *A Cradle Song*, in which the mother calls "Sweet sleep Angel mild" to "Hover o'er my happy child," here the child calls down sleep upon herself.

In innocence it is the mother's right, indeed her duty, to protect her child from "harm"; but in experience the child must cast off parental solicitude, which resolves itself into authority and even enslavement, to enter the grave of experience alone. The inability to surrender her self in this way was Thel's tragedy. The parents' weeping, in their own terms, is perfectly consistent and in character. To them, and especially to the mother, there is no other place to sleep than the maternal bosom, from which the terrors of night may be parried. The parental cry is none other than that of the nurse in *Innocence*:

> Then come home my children, the sun is gone down
> And the dews of night arise
> Come come leave off play. and let us away
> Till the morning appears in the skies.

But Lyca is no longer playing; she is taking the necessary step into life, and maternal tears can only hold her back in a realm she must leave. She is right in complaining:

> How can Lyca sleep,
> If her mother weep.

The problem here centers upon Blake's ambiguous use of the word "sleep." Throughout the *Songs of Innocence* he used it in its ordinary sense, as in *The Chimney Sweeper, A Cradle Song,* and *Night;* but in *Thel* the word took on new meaning, the basis for its ambiguity here. The "gentle sleep" of Thel's opening prayer and the reality of sleep in the grave are two very different things. Thel wanted to skip experience, to achieve an easy personal immortality, to eliminate the sleep the Bard speaks of in *The Little Girl Lost,* from which the earth will arise to seek her maker. The sleep of death and the voice of Jehovah (the voice of the grave) shatter that dream, for neither sleep is "gentle." Only to the corporeal understanding, to the earthbound senses, is sleep merely the pause between sunset and sunrise. In vision it is the passage from innocence to experience, where the mother has no jurisdiction, where the child's self achieves full stature, and where the only "protection" to be had is the human's essential divinity.[3] Thus, as Lyca says,

> If my mother sleep,
> Lyca shall not weep—

that is, if her mother sleeps in innocence, Lyca can sleep in experience[4] and welcome "Frowning frowning night," the same frowns that the mother in *A Cradle Song* beguiled away by smiles, that Thel fled from at the grave's edge.

The final section of the poem, stanzas 9 through 13, has been usually read as a picture of the higher innocence. It is a vision, to be sure, but we must not forget that Lyca remains asleep. She awakens to no higher innocence. The lions, leopards, and tigers are beasts of experience like the "devourers" of *Night.* Only the Bard, who speaks this final section of the poem, sees beyond experience to a vision of the beasts and child comparable to that in the closing stanzas of *Night.*

The role of the beasts, then, is twofold, as they are seen from the point of view of innocence looking forward to experience, and from the visionary point of view of the Bard or poet. Thus they are identified as "beasts of prey" only *after* Lyca enters the sleep of experience; but then, on finding her asleep, the Bard describes them as playing around her like the lambs of innocence. To the Bard, as to Isaiah (xi.6), in the higher innocence "The wolf also shall dwell with the lamb, and the leopard shall lie down with the kid; and the calf and the young lion and the fatling together; and a little child shall lead them." The last two stanzas, with their hints of sexuality and the darkness of the beasts' caves, then represent innocence being transported bodily into experience. Lyca of her own free will has entered experience or, at least, the half-light before complete darkness; and in this light her abduction by the beasts is perfectly right. They are playful only in the context of prophecy and vision; in reality, experience, they are still beasts of prey after all.

The erotic element here is properly uppermost, indicating woman's role in experience. In more subtle terms and with a great deal more finesse, these last two stanzas re-present Bromion's rape of Oothoon; but a further association makes them all the more powerful as a picture of the descent to experience. In *Spring* the boy and girl frolicked to welcome in the year, and in their actions lay the seed of sexual awakening:

> Little Lamb
> Here I am,
> Come and lick
> My white neck.
> Let me pull
> Your soft Wool.
> Let me kiss
> Your soft face.
> Merrily Merrily we welcome in the Year.

The shift from lamb to lion in *The Little Girl Lost* emphasizes the transition from innocence to experience, as well as suggesting the higher innocence in which the lion and lamb are one. Lyca's new year will be not the higher innocence but the dismal and terrifying darkness of experience. The lion's eyes are "of flame" and his tears "ruby tears," not the ruddy eyes and tears of gold characteristic of the lion in *Night*. These final stanzas of *The Little Girl Lost* are a fitting prelude to the magnificent terror of *The Tyger*:

> Tyger Tyger. burning bright,
> In the forests of the night;
>
> . . . .
>
> In what distant deeps or skies.
> Burnt the fire of thine eyes?

The rape of experience has begun. In the caves Lyca will become woman, parentless for all practical purposes, protected only insofar as slavery and bondage can be considered protection, and free only if she recognizes beneath her selfish human exterior the human form divine. In other words, she will become the earth of *Earth's Answer,* to whom the Bard cries his message of salvation. She will awake defiled in the worldly sense, and can be "found" only when she and her "Theotormon" realize that the soul of sweet delight can never be defiled.

2

Of the poem that always follows *The Little Girl Lost* Bronowski has written: "The child is no longer lost. . . .Now her parents wander mistakenly after a false image. . . .Their vision of fear becomes a lion, and he, god-like, becomes 'A spirit arm'd in gold' to lead them aright, to the child. For it is the parents who are found. . . ."[5] Taking into consideration Blake's shifting the poem from *Innocence* to *Experience,* Bronowski has gone to the core of the difficulty inherent in the poem's title. But simply reversing the roles of child and parents is not enough. In *The Little Girl Lost* the father played an almost insignificant role, being mentioned in only one line, but in *The Little Girl Found* he assumes an importance equal to that of the mother. The subject is "they," not "she." In addition, just as the word "sleep" occupies a central position in the ambiguous framework of *The Little Girl Lost,* the word "found" is the key to correct interpretation of *The Little Girl Found.*

At first glance, when compared with Tiriel, the weeping father of *The Little Girl Found* seems incongruous. Yet we have met him before in two places and in two vastly different situations, once in *Tiriel* and once in *On Anothers Sorrow.* The distinction to be made is between the father who becomes, or who is, a Tiriel and the father he might have been. The former usurps the role of egomaniac God by sheer force and imposes his rule upon his pliable creation, the child. But this need not always be the case. Har, for example, need not have been the "weak mistaken father of a lawless race" who "ready stands to form / The infant head," who brandishes "a whip to rouze the sluggish senses to act," who scourges "off all youthful fancies from the new-born man." Youthful fancies belong to the child as the essence of his innocence; their purgation reduces the infant joy to dry bone and sinew which, when examined in the cold light of reason, is ugly (*Jersualem,* 645). The child must wander and dance and sing, and it must be left alone by the father. His job is over at the moment of creation, according to Blake, for then the mother-protectress must hold sway. "Protection" by the father is what the world calls "law"; it leads to the tragedy, if it can be called that, of Tiriel. Thus in *On Anothers Sorrow* the father can weep with his little child, but he can do no more; the mother weeps, but she can and does also protect. It is for this reason, then, as well as the one referred to in my analysis of *The Little Boy Lost,* that no father is there for the lost boy: his mother must do the protecting and it is to her that he is returned by God.

Far from being confusion, Blake's idea is extremely precise and meaningful. Within the concept of fatherhood, as symbolized by Tiriel, there are many fathers: by venerating the self and inflating it to the realm of godhood, each father can become the law incarnate, the priest and king; by denying the self in the divine act of creation, each father symbolically recognizes his limitations and achieves god-hood as a *part* of the human form divine. Conceivably the mother has the same choice. By attempting to pursue her duties as protectress in the realm of experience she would thus restrain the energy of the child and assume the same position as the tyrant father. On the other hand, Heva's indifference to the product of her creation in *Tiriel* is a confession of the non-divinity of the act itself. In her way she is as bad as Har, for she is the mistaken mother of a lawless race. The divinity of motherhood and its concomitant responsibilities in innocence were denied in favor of the sexual passion from which motherhood emanates. The union of Har and Heva saw both devour; its product could be none other than a devourer, Tiriel.

In *The Little Girl Lost* and *The Little Girl Found* Blake clarifies the alternatives and, as Bronowski pointed out, demonstrates the role of "unfallen" father and mother in experience. He does it, typically, by means of vision, dream, and ambiguity.

One might expect, then, a connection between *The Little Girl Found* and *A Dream* of *Innocence.*[6] In addition to the clear verbal echoes, the pattern of action is strikingly similar. In *A Dream* the speaker sees a mother emmet wandering lost in the forests of the night; she is returned to her weeping children by the "watchman of the night." In *The Little Girl Found* the child is lost as well as the parents, and the latter, in search of their child, are led by the vision of a "spirit arm'd in gold" to the place where their child lies hidden.

225

And as in *The Dream* the basic conflict here is that of the parents. It stems from the fact that they cannot realize their roles in innocence have now ended; hence their search for the child, to protect her from the dews of night and experience. Their first dream makes Lyca's change of state clear to them, though they do not accept it as a valid sign: they

> . . . dream they see their child
> Starv'd in desert wild.
>
> Pale thro' pathless ways
> The fancied image strays.

With their limited "sight," the parents cannot understand that this vision is true. For Lyca innocence is no more; she is in experience with all its terror, misery, and horror. To the parents, however, their dream "proves" only that she is an innocent child strayed from the fold, a bird that cannot find its nest, a little boy lost in a fen. Just as the boy in *The Little Boy Lost* chased the "vapour" he thought was his father, and is thus led astray from his home in innocence, so in *The Little Girl Found* the "fancied image" of their child ironically leads the parents into experience where they do not belong. Not having the Bard's vision of past, present, and future, the parents can only act upon present stimulus, and their duty is protection. Fittingly Blake's emphasis at this point in the poem is on the mother-protectress: stubbornly

> Rising from unrest,
> The trembling woman prest,
> With feet of weary woe;
> She could no further go.

She can go no further because she is now on the brink of experience, where motherhood ceases and tyranny begins. This is why the father, who will become the great symbol of experience, bears the mother bodily "in his arms" on into experience.

At this point Blake makes the contrast with *The Little Girl Lost* explicit. Whereas in the previous poem the beast fawned over Lyca and gamboled and played almost ridiculously, here the couching lion bears the parents to the ground and stalks around them menacingly. The Bard's vision of the beasts of higher innocence is transformed into a vision of the present, the beast of experience in all his terror and awful power seeking for prey. At this point the parents have their second vision, this time of "A spirit arm'd in gold." Again they follow the "fancied image," which this time *does* lead them to "their sleeping child." In their limited vision they are satisfied that she is safe, even though she sleeps, significantly, "Among tygers wild." The little girl *is* found, then, but only in terms of the parents' imaginative capacity, which is limited. To the Bard (and Blake) Lyca is neither "safe" nor "found" in the true sense; but it is right that the parents give up trying to interfere.

> To this day they dwell
> In a lonely dell
> Nor fear the wolvish howl,
> Nor the lions growl.

The mother's protection has no efficacy in experience, and the father can exist there only in the guise of Tiriel. In the innocence of the present they hold full sway; over the future they can, but must not, have sway. Lyca's voluntary sleep is the sleep of death as far as they are concerned, and from it (experience) she must, of herself,

> . . . arise and seek
> For her maker meek.

As in *The Little Girl Lost,* the lion assumes the dual function of experience and the higher innocence. In his visionary role he advises the parents in perhaps the most poignant and meaningful stanza of the poem:

> Follow me he said,
> Weep not for the maid;
> In my palace deep,
> Lyca lies asleep.

In his Christ-like role, as a portion of eternity, he shows the parents their child sleeping peacefully safe from harm; as the king of beasts, a portion of experience, he makes it clear that she must not be rescued.

227

As Lyca entreated in *The Little Girl Lost,* the parents must not weep, for her sleep is actually the beginning of the way to the higher innocence. When the terrible vision of her miserable state in the desert (stanza 4) encroaches upon their dreams, the contrary vision of the golden spirit points out the other side of the picture. In both cases the lion is the agent.

Frequently the last stanza has been taken to mean that the parents rejoin their child, and all three lived happily ever after in a higher innocence. But Blake makes it clear in the second line of the last stanza that this is not so. The parents dwell in a *lonely* dell; the palace, where "Lyca lies asleep," is the same cave to which she was led in the previous poem, described here in the euphemistic language already applied to the concept of sleep. The parents, in effect, are living in a kind of transitional state between Beulah, where marriage and creation take place, and the higher innocence. Having given up their child, they live out their lives in the "knowledge" that Lyca is safe from harm. To them she is "found," as I have said, and only in this way can the child ever be found by the parents. The parents too are found, like the emmet in *Songs of Innocence,* in the sense that they remain as motherhood and fatherhood. They do not become Tirzah and Tiriel.

PART
VI

CHAPTER XII

INTRODUCTION TO EXPERIENCE

An unquiet and mysterious country
of inextinguishable desires and fears.
—JOSEPH CONRAD, *The Lagoon*

I

As befits the first song of a series which will strain to the utmost
the capacity of the lyric to carry complex thought as well as intense
feeling, the *Introduction* to *Songs of Experience* is an intricate design
in which the great hell of experience is apotheosized. Equally functional as an exordium is the immediate departure from the tone,
movement, and atmosphere of *Songs of Innocence,* so neatly foreshadowed in the *Introduction* to that series. The wandering Piper was
commanded by the visionary child to play, sing, and write songs
"every child may joy to hear"; matured into the prophetic Bard
or poetic character or genius, he commands almost arrogantly instantaneous attention. The child who listened to the *Songs of Innocence*
has now become the earth, the world of men, the reader, who must
hear the *Songs of Experience* whether they like it or not. Yet the
charge of arrogance must not be made too quickly, for the Bard's
imperative "Hear" is justified almost immediately. The situation no
longer depends upon the proper response to happy songs and sad

songs; now the ultimate fact of reality has been thrust before our eyes, the nadir of life of which we all (the earth) are a part. The songs to come are not only for our edification but for our salvation.

The past is indeed past, but it lives irrevocably in the present, and the future is made up of the two. The child's soul, Lyca's soul, has "lapsed" into the present, and it is with that lapsed soul that this poem and all the *Songs of Experience* have to do. The Piper's rural pen and its stained water have, like the miracle at Cana, become the life blood of the mature Blake, the prophetic poet, the consummation of the Piper and the cloud-borne child.

Of the many difficulties in the *Introduction* to the *Songs of Experience,* the main ones are the second stanza of the poem and Blake's erratic punctuation throughout the entire poem. If we ignore these, stanzas 1, 3, and 4 seem to embody a direct invitation to Earth to arise from the evil darkness and reassume the light of its prelapsarian state. But if such a reading were not orthodox enough to make it suspect, the subtle syllogism in the third stanza should persuade us to another reading. In similar fashion most critics, quick to point out the obvious reference in stanza 1 to Genesis iii.8,[1] ignore the fact that Genesis presents the Old Testament God, Jehovah, the cruel law-giver and vengeful tyrant, whom Blake calls Tiriel and father-priest-king. In addition, the Holy Word of Genesis walked in the garden in the *cool of day,* not to weep and forgive but to cast out and curse his children, to bind them to the soil, and to place woman in a position of virtual servitude to man.[2] In view of this, if the second stanza is read as a clause modifying "Holy Word," it is either hopelessly contradictory or devastatingly ironic. I am convinced it is the latter. Blake himself hints at the correct interpretation immediately by introducing an ambiguity into the first stanza. There are actually two voices in the poem, that of the Bard and that of the Holy Word, and the second stanza, because of its chaotic punctuation, can be read as modifying either voice, depending upon one's tone or inflection in reading.[3] The last two stanzas are the words of the voice, again twofold. Both voices are perfectly in context when the dual purpose of the poem is recognized.

Basically the pattern is not unlike that of the *Introduction* to *Innocence.* In that poem the child on a cloud spoke to the Piper;

in *Experience* the Holy Word speaks or has spoken to the Bard. In each poem the poet speaks or sings after hearing the Word, which in both poems is supramundane. Furthermore the ambiguity of the second stanza of the *Introduction* to *Experience* is an extension of the identification of child and Piper, inspiration and inspired, in the creative process at the end of the *Introduction* to *Innocence*. That is, the Piper's songs are products of the joint efforts of child and Piper. Similarly, in the *Introduction* to *Experience* both Bard and Word speak the words of stanza 2. There is this difference, however: since the Bard, unlike the Piper, already knows of "Present, Past, & Future" when the poem begins, the Word is less inspiration, which is unnecessary to the Bard, than simple stimulus.

Thus the voice of the Bard, whose ears have heard the Holy Word of Genesis, calls the lapsed soul, that is, the universal soul, all mankind; and calling, the Bard weeps in the evening dew. His weeping is, in effect, divine sympathy born of the wisdom of higher innocence. Such sympathy is the product of experience, symbolized here by the evening dew. But, as I have said, the Holy Word too calls the lapsed soul—as in Genesis Adam and Eve "heard the voice of the LORD God walking in the garden in the cool of the day: and Adam and his wife hid themselves from the presence of the LORD God amongst the trees of the garden. And the LORD God called unto Adam, and said unto him, Where art thou?" (iii.8-9) The contrast in time of day provides a further clue to Blake's intention in stanza 2 and the rest of the poem. He has juxtaposed the picture of God in the cool of his day calling to the benighted, lapsed souls of experience who are his children, and he makes those souls *the* lapsed soul, Earth. By so doing he emphasizes the patent fact that God did not come to the garden to succor the lost soul (as does the Bard) but to curse it and cast it out.

With this in mind a new and glaring light is thrown on the second line of the second stanza. The Holy Word weeps, but without pity or sympathy, and thus identifies itself with the hypocrite, Blake's archfiend. The selfishness inherent in such crocodile tears reflects the fact that the violation of Jehovah's law only means to him that his perfectly regulated and jealously guarded universe has been spoiled. Hence the rest of the second stanza, which falls into grammatical place parallel to the "that" clause ending stanza 1—that is, it is the Holy Word, "That walk'd among the ancient trees,"

> That might controll
> The starry pole;
> And fallen fallen light renew!

In the context of this contrapuntal scheme, the heavy irony of the first of these lines manifests itself. Capable of divine wisdom and understanding, Jehovah has chosen to abide by the insensate iron of his law and punishment, and thus to deny the very end which he hopes to regain, unity of creation. The scourge merely disperses the stars, as Urizen found out when, given a sceptre and crown, he sought to usurp for himself omniscient power and majesty:

> "I hid myself in black clouds of my wrath;
> I call'd the stars around my feet in the night of councils dark;
> The stars threw down their spears & fled naked away.
> We fell."[4]

The Holy Word might control the shattered firmament—that is, reorganize it—but it does not; the voice of the Bard might control it with its message of sympathy, and wisdom, if Earth will only hear.

As yet, however, the central image of the poem has not been clarified. It is shattered light reflecting the cosmic chaos. The figure in its hugeness embraces the vision of an earth torn from its axis, whirling crazily through space and scattering its vitals to the winds; in its minuteness, it pictures the dew of the evening mirroring eternal light in fragile, wavering, microscopic drops. Only when the dawn of the higher innocence breaks can the drops be reabsorbed. The contrast, then, resolves itself into an opposition of temporal and eternal, with the principal characters of each ironically having changed places. Jehovah, the God of this world, is thinking and acting in terms of the physical phenomenon of day and night, as well as the earthly morality of rewards and punishments; the Bard, mortal but prophetically imaginative, thinks and acts by eternal time and according to eternal values. As in Melville's *Pierre,* the choice must be made (by Earth) between the philosopher Plinlimmon's horologicals and chronometricals. Unlike Plinlimmon, however, Blake poses his alternatives in identical terms: both the Bard and the Holy Word call upon Earth to return, to "Turn away no more," for

> The starry floor
> The watry shore
> Is giv'n thee till the break of day.

The Bard's teaching is simple. In the past there was innocence, from which the soul in its selfhood was precipitated into experience by the encroachment of the law and its punishment. But the punishment is not eternal: another day is yet to come, just as the morning always follows the night. To achieve it one has but to see it. That is the problem alluded to in the last stanza. Enchained like Oothoon in the *Visions,* the eternal female (or Earth) comes gradually to regard all sex as sin, unless it is performed under cover of night. This coyness is a direct result of the enslavement by law that teaches "Woman's Love is Sin" (Annotations to Lavater, 88) and leads to the tragic snow-shrouded virginity of *Ah! Sun-flower.* To the dimmed eyes of the lapsed soul, sunk in the abyss of the five senses, the joy of morning light appears only as torture, a situation adumbrated in one of Blake's best early lyrics:

> Like a fiend in a cloud,
>   With howling woe,
> After night I do croud,
>   And with night will go;
> I turn my back to the east,
> From whence comforts have increas'd;
> For light doth seize my brain
> With frantic pain. (*Mad Song,* 9)

Similarly, Earth turns from the comfort of the east to remain in anguish on the "watry shore" of earthliness. Comfort is inimical to her, and she becomes an Oothoon figuratively baring her breast to Theotormon's eagles of revenge. Purgation is not the solution; rather it is the bearing of the beams of love, in full daylight, and the giving of oneself to another who can and does give as much. Sexuality per se is never sin, according to the Bard; it is only the warped single vision of Jehovah that can make it so. The soul of sweet delight can never be defiled.

But, as noted above, the teaching of the Holy Word is also voiced in the same terms. This is the act of a hypocrite. The tone of the Word, however, is considerably different from the Bard's, even to the point of patronization. Indeed one is reminded of many of Tiriel's fawning speeches and clever cajolery. Conscious of the fact that his universe, instead of being more ordered, has degenerated to chaos and confusion, Jehovah calls upon Earth to return with the dawn of a new day: the memory of what has happened at night will vanish with the light and everything will be fine. The Holy Word is thus forgiving Earth *her* sin, while at the same time inadvertently confessing the same sin:

> The starry floor
> The watry shore
> Is giv'n thee till the break of day.

Who but he has given it?—and yet he cannot understand why Earth turns away.

The curse has come full circle as it did for Tiriel. Instead of eternal day and a Garden of Eden, Jehovah has created for himself a chaos over which he himself reigns:

> Here he had time enough to repent of his rashly threaten'd curse.
> He saw them curs'd beyond his Curse: his soul melted with fear.
> He could not take their fetters off, for they grew from the soul,
> Nor could he quench the fires, for they flam'd out from the heart,
> Nor could he calm the Elements, because himself was subject;
> So he threw his flight in terror & pain, & in repentant tears.
>
> (*Zoas,* 315)

Earth's return, at God's behest, to the artificial daylight of the mundane sun would be self-exile to the vales of Har, to Thel's throne, to the abode of the weeping daughters of Albion. Only in these terms, it seems to me, is *Earth's Answer* a satisfactory answer poetically and philosophically.

In answer to the voice of the Bard-Holy Word, Earth raises up

INTRODUCTION TO EXPERIENCE

her head, "cover'd with grey despair"; the darkness of the dewy grass in the *Introduction* is reinforced by the suggestion in the third line of the *Answer* that Earth is spiritually blind.[5] "Prison'd on watry shore," "Chain'd in night," her senses closed in caves,[6] Earth hears not the voice of the eternal Bard but only the earthly admonition of the Holy Word. The latter can filter through the "narrow chinks" of her bodily cavern. These last three stanzas constitute the embittered cry of all youth, straining at the fetters of parental authority and arbitrary moral law, the same cry which gave birth to the beautiful *Ah! Sun-flower.*

Yet Earth does answer the voice of the Bard to some extent, for in her protest against the bonds of "free Love," she echoes the complaint of Oothoon in the *Visions* (192, plate 5). The emphasis throughout Earth's denunciation of Jehovah-Urizen is on the adjectives with which she characterizes him: "selfish," "cruel," "jealous," "weeping" (later deleted), and "vain." Each one not only reflects the qualities inherent in the Holy Word of the *Introduction* but also serves to crystallize the image patterns of both poems. Thus, selfishness and cruelty encompass the vision of Jehovah walking in the garden in the cool of day to chastise Adam and Eve; jealousy capitalizes upon the significance of the star-dew image, which was so central in the *Introduction,* through Blake's coinage of a new phrase, "Starry Jealousy"; the weeping and vanity bring together the hypocritical concern of Jehovah for the children of his curse and his forgiving Earth the crime more accurately attributable to him; and finally, the fear of the creator is made explicit in stanza 3, the fear of his own Tirielistic curse now descending upon his head.

Within that context Earth is right in turning away: love in a secret place (night) can never produce virgins or joys of morning light.

> The virgin
> That pines for man; shall awaken her womb to enormous joys
> In the secret shadows of her chamber; the youth shut up from
> The lustful joy. shall forget to generate. & create an amorous image
> In the shadows of his curtains and in the folds of his silent pillow.

Following this passage in the *Visions* Blake went on, in Oothoon's words, to propound the basic dilemma of this world. For Jehovah, the jealous, wrathful God of this world, the pragmatic view of the creation is acceptable only so long as the process or act of reproduction is kept hidden. That is what the night is for. Oothoon cries:

> Why dost thou seek religion?
> Is it because acts are not lovely. that thou seekest solitude,
> Where the horrible darkness is impressed with reflections of desire.

And in the last stanza of *Earth's Answer,* the chain is Bromion's chain, given life and power by the law of the father of ancient men:

> Forgetfulness, dumbness, necessity,
> In chains of the mind locked up,
> Like fetters of ice shrinking together,
> Disorganiz'd, rent from Eternity. (*Urizen,* 228)

Earth's situation is also analogous to Ahania's in *The Book of Ahania,* indicating the recurrence in Blake of a favorite pattern that underlies his whole conception of the cosmic ailing and its cure:

> Deep groan'd Urizen! stretching his awful hand,
> Ahania (so name his parted soul)
> He siez'd on his mountains of Jealousy.
> He groan'd anguish'd, & called her Sin,
> Kissing her and weeping over her;
> Then hid her in darkness, in silence,
> Jealous, tho' she was invisible. (249-250)

Earth *can* return, but only through the medium of a Christ, a Milton. Urizen, the selfish father of men, cannot break the chain, for with it would go his identity, the way of Tiriel at the end of *Tiriel.* Like Oothoon, Earth must realize her own purity despite the whoredom of experience. It is this vision that forms the essence of the voice of the Bard. That Earth hears it not is tragic; that she must hear it is certain as long as the cunning and hypocrisy of Urizen is not submitted to.

One further word: in terms of the *Introduction* and *Earth's Answer,* the *Songs of Experience* can now be viewed in their proper perspective. The Bard who sees the present as it is, knows of the past and how it works in the present, will sing of experience and look with sure vision at the state beyond (*Jerusalem* and *Milton*). The listener is Earth, and we too listen, not to joy, as in *Songs of Innocence*, but to find *our* way.

2

The next poem to be considered in this "introduction" to the state of experience is something of a curiosity. Infancy has been heretofore the exclusive property of innocence, and yet here is an "infant sorrow" in the state of experience. The exact nature of the antithesis Blake envisioned between *Infant Joy* and *Infant Sorrow* can be made clear by a famous passage in *Jerusalem*:

> The Infant Joy is beautiful, but its anatomy
> Horrible, ghast & deadly! naught shalt thou find in it
> But dark despair & everlasting brooding melancholy! (645)

"Infant joy" was beautiful, but dissected by the rationalistic approach of experience it stands revealed as "infant sorrow."

The violent contrast with the innocence of "infant joy" is seen at once in the first stanza of *Infant Sorrow:* the mother groaning, the father weeping, and the child crying in a dangerous world where he feels like a fiend in a cloud. The mother's groans, of course, are due to the fact that she no longer has any place in the child's life. Her role as protectress is over, and the child, though helpless, is on its own. The father, however, as a product of experience, weeps tears of jealousy, the earthly counterpart of pity, because experience relies upon mutual fear for its existence.[7] Experience is the father's home ground, so to speak, and the infant sorrow a dangerous trespasser:

> Into the dangerous world I leapt:
> Helpless, naked, piping loud:
> Like a fiend hid in a cloud.

The dangerous world recalls something of Thel's "secret air" which she sought with trepidation; and the fact that the infant leaps into it definitely associates him with Thel whose descent into the grave was in sharp contrast to her fervent desire to gently fade into the higher innocence. And, like Thel, the infant is helpless in the face of this danger. She fled, and though the infant merely pipes loud, he too will approximate that desperate flight in the last stanza. He is helpless, of course, because the mother can no longer protect, because the father's dominion is upon him, because he is most definitely human. His nakedness now loses all of the spiritual glory it had in innocence and will have again in the higher innocence; it merely reiterates his help-lessness. And that helplessness will become soon enough the child's damnation, as it is the nurse's of *Nurse's Song,* the rose-tree's of *My Pretty Rose-Tree,* and the speaker's of *The Angel,* all of whom learn to "get along" in this dangerous world.

The remainder of the first stanza is a cruel reminder of the Piper who piped so merrily down the valleys wild; the infant sorrow pipes only loudly, not a song of joy but the cry of terror Blake wrote of in *London:*

> In every cry of every Man,
> In every Infants cry of fear.
> In every voice: in every ban.
> The mind-forg'd manacles I hear.

The child of the Piper's vision no longer sits calm and lovely on the cloud but, in the infant sorrow's vision, is hidden in dark clouds, a fiend of reason and experience, as in *Mad Song:*

> Like a fiend in a cloud,
>   With howling woe,
> After night I do croud,
>   And with night will go;
> I turn my back to the east,
> From whence comforts have increas'd;
> For light doth seize my brain
> With frantic pain. (9)

The recalling of *Mad Song* is most apt for Blake's purposes, since experience involves the loss of light or imagination as well as an increase in "howling woe," a decrease of "comforts."[8] Further, the Piper's child-inspiration sat *on* the cloud, while the fiend hides *in* the cloud—one free, open, bright; the other enclosed, trapped, imprisoned, dark. Reason, the human brain of *The Human Abstract,* has usurped the place of vision and imagination.

The second stanza of *Infant Sorrow* pursues this idea vigorously. The child struggles in the father's hands just as in *Tiriel,* when "The child springs from the womb. the father ready stands to form / The infant head." To "get along" in such a world is easy (like Thel's retreat from the grave's edge); it can best be done through rational analysis, humility, and hypocrisy. So, in *Infant Sorrow:*

> Bound and weary I *thought* best
> To sulk upon my mothers breast.[9]

Implicit in the last line is the mother's indifference and impotence. She cannot save the child from the father, she cannot cajole away the sulk, and, moreover, she does not care. In *Tiriel,* we recall, "the mother idle plays with her dog on her couch." Most important, however, is the child's surrender to the world, sacrificing vision and faith for the sake of present convenience, here survival. The immediate consequences, unnecessary in the poem as it stands, are in the deleted third stanza:

> When I saw that rage was vain
> And to sulk would nothing gain
> Turning many a trick & wile
> I began to soothe & smile. (167)

A new Tiriel is born, paradoxically and most powerfully in the same form as the symbol of innocence, a child at the mother's breast.

In the same way *The Divine Image* of *Innocence* is perverted in experience to *The Human Abstract,*[10] in which

> Pity would be no more,
> If we did not make somebody Poor:
> And Mercy no more could be.
> If all were as happy as we;
>
> And mutual fear brings peace;
> Till the selfish loves increase.

And, in addition to these new "virtues of delight" "Cruelty" and "Humility" combine to produce the tree of Mystery, which "bears the fruit of Deceit."

> The Gods of the earth and sea,
> Sought thro' Nature to find this Tree
> But their search was all in vain:
> There grows one in the Human Brain.

Such a rational "holiness" leads us directly to the "holiness" of *Holy Thursday*, the "heaven" of *The Chimney Sweeper*, the "Church" of *The Little Vagabond*, the "mystery" of *A Little Boy Lost*, and the "Christian forbearance" of *A Poison Tree*.

CHAPTER XIII

THE WINTER OF HOLINESS

ફ

The true church of Christ has no law!
—JACOB BOEHME, *Of the Incarnation of Jesus Christ*

I

In the *Holy Thursday* of *Songs of Innocence* Blake introduced
the religious element of his triune tyrant; in *The Divine Image* he
delineated his concept of holiness and amplified it in *The Marriage*
and the *Visions. The Human Abstract* is the perversion of that concept in experience, the key figure the priest, perhaps best represented
in *The Garden of Love.* The similarity of *The Garden* to the "perilous
path" of "The Argument" to *The Marriage* is important, for both
of these poems lead directly to the aridity of the *Holy Thursday* of
Experience, in which the priest, though never actually present, is
ever present.

The two main questions (the first two stanzas) with which this
Holy Thursday begins are not as simply rhetorical as they seem. The
omniscient, eternal Bard is speaking, and it is in terms of his wisdom
that the questions and answers must be interpreted. The first question awkwardly juxtaposes the concepts of holiness and of physical
health and well-being. But the awkwardness is clearly functional. On
the surface it is not a "holy thing" to see children starving in a land
of plenty; it is merely unfortunate. But in the context of worldly

morality and material values, the very fact that the babes are fed at all is "holy," regardless of the richness of the land in which they starve. The point is a basic one. No question is made by "cold and usurous" man into the origin of the terrors of experience, of human enslavement (for its origin is man himself, whose heart has been petrified by moral, religious, and penal codes); but given that slavery and misery, an attempt is made, however feeble, to alleviate it. That is holiness. For the Bard, however, holiness is not a question of richness or poverty, but one of attitude, of heart, and of mind. "Poverty the mind appall[s]," says Blake, but he means only the spiritual and emotional poverty reflected in the "beneficent" cold and usurious hand of stanza one. To the beadles and the grey-haired men of *Holy Thursday* in *Innocence* the feeding of the miserable babes is a holy thing to see; to the Bard the very fact that the children are fed as they are appalls.

Even this, however, does not explain completely the powerful condensation of the stanza. For that, as well as for the emphasis on the hypocrisy that underlies the whole idea of charity as Blake saw it, the last line is largely responsible. In a rich and fruitful land, babes can be reduced to misery only by some agent, for the last stanza proclaims the eternal truth of rich and fruitful lands. The agent, of course, is the usurious hand, ironically feeding the very mouth from which it steals its opulence. The hand is also cold for it lacks the love inherent in Blake's symbolic sun. The transferred epithet at the end of the fourth line thus unites the concepts of hunger and poverty which form the foundation for the poem's whole structure. The all-grasping, omnivorous hand symbolizes for Blake the very material values and hypocritical benevolence described in glowing terms in line 1 ("holy thing") and line 2 ("rich and fruitful land"), which are, in their turn, the cause of the babes' reduction to misery.

The second stanza asks the second ambiguous question:

> Is that trembling cry a song?
> Can it be a song of joy?

The song is the cry of miserable children, but it is also a song of joy like that in the *Holy Thursday* of *Innocence.* Impoverished, the children still know the way to God, and as in *Innocence,* this merely serves to point out the essential emptiness, corruption, and poverty of the hand that purports to help. Like Earth the children are bound; and also like her they know what the chains consist of. Blake states it in his remarkably effective eighth line: "It is a land of poverty." This is the key line of the poem, containing all that comes before and foreshadowing all that follows. It is a land of poverty materially and spiritually; it is not a rich and fruitful land, for there are "so many children poor." It is not a holy thing to feed them and treat them as they are; it is hypocrisy. The poverty, of course, includes lack of richness, lack of fruitfulness, lack of joy, and lack of warmth, all of these terms now pertinent to the worldly as well as the spiritual scheme of things. The third stanza amply demonstrates this. There is now no alternative answer to a question: there is only flat statement of fact. The dilemma of Earth, this land, these children is symbolized in the children of experience:

> And *their* sun does never shine.
> And *their* fields are bleak & bare.
> And *their* ways are fill'd with thorns.
> It is eternal winter *there*. (my italics)

Even the echo of "their" in the last line is functional: "there" is in the child's heart, and as the last word of the stanza it contrasts sharply with the elsewhere of the last stanza, the "where-e'er." Elsewhere the sun and the rain produce not the empty richness and poisonous fruit[1] of the first stanza, but the higher innocence where poverty and hunger do not even have meaning—just as harm in innocence has no validity as a deterrent to action. Productiveness, creation, is all, the love and pity whose essential characteristics are symbolized by sun and rain.

The last stanza, Blake's powerful answer to all the questions, is a superb climax and summary of the image and associational echoes of the first three stanzas. Through the child of experience, who assumes the burden of central symbol in the poem, Blake leads directly to the state to which that child aspires; the material values are thoroughly translated into the spiritual realm, into the "holy thing" that is so grimly ironic in the first stanza. Though one is scarcely conscious of the transitions that align the whole poem inevitably toward this stanza, Blake has nevertheless pointed the way with exquisite artistry. The first line of the stanza is precisely parallel to the first line of stanza 3, but with a significant shift from the heavily accented "never" to the equally stressed "does"; and, with its Blakean connotations of warm, heavenly love, the line contrasts sharply with the calculated beneficence of the usurious hand and the "eternal winter" of the bones.[2] Line 2 of the last stanza completes the background transition by drawing together the ironic "rich and fruitful" of stanza 1 and the realistic "bleak & bare" fields of stanza 3. The third line is a structural masterpiece. Pitched on a high key, the heavy initial accent carries through the entire length of the line and falls with equal emphasis on the other key word, "there." The babe is the child of experience, encompassing all the babes of stanza 1 (note its comparable position in the line) and the children of stanza 2. The second word recalls the equivocal, hesitating question of line 6, now transposed into a resonant assertion. The third word echoes its negative counterpart in the first line of stanza 3, again sharply reversed. The fourth word recalls both the cruel hand that feeds in stanza 1 and the frigid drouth of stanza 3, and it negates their efficacy in the world of light. And the fifth word identifies the child with the higher innocence by merging the "their" and "there" of stanza 3, the wisdom and love inherent in the human form divine, to which material poverty or riches are but empty, meaningless terms substituted by enslaved man for the true virtues—mercy, pity, peace, and love.

The last line returns to the ambiguity of the first two stanzas and resolves them into their true perspective. Poverty appalls the mind, but it is the mind of the usurious giver, the indifferent passer-by, the pitying onlooker who weeps and then turns away to glut his appetite. To the man with greater vision, to the imagination, to the Bard, the song is a song of joy, and the real poverty rests in the bosom of the "rich and fruitful" land where love is bought and sold, where

> . . . the youthful Harlots curse
> Blasts the new born Infants tear
> And blights with plagues the Marriage hearse. (*London*)

It is at this that the Bard's mind—and the reader's—is appalled, for in the usurious heart the sun never *can* shine.

One word more. If the poem is read as conventional social protest, as it is more often than not, the last stanza seems to me to require extensive apologetics. Of course where the sun shines and the rain falls there will be plenty of food for all, and charity will not be necessary. There is no question; there is no poem. Until Blake's subtle distinction, and subsequent blending, of natural and spiritual is discerned, the poem remains but a poor counterpart to the *Holy Thursday* of *Innocence*.

2

Like *Holy Thursday*, *The Chimney Sweeper* is one of the seven or eight songs in *Experience* that are most closely connected with their similarly named counterparts in *Innocence*. Each of them, however, has been modified or translated consistent with the shift from the state of innocence to experience. In *The Chimney Sweeper* the shift is mainly one of character, as in *Infant Joy* and *Infant Sorrow*. In *Innocence* the sweeper dreamt of an angel with a bright key which transported him to the realm of innocence in which he really, imaginatively, dwelt. As yet he had not reached the forests of experience, nor had he come under the dominion of the earthly tyrants, mother and father. In *Experience* the sweeper not only reaches the forest, but succumbs to its darkness and its tyrants. This change of character depends upon several details absent from *The Chimney Sweeper* of *Innocence*, which were developed by Blake either in the interim poems between the earlier and the later *Songs* or here in *Experience* itself: (1) the father and mother of experience; (2) the church and its relationship to Blake's idea of father, God, priest, and king; (3) the concept of harm or injury, anticipated in *The Chimney Sweeper* of *Innocence* and an important element in Tiriel's first visit to Har and Heva; and (4), of course, earthly morality and values.

Though *The Chimney Sweeper* begins on the same note as its counterpart in *Innocence*, a contrast is almost immediately apparent: in the earlier poem the mother was dead and the father not present, while here both parents are living and have gone "to the church to pray." Blake's irony is almost too mechanical. The innocent child had no mother in the realm of motherhood and the child of experience has both parents in a realm where neither should be. The sweeper of innocence relied on his soot-covered body to shield him as the shade tree shielded the little black boy, and he attained his rightful place in innocent joy through vision. The sweeper of experience, though he has both parents, has no such shield. Even more disastrous, he has no vision, as we shall see in a moment. Thus, a further contrast is evident—between the weeping parents of "the little girl lost," who in their ignorance sought to prolong their protective function through experience, and the indifferent parents of the sweeper of experience. Ignorant of the divinity of their own creation, the parents, like Har in *Tiriel,* scourge the youthful fancies from their child and then with the coolness of villainy praise the God which makes this possible. The condemnation of father-mother is most explicit, but the attack on God himself remains only implicit until the last stanza.

The church itself has a major function in the poem, related somewhat curiously to the grave in which the mother of the sweeper in *Innocence* lies. This relationship is suggested by the sweeper's description of his parents' treatment of him: "They clothed me in the clothes of death." The inference is that the clothes of death are sanctioned by the church, to which the parents go with songs of praise instead of remaining to help their child. Thus, whereas the mother of the sweeper in *Innocence* is dead, wrongfully, the mother of the sweeper in *Experience* lives, also wrongfully. The former, however, lives for the innocent sweeper in vision; he finds the comfort, warmth, and protection which are his due in the dream of the angel with the bright key. On the other hand, imaginatively the mother of experience is dead to her child, for in place of her protective warmth has arisen the spectre of authority which retains the name of mother but has corrupted its significance. The church has become the grave, the mother's prayer a profanation. The God to whom the parents pray will be equated to priest and king and, by extension, to the parents themselves. On this note of selfishness and hypocrisy Blake writes the rest of his poem, the point of view and the words, of course, being the sweeper's.

The first two lines of stanza 2 are a direct reference to *The Chimney Sweeper* of *Innocence,* who despite his plight can smile and be happy in the imaginative knowledge of his own innocence. In experience, however, the child loses his imaginative capacity, his perspective becomes confined to worldly images and, in turn, to rational concepts. He must now make the best of his new world (as infant sorrow does) under the tutelage of his indifferent, equally limited parents. It is they who bind him in clothes of death and teach him to sing the notes of woe. These clothes contrast sharply with the sweeper's naked whiteness in the vision of *Songs of Innocence,* Tom Dacre's whiteness being the ultimate reality of his condition, the soot merely the protective shade which must be imagined away. For the sweeper in *Songs of Experience,* however, there is no vision, no angel with a bright key, no rivers to cleanse, no sun to warm. The clothes of death are the ultimate reality. This is significant in two ways. First, the parents clothe the child: he does not assume his position willingly; and by that act, the parents follow in the footsteps of Har and Heva, who "humble the immortal spirit" of Tiriel. By molding the sweeper to their wishes, the parents *sous tous les rapports* weave his winding sheet and compose his dirge, which, in effect, is the poem itself. By far the most important word (or phrase) of this dirge is "death" ("the clothes of death"). In *Innocence* "death" is unknown to the children; in *Experience* it is "taught."[3] Death for Blake had validity as a concept only in worldly terms. Otherwise there is only life and then a greater life.[4] The chimney sweeper's real tragedy, then, is a loss of imagination and vision, a surrender to "mind-forg'd manacles."

Thus in the last stanza of the poem we should not be surprised to hear the sweeper analyzing his situation in terms of physical "injury" and discomfort:

> And because I am happy. & dance & sing.
> They think they have done me no injury:
> And are gone to praise God & his Priest & King
> Who make up a heaven of our misery.

Molded and taught by the parents, the child falls rapidly into the straight and narrow path which leads but to the grave, the same path Blake wrote of so damningly in "The Argument" to *The Marriage of Heaven and Hell.* The sweeper confesses his misery and winces from his injury; life has become a matter of blackness and whiteness, the former evil and the latter good, the former hazardous, the latter safe from harm. Unlike the sweeper in *Innocence* the one in *Experience* does not cry. Rather he curses, in indirect fashion to be sure, God and priest and king for profiting by his low state.[5] Blake's point is that physical discomfort is meaningless to the free, imaginative man. To the sweeper, however, his misery is important and his parents are evil for allowing it to happen. The clothes of death have shrouded him in their folds; he has indeed been fashioned in his parents' image. As noted above they praise the infinite God through his priest and king for the blessings of this world; they do not feel they have done the child injury because survival in this world demands that he work. Besides, he dances and sings, and that is corroboration enough of their own righteousness. To enable him to live in this world, then, the parents smother his soul, and neither they nor the child is cognizant of that all-important fact. The world, life, and material richness are all dazzling and attractive to the corporeal eye, but when the grave is opened (as in *Thel*) and the twisted roots of corruption are bared, the soul of life is seen to shrivel up like a burnt cinder. God and his priest and king lay down the laws on how to get along on earth, but the process inevitably involves the strangulation of all desire and energy.

The last line of the poem sums up Blake's comment on the whole situation: God, priest, and king "make up a heaven of our misery." It is Swedenborg's heaven, of course, and for Blake it is death: the death of the parents, just as Tiriel died by his own curse, and the death of the chimney sweeper whose desire for freedom was weak enough to be restrained. The sweeper's rational analysis of his miserable condition parallels Thel's complaint about her earthly evanescence. The decalog has been invoked so that the vision of an angel with a bright key is no longer possible. Even the imagination has been stultified; the sweeper is no longer the innocent child but the worldly spectre.

The poem, I think, is inadequate to say all this, and especially it leaves a key question unanswered: if the sweeper is actually enslaved through his own weakness, what could he have done to avoid it? Weren't the circumstances against him? Blake himself answered a similar question in a letter to Butts: "If we fear to do the dictates of our Angels, & tremble at the Tasks set before us; if we refuse to do Spiritual Acts because of Natural Fears of Natural Desires! Who can describe the dismal torments of such a state!—I too well remember the Threats I heard!—If you, who are organized by Divine Providence for Spiritual communion, Refuse, & bury your Talent in the Earth, even tho' you should want Natural Bread, Sorrow & Desperation pursues you thro' life, & after death shame & confusion of face to eternity" (813). Circumstances can *never* alter the soul; the soul of sweet delight can never be defiled. The chimney sweeper, however, surrenders his soul and in effect, like his parents and god-priest-king, he makes a heaven of the misery which is actually a hell to him. He could have gone naked, but he tacitly accepted the clothes of death;[6] he could have sung a song of joy, but the notes of woe came easier; he could have made a real heaven of his misery, but he did not see that that heaven—and all deity—resided in his own breast.

3

Earlier in this study I explained that innocence itself, though basically selfish, irresponsible, even hedonistic, nevertheless did not recognize or conceive of the self as an entity. The innocent child merely existed and was innocent without speculation as to the reason for such existence. But beyond a certain point—never precisely defined by Blake—this innocence could not continue; the child (or adolescent) had to choose whether to retreat from the gaping grave of the empirical world or advance like Lyca in *The Little Girl Lost*. An advance meant the recognition of self as such, the assumption of a sentience commensurate with an advance in age, in intellect, and in passion.

The lesson of experience, as Blake saw it, was to transform that selfconsciousness into total consciousness—that is, to see the self as only a part of the great self, the human form divine. The love that was innocently devoured by the child in innocence must now be given in equal measure. But love in experience, the love of the pebble in *The Clod and the Pebble*,

> . . . seeketh only Self to please,
> To bind another to Its delight;
> Joys in anothers loss of ease,
> And builds a Hell in Heavens despite.

By so doing, the adolescent-experience deifies his newly recognized self, or spectre, for, as his Bible tells him, man was created in God's image. This usurpation of divinity, based on a concept of ineffability inherent in rational interpretation of scripture, constitutes selfhood.

"Another" exists only to be bound to self, something to trap and use, something to cajole and deceive, something to nourish the oyster that is "mine." This is what Blake means by pride, the cosmic sin of Urizen—not pride in what one is, but pride in what one hopes to be or forcibly makes oneself to be. As for the self, it takes the form of guile, deceit, hypocrisy, and tyranny, for the question now is not one of remaining innocent but of bodily existence. Death becomes the great enemy, as it was to Thel. It is quite understandable, then, that the spiritual qualities or aspects of pride and self are obliterated; the spiritual has become the physical, religion is self-preservation, and divinity self. In fact, Blake would say the way to spiritual values has been barred, ironically because the paths of sensual enjoyment, the windows of the soul, the freedom of the spiritual self, have all been obliterated.

The corrective for all of this worldly "evil" is not humility, for humility is the same as hypocrisy. "Sneaking submission can always live," Blake wrote in *The Everlasting Gospel* (752). The remedy is a kind of pride that is the greatest humility—that is, recognizing the self to be but a part of the greater, divine self and seeing in all others the human form divine. "God only Acts & Is, in existing beings or Men," he wrote in *The Marriage;* and, in *The Everlasting Gospel,*

> Thou art a Man, God is no more,
> Thine own Humanity learn to Adore. (750)

In these terms there is no greater God than self, indeed no other God at all. At the same time, self is merely a particle of eternity, and to recognize it as such is to keep one's self-consciousness within the limits of world consciousness. Self is only divine if the human form divine as a whole is divine; "All deities reside in the human breast" (*Marriage*). To see that relationship is divine wisdom; to manufacture the divinity of self at the expense of others is the ignorance of experience, of mystery, of religion and priest.

It is with these sharply contrasting attitudes that Blake deals in *A Little Boy Lost.* The words of the child in the first stanza of this poem seem to indicate that he has achieved both self-identification or self-consciousness and imagination or omni-consciousness. Since there is no greater God than that which resides in the human breast, than that which "Acts & Is, in existing beings or Men," the third and fourth lines of the stanza are "true." The child recognizes his self as divine; he has learned his "own Humanity . . . to Adore." Such love of self is admirable and right in Blake's eyes and abhorrent, of course, to the priest and the child's parents. But what the child has not yet gained is complete spiritual wisdom, the realization that his self is not divine per se but only because it is part of something greater. Consequently in the first two lines of the stanza he sets up love of self as all-powerful. Not having completely opened the windows of his soul, the child still languishes in experience; but he approaches the higher innocence in the second stanza:

> And Father, how can I love you,
> Or any of my brothers more?
> I love you like the little bird
> That picks up crumbs around the door.

He can love his father and brothers only as much as he loves the divine in his own self, and that self's partial divinity is emphasized by its coequality with that of the little bird (perhaps a recollection of the child-bird identification in *Innocence*).[7]

The priest, of course, cannot understand the real meaning of the child's speech. He calls it "reason," the very foundation in Blake's terminology of religion and mystery, something created by man to dupe man. To the priest, the child is judging the religious mystery, God, whereas it is actually reason that judges the child, and metes out punishment according to the law reason created. Blake's subtle repetition of the word "holy" is most effective in accentuating this point, applying it as he does both to the "Mystery" itself and to the place in which that kind of holiness destroys true holiness.

Reason for Blake is the very faculty that analyzes love and decides how much should be given to father, brothers, birds, and God. Thus the priest-father demands greater love since to love him is supposedly to love God. The child and Blake would agree with this last idea, of course, with the exception of the quantitative division. In such measuring lies the rational element of mystery, and the terror of experience made manifest in the burning. The child is executed like a heretic in the ritual of the witch-hunt, his only heresy being that he did not conform to the laws of behavior and the rules of religion and love. Such things *are* done "on Albions shore."

The parents' roles in this martyrdom must be read in terms of the parental concept elsewhere in *Songs of Experience* and in *Tiriel*. Originally Blake introduced them into stanza 3 in very significant fashion. As the third and fourth lines of the stanza, to complement the priest's furious seizure of the child-heretic, Blake wrote:

> The mother followd weeping aloud
> O that I such a fiend should bear. (177)

Though Blake elected to omit these lines in his final version—probably because they were too blatant a condemnation of the mother—they do provide strong evidence for my reading of the parents' role in the last two stanzas.

> The weeping parents wept in vain:
> They strip'd him to his little shirt.
> And bound him in an iron chain.
>
> And burn'd him in a holy place
> Where many had been burn'd before.

The key word is "They," for upon it the following four lines depend. Since previously only the priest speaks, condemning the child, "They" must mean, then, the parents too—or perhaps only the parents. Such parental cruelty is perfectly in character in view of Blake's prevailing conception of their roles in experience, and in the light of the deleted line in which the mother regrets bearing "such a fiend." In complete agreement with the blind judgment of the priest, the parents strip, bind, and with ruthless cruelty even burn the child, as punishment for his "sins," perhaps even as an offering to the god of this "holy Mystery." But still Blake is not through with them. They weep again, the prosaic repetition emphasizing the lack of novelty in such a ritual, and then, with all the naiveté and innocence they can muster, they cry, "Are such things done on Albions shore." The line is richly ambiguous: (1) it is the parents' denial of their own ignorant brutality in executing their child; (2) it is their justification for the act through an expression of horror that "this," the child's heresy, could happen on Albion's shore; (3) it is Blake's, or the Bard's, cry of despair that such ignorance and depravity could exist in this world. For in experience such things *are* done, and the spark of imaginative wisdom visible in the child's love is allowed to burn only after death. The devourer is still in the ascendancy.

Such "Christian" policy is defined in still another way in *A Poison Tree,* a most interesting poem in that it is the first since *Tiriel* to present restraint and hypocrisy in almost exclusively human terms Tiriel was man, god, and father at one and the same time, an outstanding example of the Blakean symbol. In *A Poison Tree,* however, there is a different kind of symbolization which encompasses the speaker, God, and somewhat strangely the apple. In this light Blake's original title for the poem, "Christian forbearance," is more readily and completely understandable. "Christian," of course, refers both to the Christian God and the virtues which he inculcated or desired in man; "forbearance" is one of those virtues. With the poem firmly emplaced in *Experience,* Blake thus identifies the incident in the poem with such Christian virtue. The result is a vicious attack on the earthly Christian ity fostered by a man-made god who is the deification of self. His manifestation in man's hypocrisy and the law's discipline forms the basic tenet of the poem.[8]

Wrath itself is not wrong; it is merely one of the contraries. Love is another. Without the tiger and the lamb can be no progression, and to deny either is to deny existence. Each is equally divine within its own sphere, like the prolific and the devourer, but they can only be divine if they are expressed. Wrath unexpressed produces the poison tree;[9] love unexpressed produces a Theotormon (in *Visions of the Daughters of Albion*), or, even more extreme, the tyranny of self-love seen in *The Angel* or *My Pretty Rose-Tree.* Accordingly it is not surprising to find in *The Angel* a line closely parallel to the opening lines of *A Poison Tree:* "And hid from him my hearts delight." In *A Poison Tree,* though the speaker does not love as does the speaker in *The Angel,* the action is fundamentally the same:

> I was angry with my foe:
> I told it not, my wrath did grow.

This is "Christian forbearance," by which the speaker remains sinless and pure in his magnanimity, and the foe remains ignorant of the speaker's intentions or attitude. Perhaps this is what Blake meant in *The Human Abstract* when he wrote:

> And mutual fear brings peace;
> Till the selfish loves increase.
> Then Cruelty knits a snare,
> And spreads his baits with care.

In *The Abstract* selfish loves increase; in *A Poison Tree* wrath increases. Both "increases" are of a piece, involving inhibition and fundamental selfishness; and both of the strategic schemes evolved originate in the same way. In *The Human Abstract* Cruelty

> . . . sits down with holy fears,
> And waters the ground with tears:
> Then Humility takes its root. . . .

In *A Poison Tree* "I waterd" my wrath "in fears,"

> Night & morning with my tears:
> And I sunned it with smiles,
> And with soft deceitful wiles.

The deception is all the more powerful as Blake fuses the almost unconnected tears and fears of *The Abstract* into an image. Out of context "fears," "tears," and "smiles" for something other than self recall most vividly the mother's careful protection of and solicitude for the innocent child. But in experience the selfless mother has become the selfish speaker, and the child has become growing wrath:

> And it grew both day and night,
> Till it bore an apple bright.

This is the same fruit of deceit seen in *The Human Abstract*, bait for the trap which Cruelty set, but it is also much more. By means of the apple Blake enlarges his scope to draw into the vortex of human passion the Christian God himself. Thus while the speaker exercises Christian forbearance, at the same time he ironically usurps the role of the very God who decreed that forbearance. The first hint of self-deification comes in the second stanza where the speaker performs all of God's roles in the Creation, from the seed (here, of wrath) to its nourishment by rain and sunshine. The sun, of course, had greater meaning for Blake since it dispensed both light and heat, the comfort and love of the Blakean God. In *A Poison Tree* that divine love is introverted so that hate, the abomination of love, receives the nourishment.

The culmination of the man-God identification comes with the bearing of the apple, an instrument of temptation in the context of both Genesis and *A Poison Tree*. To this fructification, however, Blake has already added a generous helping of deceit, so that the identification now appears in a somewhat lurid light. God's creation of the tree of good and evil was merely a subterfuge to effect the destruction of his only rivals in the universe, Adam and Eve; *A Poison Tree* merely presents man in the same "Christian" role, creating his own tree and his own apple of deceit. In both situations

> . . . my foe beheld it shine,
> And he knew that it was mine.

Eve and Adam knew, but they were tempted and their paradise was destroyed. So in *A Poison Tree* the speaker's foe

> . . . into my garden stole.
> When the night had veild the pole;
> In the morning glad I see;
> My foe outstretchd beneath the tree.

This is not to say that Blake deliberately attempted to paraphrase Genesis; but it is clear that the idea of God as selfish creator and destroyer was not far from his mind when he wrote *A Poison Tree*. My simplification of the relationship between the two is merely to point up the power Blake could infuse into a simple image. And he did not stop even with the man-God relationship, for the poem also explores a kind of Tirielistic hypocrisy. Apparently "ruddy and sweet," as Blake described it in *The Abstract,* the apple is in reality a death potion, the tiger masquerading in the lamb's skin. Now the line in *The Tyger,* "Did he smile his work to see," is given terrible meaning, twisted to fit the particular circumstance which here characterizes the tiger's environment, the forests of experience. The speaker of *A Poison Tree* does smile his work to see, "My foe outstretchd beneath the tree." This does not obviate Blake's tiger and lamb as contraries necessary for existence; it does accentuate the subversion of one of those contraries to effect the domination of the other. When wrath prevails, the devourer is in the ascendancy, and the days of the animal, of survival of the fittest, take over the earth. Man is no more; only the hypocrite and God exist.

On the other hand, as the first two lines of *A Poison Tree* suggest, wrath told *is* divine.

> To be in a Passion you Good may do,
> But no Good if a Passion is in you. (*Auguries,* 433)

Even as early as his annotations to Lavater Blake was convinced of this. To the aphorism, "If you see one cold and vehement at the same time, set him down for a fanatic," Blake added in the margin, "*i.e.,* hypocrite" (73). And to a similar aphorism he cried "Bravo!" and heavily underscored as follows: "The most stormy ebullitions of passion, *from blasphemy to murder, are less terrific than one single act of cool villany: a still RABIES is more dangerous than the paroxisms of a fever—Fear the boisterous savage of passion less than the sedate grin of villany*" (68). "Lie," he said, "is the contrary to Passion" (74); the wrath of *A Poison Tree,* then, could not be divine. The growth of the tree and the yielding of the fruit are both lies, not passion. True passion is seen in the first two lines; mendacious passion is restrained yet secretly fostered under the guise of sunny smiles until the calculated trap is baited and sprung. The resultant murder is the prevention of act in another, just as act was prevented in self. That for Blake was the only kind of evil, a negation.

CHAPTER XIV

THE SILENT PILLOW

ॐ

My grave is like to be my wedding-bed.
—WILLIAM SHAKESPEARE, *Romeo and Juliet*

I

With the pattern of desire and restraint thus solidly before us in terms of "Christian" inhibition and a kind of perverted "holiness," we can now turn more confidently to the crux of Blake's state of experience, the suppression of man's divine desire to love "another as itself," and thus to build "a Heaven in Hells despair" (*The Clod and the Pebble*). For in the hell of experience "Love! sweet Love! was thought a crime" (*A Little Girl Lost*), and "the Youth pined away with desire," "the pale Virgin" was "shrouded in snow" (*Ah! Sun-flower*). Both of these tragic figures Blake introduced in *Visions of the Daughters of Albion* as Theotormon and Oothoon. The latter, we noted, had made some progress over the blind vanity and incapacity of Thel, since, despite the basic parallelisms, Oothoon loved Theotormon while Thel loved only herself. More important, Oothoon loved him in the light of day, unashamed. Again, though Oothoon fled like Thel from the horrible prospect of the grave of experience, she did not allow herself to be trapped in her escape. Instead, after plucking Leutha's flower, she turned her face "to where [her] whole soul seeks." Except for Bromion's interference she might have reached her goal and eventually the higher innocence. But Bromion was there and is always there in experience; Blake insists on this point. So in *A Little Girl Lost* the father is there.

The variation in this poem on the pattern of the *Visions* is clearly not very great. The maiden, who like Oothoon trembles in her virgin fears, does not flee but rather plucks Leutha's flower (sexual experience perhaps) by meeting the youth in the "garden bright." And, like Oothoon again, her love is apparently unashamed in the "holy light" of "rising day." She seems to have reached the place where her "whole soul seeks," her Theotormon. The time of day is appropriately dawn, innocence, the birth of passion we saw briefly in a song of innocence, *Spring*. But then as "Nativity, once in the main of light / Crawls to maturity,"

> There in rising day,
> On the grass they play:
> Parents were afar:
> Strangers came not near:
> And the maiden soon forgot her fear.

Innocence is fading, the protective mother has become a threat, secrecy is now necessary. Thus isolated from prying eyes "the maiden soon forgot her fear," the fear, we recall, that is present only in experience with its inhibitive Christianity, morality and law.

Though they act as if they were free, then, the maid and youth secure that freedom by hypocrisy and secrecy, qualities most logically exhibited at night. As the nurse says cynically in *Nurses Song (Experience)*,

> Your spring & your day. are wasted in play
> And your winter and night in disguise.

Whereas dawn and day in *A Little Girl Lost* are treated and reacted to in terms of innocence, the irrevocable fact of experience forces the postponement of love's consummation ("Tired with kisses sweet") until the night in which experience flourishes.

To follow this powerful statement of the effect of experience on new love, Blake immediately presents the father, the supreme hypocrite, the teacher of love's suppression. His "enslavement" of the maiden is implicit in her docile return to him before she consummates her love. "His loving look" with crushing irony exudes the hard and fast law of the "holy book" and the earthly morality to which man's ignorant reading of it has led. In *The Little Boy Found* God appeared like the boy's father in white and led him back to his mother; here the father appears, like God, in white, thus uniting the earthly concept of God and the self-manufactured godhood of the father himself. His "love" is possessive and selfish, proffered only to one who can be molded like clay to suit the potter's fancy. The whole is a dramatization of the "curtain of flesh" which is ever "on the bed of our desire" *(Thel)*. For the first time Ona sees that curtain; the fear she lost momentarily in the secret amour now returns tenfold in the face of the real reason for that fear.[1]

The father's role in the poem, then, is much the same as Bromion's in the *Visions;* parallel to Oothoon's fate, Ona is ravished intellectually, or perhaps spiritually. Her fate is that of the speaker in *To Tirzah:*

> Thou Mother of my Mortal part.
> With cruelty didst mould my Heart.
> And with false self-decieving tears.
> Didst bind my Nostrils Eyes & Ears.
>
> Didst close my Tongue to senseless clay
> And me to Mortal Life betray.

The last line of *A Little Girl Lost* is puzzling. I suggest that Blake was here alluding, rather awkwardly, to the tree of mystery and humility so prominent in *The Human Abstract*. Like Tiriel, Ona's father is that tree, for "there grows one in the Human Brain"; in its confining shade (law, parental authority, the "holy book") "Love! sweet Love! was thought a crime." In *Visions of the Daughters of Albion* Oothoon defied it (194, plate 7). Ona, on the other hand, surrenders, her father, "grey and hoary, dark," standing solidly between the lovers like a curtain of flesh.

Such enslavement tragically multiplies, as we have already seen in the *Visions.* When Oothoon's love for Theotormon is rebuffed she finally resorts to enslaving others for her own delight by means of coyness, modesty, deception, and secrecy.[2] Enslave or be enslaved; such is the nature of experience. By restraining desire (or perverting it) the woman, in effect, becomes devourer instead of prolific; she accretes secret joys unto herself instead of giving herself to attain eternal joy. Blake expressed this idea most succinctly in his manuscript book:

> He who binds to himself a joy
> Does the winged life destroy
> But he who kisses the joy as it flies
> Lives in eternity's sun rise.[3]

Similarly in *The Sick Rose* the invisible worm (associated with both jealousy and "secret love")[4]

> Has found out thy bed
> Of crimson joy:
> And his dark secret love
> Does thy life destroy.

The night and the howling storm in which the worm "flies" is, of course, the terrible night of experience, the night in which enslaved man (and woman) secretly practise the joys of day. As Blake wrote in the *Visions,*

> ... the youth shut up from
> The lustful joy. shall forget to generate. & create an amorous image
> In the shadows of his curtains and in the folds of his silent pillow.[5]

These are the self-enjoyings of self-denial, the consequences of thinking that "acts are not lovely." Just as jealousy, invisible in the clouds of doubt and rationality, can destroy the innocent love of maiden, so modesty, inculcated by experience in the experience-ravished woman, can destroy all love—and hence life. The woman wakes to dissemble all the secret joys of night and passes herself off as virgin to the world. Blake's *The Sick Rose* does not merely reveal love (the spiritual) corrupted by the flesh (the mundane), although that is certainly part of the idea. More accurately love is sick without the vision necessary to see what love really is. Without this knowledge, true love is betrayed and cursed as irrational, and in its place grows the tree of religion with roots in the love of self. Both jealousy and death are involved, and both are united in the image of the worm; the bed on which the secret joys are performed differs little from the grave Thel refused to remain in. And just as surely as the eternal worm rings itself around the mortal remains, jealousy crushes the life from the object of his perverted love.

In a better poem, one not quite so bitter as *The Sick Rose,* Blake clearly illustrates the distinction between loves that I have been trying to make, and the tone of it is a fitting postscript to *The Sick Rose:*

> Silent Silent Night
> Quench the holy light
> Of thy torches bright
>
> For possessd of Day
> Thousand spirits stray
> That sweet joys betray
>
> Why should joys be sweet
> Used with deceit
> Nor with sorrows meet
>
> But an honest joy
> Does itself destroy
> For a harlot coy (Untitled, 168)

2

A new chord within this same thematic context is struck by Blake in *The Angel,* which is particularly interesting in that it is the only dream-poem in *Experience.* In *Innocence* we saw that dreams (like that of the chimney-sweeper, for example) often re-established the fact of the dreamer's innocence; in *Experience* perversely they establish the dreamer's state as experience.

The opening lines immediately ally *The Angel* to *The Book of Thel,* in which the "maiden Queen" Thel, after refusing to face the fact of her own experience, gradually discovered that she could not blandly maintain her innocence and gently fade into the higher innocence. The dream in *The Angel* reflects the sleeper's similar predicament: to continue being an "innocent" maiden, surrounded by guardian angels like those in *A Cradle Song* and *Night,* or to try to "get along" in experience. Like Thel, upon entering experience she cannot conceive of what she must do to get to the other side of the forest. Again like Thel she sees herself as a "maiden," unravished by experience, and the prospect of losing her chastity openly, though it has not yet been brought home to her, is most distasteful. In the dream this attitude takes the form of the guardian angel, who will keep her safe from harm. The angel cannot be considered other than as a euphemism for mind-forged manacles and conventional morality. As an integral part of the speaker's fear, as well as her desire to remain in the state of innocence, she sees the angel guard against her tears and wipe them away as the mother did in *A Cradle Song.* But in experience we have seen that the mother has become part of Blake's multiple tyrant father-priest-king. Consistent with dream logic, then, Blake gradually merges his conception of the mother-protector and the lover-protector until the angel becomes a kind of Theotormon in relation to the dreamer's Oothoon. The dreamer's tears do not cease, however, for they are tears of self-pity, and in experience such tears divide the soul and give rise to a self which can only survive in experience through secrecy, hypocrisy, and woman's wiles:

> And I wept both day and night
> And hid from him my hearts delight.

The witless woe of the first stanza has become earthly knowledge—how to get along in the hard, cruel world. The best way is introversion, playing the cards close to the vest, keeping as much of the self unto self as is possible. The result, of course, is the immediate alienation of the lover; in effect he is closed out from the very joy which should be opened for him:

> So he took his wings and fled:
> Then the morn blush'd rosy red:
> I dried my tears & armd my fears,
> With ten thousand shields and spears.

Fear has taken over, and in the first blush of day (akin to the crimson joy of *The Sick Rose?*) some protection other than the fled angel must now be resorted to. The dreamer consequently arms herself with modesty, coyness, and all the female wiles with which she thinks she can combat any worldly threat to her virginity. To her virginity is life.

When the angel-lover comes again, therefore, it is completely in vain. He can no longer protect, for his lover is armed, and he cannot love because she is coy and guardedly chaste. That situation, that stalemate, is Blake's equivalent for old age in the physical sense. The parallel with *Thel* has now come full circle:

> For the time of youth was fled
> And grey hairs were on my head.[6]

Instead of the sensual woman there is a hollow shell, devoid of feeling and emotion and imprisoned within the bony walls of ratiocination and convention. Blake's (and the Bard's) own feelings about this are implicit in the poem of course, but in a manuscript poem his attitude is made explicit:

> Pitying I wept to see the woe
> That Love & Beauty undergo,
> To be consum'd in burning Fires
> And in ungratified desires.[7]

3

Nurses Song is in many ways the most difficult poem of this group,[8] but it is also an excellent summation of conventional holiness and desire restrained, and especially it is the only poem in *Experience* that dramatizes the mother's "conversion."[9] It seems to me to reveal Blake's most mature art in its almost perfect blending of simplicity, lucidness, depth, and complexity of meaning and association. The complicated at once merges with and emanates from the uncomplicated. That this technique is intentional is apparent from the fact that the first line of the first stanza and the first two lines of the second are taken quite deliberately from the pleasant, joyful *Nurse's Song* of *Innocence*. But although line 2 of the first stanza remains in the same pattern as that of the earlier song with a slight change of wording and a subtle, almost absurdly small, modification of the rhythm, the line becomes a parody of innocence. Instead of the lilting "And laughing is heard on the hill," we have "And whisprings are in the dale." The obvious difference in diction immediately introduces the theme of secrecy, but what is not so obvious is the absence of the word "heard" in the *Nurses Song* of *Experience*. It is a key word. Without it a contrast develops between the openness of the action and its clear apprehension by the speaker in line one, and the fact that although the "whisprings" are not *heard,* the speaker asserts that they are there. The accent falls heavily on "are"; in the earlier poem "are" is merely a weak auxiliary. Who, then, is the speaker and what is Blake's intention in having her vary her speech? There are several answers, all of which illustrate Blake's sure control of the reader's associative process. Whereas the nurse of the earlier poem was a variant of the protective mother of Beulah, the nurse in the later poem observes the echoing green with somewhat more than a solicitous eye. The voices are still heard, it is true, but in addition she knows, or thinks she knows, that "whisprings are in the dale." Though the children in the first line seem to be innocents, in the second line the nurse sees them as secretive, close-lipped. This may overstate the case, but at any rate the opposition is there, in the poem and in the nurse's mind. As we have seen in *Tiriel,* Har and Heva constituted vivid symbols of the debilitating power of memory and unfulfilled desire; the nurse, in terms of her memory, now corrupted, interprets as something hidden the innocence we have seen to be joyous, unrestrained, and completely guileless. The whisperings are not heard because they are not there; but in the nurse's mind they must be there. Her experience tells her so. Complete freedom and lack of inhibition are inconceivable to her. Happiness is a thing stolen and hidden away, and crushed into nonexistence; laughing in experience is not heard on the hill in the face of the bright day, but there are snickers in the covertness of the dale.

Recalling her innocent past while at the same time interpreting that past in terms of her enslaved present condition, the nurse merely accentuates her enslavement when she confesses:

> The days of my youth rise fresh in my mind,
> My face turns green and pale.

For a moment she envies the children their play,[10] and her days of innocence flash before her eyes. But the moment is fleeting, and only the paleness of fear is left to take its place. Once again Blake draws on the earlier *Nurse's Song* to reinforce and enrich his picture. The last two lines of the first stanza of that poem read:

> My heart is at rest within my breast
> And everything else is still.

In innocence her heart *was* at rest simply because she was performing her divine function, protecting and caring for the innocent children. The nurse in *Experience,* however, is disturbed by the children on the green. Far from being still for her, everything is in a silent uproar as she contemplates what seems to her a waste of life.

The beginning of the second stanza, then, with its two lines verbatim from the earlier *Nurse's Song,* takes on a power not half-realized if the poem is treated only as a simple antithesis to the earlier poem. In innocence the nurse called the children home to protect them, not from the night of experience which as yet is afar, but from the night of innocence which holds comparable terrors (as in *The Little Boy Lost*) only if the child is separated from his mother. Thus in innocence the nurse called:

> Come come leave off play. and let us away
> Till the morning appears in the skies.

In experience the nurse warns the children of the terrors of experience, but the fact that her cry *is* a warning and that she has less regard for protecting them than for judging them is symptomatic of the great change that Blake has wrought here. In innocence the morning does appear in the skies, and the birds are once again free to fly from their warm bosomy rest; in experience, as we saw in *Earth's Answer,* the dews of night foreshadow the watery shore on which one is enslaved and from which the escape to morning involves something more than a sunrise. Actually the nurse in experience is convinced that the children too are already in experience, as the whispering in the dale emphatically proves, and this merely provokes her to reprimand them for the folly they mistake for happiness: "Your spring & your day. are wasted in play."

If the close parallels with the earlier *Nurse's Song* contribute significantly to Blake's theme, the absence of parallel should also be expected to add its "negative" richness. For example, to emphasize the fact that the night of experience is already upon the children in the poem—that is, in the second stanza, not the first—Blake omits the objections to coming home which the children voice in the earlier poem. The reason is obvious. Those objections make it clear that night has not yet come, innocence is still innocence, and the hills and the green still echo:

> No no let us play, for it is yet day
> And we cannot go to sleep.

And hearing no objection the nurse in the later poem, of course, does not answer as the nurse in the earlier one does:

> Well well go & play till the light fades away
> And then go home to bed.

Instead she accuses the children of wasting the very freedom she now lacks.

The last two lines of the *Nurses Song* of *Experience* also contrast sharply with the first stanza: the reference to the children's spring certainly looks back to line one, but it also recalls *The Ecchoing Green* and *Spring*. The children's day is expressly contrasted to "the days of my youth" of line 3, thus bringing together the fact of innocence and the nurse's present point of view toward that fact. But innocence can only be wasted in terms of self, in rational terms. The mind can conceive of something more profitable to do with youth, something from which a richer joy, in the worldly sense, can emerge. And that "richer" joy can only be at the expense of a spiritual joy that should know no bounds. Since the latter involves a denial of self, the secretive whisperings, which conceivably reflect a certain privacy and hence self-satisfaction, can only occur in the dale, not in the light of the sun. True joy is selfless and therefore to the nurse wasted, because nothing in a tangible sense accrues to self. The last line is a kind of prophecy, then, as well as a summation, which reveals the essentially benighted mind of the nurse. For Blake spring and day are never wasted; play is energy unrestrained, the very core of innocence. On the other hand winter and night can be wasted, but only in disguise—that is, with energy restrained. Such waste is a product of the state of experience, the state in which the jealous nurse prevails, the state in which she wastes *her* energy through repression. The restraints of experience are not avoidable, but they can be invalidated by "the lineaments of gratified desire," by "an improvement of sensual enjoyment." Since the nurse has experienced neither of these, in her view of both innocence and experience she can make the most devastating of all comments on her own state. Enslaved, she calls the children from the very freedom in which their salvation lies to the bondage in which she now merely exists.

In other words, she has not learned the lesson of experience. Clandestine joy to her is all the sweeter, and even though it leads to the edge of non-entity, the fact of her own tragic ignorance cannot penetrate the mind shaken by fear and trapped in the web of rationality and worldly morality. It is in this sense only that Wicksteed's judgment of the poem as the "tragedy of innocence that leads to nothing" is accurate. Innocence is only tragedy to the non-innocent. The nurse's reproach to the frolicking children reveals the wisdom of Blake's proverb: "Listen to the fool's reproach! it is a kingly title!" (*Marriage*) And it is most apt that Blake in his manuscript book followed *Nurses Song* with:

> Are not the joys of morning sweeter
> Than the joys of nigh
> And are the vigrous joys of youth
> Ashamed of the light
>
> Let age & sickness silent rob
> The vineyards in the night
> But those who burn with vigrous youth
> Pluck fruits before the light (172)

4

Finally, we have the song of the earthly mother, a song whose opposite or contrary cannot be found in any one song of innocence but in the concept of innocence as a whole. She is the mother of "infant sorrow," of the little vagabond, of the chimney sweeper; she is the female Tiriel "who by hypocrisy and selfishness continues the delusion of our mortal bodies."[11] And for Blake the confirmation of that delusion constitutes selfhood. Thel's desire for physical immortality, the selfish pride of earthly beauty and estate, Blake directly attacks in words that are spoken *To Tirzah*[12] by the imagination, perhaps by an Oothoon, in an attempt to gain the higher innocence. The self, which is a product of the merciful creation, must be consumed in experience, must be recognized for what it is and then denied.[13] With that denial the escape from generation is achieved and regeneration is attained. Therefore the speaker will have nothing to do with the mother of self now that experience has been reached. The mother's blessed protection prolonged into experience is a curse, an enslavement, a cruel hand that molds the heart and binds the senses to keep the child free from "harm." As Blake put it in *The Four Zoas* in Tirzah's own words:

"O thou poor human form! O thou poor child of woe!
Why dost thou wander away from Tirzah? why me compell to bind
    thee?
If thou dost go away from me, I shall consume upon the rocks.
These fibres of thine eyes that used to wander in distant heavens
Away from me, I have bound down with a hot iron.
These nostrils that Expanded with delight in morning skies
I have bent downward with lead molten in my roaring furnaces.
My soul is seven furnaces. . . ." (348-349)

Along with the creation, however, God also supplies the way out, the way to regeneration:

> . . . Mercy changd Death into Sleep;
> The Sexes rose to work & weep,

the sexes which "sprung from Shame & Pride." When Urizen in his pride broke away from the primal hermaphroditic unity, the first thing that was revealed was his sex manifestation. In his shame, which is the same as pride since it is "Pride's cloke" *(Marriage),* the female was born and sexual strife began. Their constant seeking for each other and their equally constant rebuffs constitute the living death of chaos. To save man from complete destruction God made a limit to the "contraction"; only in that way could the sexes have the opportunity to work and weep through experience and to achieve a higher innocence again in hermaphroditic form, the human form divine.

Accordingly "The Death of Jesus" set man free to choose the way up or the way down. The decision depends on the denial of the great bar to that freedom, earthly restraint, the law, the father, the mother-Tirzah. But let me put it another way. By being born we are *ipso facto* imprisoned, from the womb to the parents' molding hands to the law's mind-forged manacles. Yet, by being born we are also free because Christ died for us, died to make that very birth and existence possible. Given that existence, the choice must be made between mere existence, Thel's, and imaginative existence, the Bard's and Jerusalem's. With the pressure of the womb thrown off, there are further pressures to resist, the main one of course being the grave of self. Out of that grave only the imagination can raise us, out of generation into re-generation: "Then what have I to do with thee?" These are the words of Christ to *his* mother immediately before he performs the first miracle at the marriage in Cana: changing water into wine, changing the "Mortal part" so that "It is Raised a Spiritual Body."[14]

That spiritual body is the "Image of truth new-born" proclaimed by the "Voice of the Ancient Bard":

> Doubt is fled & clouds of reason.
> Dark disputes & artful teazing.
> Folly is an endless maze,
> Tangled roots perplex her ways,
> How many have fallen there!

Now, however, it is the "break of day" mentioned by the Bard in the *Introduction* to *Experience*. With a look back at the tangled maze of experience through which he has just brought us, Blake announces his millennium. And yet it is really only a prophecy after all, as far as his poetic development is concerned. The lyric form somehow did not seem right to him to portray such a millennium. Although for this decision there were probably several reasons which one can only guess now, guessing at this point of my study is not only apropos but essential. The following chapter is an attempt to ascertain the reason for Blake's abandonment of the lyric,[15] as well as a suggestion as to how the prophecies may be read in terms of the *Songs of Innocence and of Experience*.

P·A·R·T

VII

CHAPTER XV

A VIEW OF PROPHECY

ह्र

A poet participates in the eternal, the infinite,
and the one; as far as relates to his conceptions, time and place and number are not.
—P. B. SHELLEY, *A Defence of Poetry*

I

Having created the states of innocence and experience, Blake was
next to dramatize the higher innocence, the "heaven" of his system.
"The question for him," as Max Plowman has put it, "was not whether
men went to hell, but how they got out of it."[1] That heaven, as we
have seen, involved the union of all partial divinity in the human
form divine. The millennium was to be cosmic. The system existed, but
there was no myth to prove its validity. Though the Bard of the
Introduction to *Experience* knew and sang of "Present, Past, & Future,"
such a concept of time was applicable only to man. If man was created,
fell, and arose, the cosmos of which he was only a microcosmic reflection must also have progressed through its versions of innocence
and experience to a higher innocence. Though each man is capable of
a last judgment, the Last Judgment involves all men and all creation.[2]
The restrictions of time and space were now to give way to timeless
eternity and the wars and passions of the "eternals." The contraries
were established; it now remained to explain how the contraries began.

275

Such an explanation could not be other than epic in proportion or even greater. It is of prophetic magnitude.

The variegated elements that went to make up the lyrics will now be given a habitation and a name: Blake's emphasis will shift from the outside to the inside, from the actions to the motives, from the phenomenal to the noumenal. The major symbol of innocence, the child, will become the divine human or Albion or Milton, and all the songs of innocence, which contributed to the child's symbolic stature, will become characters, places, and symbols of vast scope. The father-priest-king is no longer the only tyrant; he is Urizen and the spectre of every symbolic character Blake develops to portray the cosmic ailing and cure in all its detailed profusion. Two central characters are prerequisite to Blake's scheme, a protagonist fighting for liberty and an antagonist defending tyranny. They "must derive," writes Frye, "from his conception of tyranny as the defense of the fallen world and of liberty as the effort of the imagination to recover the state of innocence."[3] It is therefore out of innocence and experience that the two great figures of Orc and Urizen emerge. The other prophetic characters are variations on the theme. Together they make up the myth to prove the system.

Into that myth Blake tried to cram everything he knew and felt, incidents in his own life, his quarrels and grievances, people he knew and some he didn't know, his attitude toward contemporary society, politics, and art. The precise discipline of the lyric was now no longer his concern because his mind was expanding—even bursting—with the myth. He was apparently interested less in the coherence of his theme than in the rich profusion of its ingredients. He wanted to get everything in. In effect the complexity of the superbly controlled lyric was giving way to complexities within complexity. In no other way could Blake conceive of presenting the history of man and his universe.

"Eternals!" Blake cries in the "Preludium" to *The First Book of Urizen,*

> Eternals! I hear your call gladly.
> Dictate swift winged words & fear not
> To unfold your dark visions of torment. (222)

The torment is still the state of experience, as eternity is innocence, but the resolution of that torment in the higher innocence encompasses both the eternals and man. The lyric could sustain song; it could not embody such a triumphant scene as the great conclusion to *Jerusalem* (744-747). The lyric is a passionate art form, but its passion is of a different order than prophetic fervor. Man in relation to other men generates passion; the loves and wars of human faculties and states of being provoke prophetic fervor. The lyric presents its human passion; prophecy explains passionately why and how that human passion exists. The lyric is the gospel according to Matthew, Mark, Luke, and John; prophecy is Genesis, Exodus, and Revelation.

The lyrics of *Songs of Experience* saw a great increase in intellectual content and didacticism, and, as we have seen, not all of them were capable of bearing the load. Blake wanted now a form that could include lyric intensity as well as prosaic expatiation. To do that meant to escape almost completely from prosodic restrictions. Unfortunately too often that freedom constituted a kind of chaos. Nevertheless the chaos is seldom without some control. Though the prophecies are fundamentally narratives, they eschew for all practical purposes the normative controls of time and space; rather they rely for what unity they have on images, symbols, characters, and acts already established to some extent in the lyrics. The almost endless proliferation of these basic elements is the narrative. In other words, if the myth enacts the system and provides a basis for its very existence, the human elements of the system already dramatized should provide an invaluable aid to interpreting what is essentially an expansion of the human level. For example, though *The Tyger* and *The Four Zoas* are two vastly different poems, basically there is a thematic similarity between them. *The Tyger* concerns the forests of experience in which roam the fears and sorrows of the created universe; those forests are bounded by error, circumscribed by the cold light of reason, and permeated with pale religious lechery. As Blake's concept of experience evolved from the ominous hints in the *Songs of Innocence* to the specific terror of *Tiriel* and the multimodal darkness of the *Songs of Experience,* it centered about the ideas of contraction, restraint, enslavement, and stultification. These "evils" were self-induced by the weakness of desire and its consequent surrender to the moral precepts of the mind-created god. Yet within experience, inherent in the very fact of its earthly existence, lay the divine, for it was an act of divine mercy that prevented man from eternally falling through abysmal chaos into non-entity. Paradoxically the tiger's creation is at once an act of mercy and a menace.[4] Both are divine, just as heaven and hell are divine. Man himself, of himself, must deny himself—and the efficacy of the tiger's terror—and by means of the tiger's energy, wrath, and imaginative thought dispel the night's darkness. The consequent immortal day, expansive, unrestrained, free, and vigorously healthy, will see the tiger, lion, and lamb lie down together, portions of eternity once again united in the all-embracing human form divine.

From this point of view the universal chaos of Blake's prophetic books merely expands the personal chaos of man in experience. The two are actually inseparable to the poet. The link which joins them is the link of motivation, of character not person, of idea, if you will, not fact. Tiriel is as much Urizen as the lamb is Milton; only the context varies to give an ever more detailed analysis, or vision, of the cosmic ailing and divine cure. Each man, beast, and insect must find the ailing and the cure in his own breast. If the tiger was a powerful symbol to Blake, it was still only the symbolic stimulus for the creation of a greater symbol, the hammer, forge, and furnace of the "immortal hand" that made the tiger. To present that tremendous process of creation, the creation which for Blake was the cataclysmic mushroom of his own mythographical atomic bomb, Blake conceived *The Four Zoas*. And to that poem of the greater creation-chaos *The Tyger* ominously points.

To attempt a comparative explication here is not my purpose; rather I should like to suggest, by fairly extensive quotation, the similarity of the poems in plan, image, tone, and over-all pattern. As I have said, they are not the same poem, so that one should not expect Blake to quote himself (though he does occasionally). Nevertheless the following I believe will make it clear that one must know *The Tyger* (in its context as a song of experience and in its relation to the poems which nurtured its creation) in order to approach *The Four Zoas* with sympathy and perceptiveness.[5]

2

In the second night of *The Four Zoas* the fall into division has already taken place: Luvah and Urizen have hatched the plot and burst the human form divine into infinitesimal particles. The cosmic state of experience has been inaugurated. As the divine imagination looked down upon man's division into spectre and emanation and saw the sun repelled by the dark secrecy of the lover's inner chamber, the divine hand created the tiger; or, diabolically like Circe, he turned his gentle lamb into a ravening, wrathful force of terrible aspect. Then

Terrific Urizen strode above in fear & pale dismay.
He saw the indefinite space beneath & his soul shrunk with horror,
His feet upon the verge of Non Existence; his voice went forth:

Luvah & Vala trembling & shrinking beheld the great Work master
And heard his Word: "Divide, ye bands, influence by influence.
Build we a Bower for heaven's darling in the grizly deep:
Build we the Mundane Shell around the Rock of Albion."

The Bands of Heaven flew thro' the air singing & shouting to Urizen.
Some fix'd the anvil, some the loom erected, some the plow
And harrow form'd & fram'd the harness of silver & ivory,
The golden compasses, the quadrant, & the rule & balance.
They erected the furnaces, they form'd the anvils of gold beaten in mills
Where winter beats incessant, fixing them firm on their base.
The bellows began to blow, & the Lions of Urizen stood round the anvil
And the leopards cover'd with skins of beasts tended the roaring fires,
Sublime, distinct, their lineaments divine of human beauty.
The tygers of wrath called the horses of instruction from their mangers,
They unloos'd them & put on the harness of gold & silver & ivory,
In human forms distinct they stood round Urizen, prince of Light,
Petrifying all the Human Imagination into rock & sand.

  .   .   .   .

Aloft the Moon fled with a cry: the Sun with streams of blood.
From Albion's Loins fled all Peoples and Nations of the Earth,
Fled with the noise of Slaughter, & the stars of heaven fled.
Jerusalem came down in a dire ruin over all the Earth. . . . (280-281)

There is of course a considerable difference between the creative power of the tiger's maker and Urizen, the builder of the "Bower"; the cosmos is the former's realm, the poor earthly substitute the latter's. Urizen is the Divine only insofar as this world views him as such through its cataractic eyes, and only insofar as God allows him to be seen as such.

279

The creation, in which Urizen is involved in the above quotation, was an act of mercy so that the eternal creation could be renewed. Given his position, however, Urizen like Milton's Satan will reign in hell rather than serve in heaven. The selfhood will be exalted and hence reflected in the broken bits of eternity called father, priest, king—and tiger.

The keynote of the creation, then, is restraint, the compression of the shattered divine into finiteness, the retention of the fallen earth's watery shore (which reflects the broken lights of eternity) instead of the void of non-existence. The hand that created this, in line 3 of *The Tyger,* is as immortal as the creation is mortal, and yet within that very mortality, buried within its darkness, the eerie light of the tiger flickers as the spark of divinity within the human breast which can never go out. But the incontrovertible fact of repression remains to join this passage from *The Four Zoas* to the lyric: from the forests of the night to the iron sinews of the heart to the hammer, chain, furnace, and anvil, and finally to the fear itself inherent in all of this, Blake's images reflect the basic process of shrinkage. It is the change from human form divine to human form human. Blake put it a different way, more closely allied with other songs of experience, in a speech by Luvah:

"They have surrounded me with walls of iron & brass. O Lamb
Of God clothed in Luvah's garments! little knowest thou
Of death Eternal, that we all go to Eternal Death,
To our Primeval Chaos in fortuitous concourse of incoherent
Discordant principles of Love & Hate. I suffer affliction
Because I love, for I was love, but hatred awakes in me,
And Urizen, who was Faith & certainty, is chang'd to Doubt. . . ." (282)

Though the tone and circumstance of this speech deviate from the speaker's words intoning the solemn notes of *The Tyger,* the essence of Luvah's appeal to the lamb seems to me peculiarly similar to "Did he who made the Lamb make thee?" The tremulousness and awe with which the question is asked in *The Tyger* is accentuated by the rest of Luvah's speech, which in turn reinforces the deep despair and paradoxical chaos of creation. There eternal death and fear have become living realities to torment the human body. Affliction becomes the reward of love; the sun and the moon go out, as Blake warned in *Aug-*

uries of Innocence, when faith is changed to doubt. The forests of night envelop the earth:

For Urizen beheld the terrors of the Abyss wandering among
The ruin'd spirits, once his children & the children of Luvah.
Scar'd at the sound of their own sigh that seems to shake the immense
They wander Moping, in their heart a sun, a dreary moon,
A Universe of fiery constellations in their brain,
An earth of wintry woe beneath their feet, & round their loins
Waters or winds or clouds or brooding lightnings & pestilential plagues.
Beyond the bounds of their own self their senses cannot penetrate:
As the tree knows not what is outside of its leaves & bark
And yet it drinks the summer joy & fears the winter sorrow,
So, in the regions of the grave, none knows his dark compeer
Tho' he partakes of his dire woes & mutual returns the pang,
The throb, the dolor, the convulsion, in soul-sickening woes. (314)

And with the ultimate soul-sickening woe, the beauty of the human form becomes the fearful symmetry of the beast. So Urizen in his wanderings

. . . came . . . among fiery cities & castles of burning steel.
Then he beheld the forms of tygers & of Lions, dishumaniz'd men.

. . . .

He knew they were his Children ruin'd in his ruin'd world. (314-315)

Perhaps the most striking passage of all regarding the attitude of the creator of this desolation—and of the tiger—occurs also in "Night the Sixth": hidden in a cave to protect himself from his own creations, Urizen tries to recoup "his obstructed powers with rest & oblivion."

Here he had time enough to repent of his rashly threaten'd curse.
He saw them [his "children"] curs'd beyond his Curse: his soul melted
            with fear
He could not take their fetters off, for they grew from the soul,
Nor could he quench the fires, for they flam'd out from the heart,
Nor could he calm the Elements, because himself was subject;
So he threw his flight in terror & pain, & in repentent tears. (315)

Simultaneously, the differences and similarities between Urizen and God are apparent when what seems to be God's creation in *The Tyger* is compared with Urizen's comment on the creation in *The Four Zoas*. While a part of the divine, Urizen broke away from the primal cosmic unity, so that although the creation can be envisaged in and through him, the hand of the divine is the only one that "dare sieze the fire." In other words Urizen is at once creator (the earthly god) and created (a particle of the creator). His usurpation of the divine prerogative along with Luvah constituted the creation of a self which he then elevated to a god. Though the pristine innocence of the cosmos cracked at the act, the creation of the universe, especially of earth, provided Urizen with the seat which he attempted to grasp by force from God. Thus God still reigned in heaven, as Milton's God did, while Urizen set up shop in hell.

The parallel with *Paradise Lost,* then, assumes great importance, the more so when it is examined in conjunction with *The Marriage of Heaven and Hell*. In that work Blake makes the conventional hell his heaven and Satan its god, for only in that hell do the divine fires, including the "Tyger burning bright," rage without cessation or restraint. Therefore, as the self-created god of the earthly universe, Urizen has within himself the seeds of his own destruction. The blossoming of those seeds is the redemption of the world. Though closely hedged in by the sunless and moonless firmament, the forests of night nevertheless nurture the divine spark of wrath and rebellion from which the reformation of innocence can and does emanate. So, in the passage quoted above, Urizen can be subject to the torments of the very elements which he himself created through his selfish act and God's selfless mercy. Urizen acknowledges his fundamental dependence in the fifth night of *The Four Zoas:*

> "O Fool! could I forget the light that filled my bright spheres
> Was a reflection of his face who call'd me from the deep!" (310)

This is so like the second stanza of *The Tyger* that the similarity of Blake's basic patterns cannot be denied:

> In what distant deeps or skies.
> Burnt the fire of thine eyes?

In his supremely brazen selfhood Urizen had convinced himself that his light and majesty and very existence were self-induced. On that

basis he balked at God's request to "'Go forth & guide my Son who
wanders on the ocean.'" Instead, with the catastrophic loss of divine-
given light, he hid himself in black clouds of wrath, ultimate source
of the forests. Then, Urizen recalls,

> "I call'd the stars around my feet in the night of councils dark;
> The stars threw down their spears & fled naked away.
> We fell." (311)

In *The Tyger* Blake puts it this way, in one of his most famous passages:

> When the stars threw down their spears
> And water'd heaven with their tears:
> Did he smile his work to see?
> Did he who made the Lamb make thee?

The lines are double-edged. On the one hand, as Schorer, Erdman,
and Nurmi have convincingly shown,[6] they indicate the defeat of the
rational power at the hands of the divine. On the other, the defeat
is a victory for Urizen for it enables him to build his own heaven, this
world. The firmament has crumbled and fallen in tiny pieces to make
up the starry shore, and on it the enslaved of *Earth's Answer* rest. On
it Urizen too will suffer. The stars' surrender, then, is the failure of
what Erdman calls the "armies of counterrevolution," but their weeping
also reveals their fear and sorrow at their lamentable condition.

Let us examine now in more detail the concept of experience as it
is revealed in both *The Tyger* and *The Four Zoas*. In the third night
of *The Zoas* Ahania upbraids Urizen and, in so doing, describes the
devastating night of experience in terms which reflect the contrast
between *The Tyger* and *The Lamb,* or better the *Songs of Experience*
and the *Songs of Innocence:*

> "Why didst thou listen to the voice of Luvah that dread morn
> To give the immortal steeds of light to his deceitful hands?
> No longer now obedient to thy will, thou art compell'd
> To forge the curbs of iron & brass, to build the iron mangers,
> To feed them with intoxication from the wine presses of Luvah
> Till the Divine Vision & Fruition is quite obliterated.
> They call thy lions to the field of blood; they rouze thy tygers

Out of the halls of justice, till these dens thy wisdom fram'd
Golden & beautiful, but O how unlike those sweet fields of bliss
Where liberty was justice, & eternal science was mercy." (292)

But there is still another aspect to the creation, Blake's insistence
on the higher innocence inherent in experience. I have already spoken
of the tiger's fire both as an agent of terror and as the energy inherent
in the divine imagination. Within Urizen's world exists the seed of,
or the driving force for, the immortal world. In Blake's prophetic books
the figure of Los, the spirit of prophecy, embodies that force. He is the
"divine artificer," the divine good in moralistic terms, to counter the
divine evil. It is Los who binds Urizen in the web of the latter's
making; it is Los who enchains Urizen with the iron links of spiritual
death which Urizen's own selfish furnaces have forged; it is Los's
hammer that continuously strikes the spark to light the way out of
Urizen's forests of night. Los binds Urizen with time, and "Eternity
is in love with the productions of time" (*Marriage*); "The Ruins of
Time builds Mansions in Eternity" (Letter to Hayley, 797). In other
words experience and its sense-bound, clock-controlled, walled-in existence is necessary to the attainment of the higher innocence; and, contra-
riwise, the higher innocence depends for its existence on the life of
experience. Thus when Los saw the ruins of Urizen and his creation, it
was not enough that earth be created to limit the fall into the abyss. It
was also necessary to give form to the time in which that earth existed.
And in terms strongly reminiscent of *The Tyger* Blake pictures Los
working furiously at his temporal furnaces:

> . . . in his hand the thundering
> Hammer of Urthona forming under his heavy hand the hours,
> The days & years, in chains of iron round the limbs of Urizen
> Link'd hour to hour & day to night & night to day & year to year,
> In periods of pulsative furor. . . . (302)

This passage is perhaps of more interest than the others I have quoted
in connection with *The Tyger* since it seems to me that Blake, whether
wittingly or not, has given us here the most succinct description of that
memorable lyric: "periods of pulsative furor." Though one can hardly
describe the chopped phrases of *The Tyger* as rhetorical periods, they

nevertheless pound as the resonant strokes of Los's hammer pound out the minutes and hours with pulsative fury. The whole lyric fairly beats with the awesome life it portrays.

In the same section of *The Four Zoas* Los continues his labor in a passage which ties this aspect of creation even closer to the enslavement theme of *The Tyger:*

> The Prophet of Eternity beat on his iron links & links of brass;
> And as he beat round the hurtling Demon, terrified at the Shapes
> Enslav'd humanity put on, he became what he beheld.
> Raging against Tharmas his God, & uttering
> Ambiguous words, blasphemous, fill'd with envy, firm resolv'd
> On hate Eternal, in his vast disdain he labour'd beating
> The Links of fate, link after link, an endless chain or sorrows.
>
> The Eternal Mind, bounded, began to roll eddies of wrath ceaseless
> Round & round. . . .
> .   .   .   .
> Forgetfulness, dumbness, necessity, in chains of the mind lock'd up,
> In fetters of ice shrinking, disorganiz'd, rent from Eternity,
> Los beat on his fetters & heated his furnaces,
> And pour'd iron sodor & sodor of brass. (302-303)

This, then, is the finite world, ruled over by Urizen who caused its finiteness, the world of experience and tigers. Even Urizen himself questions it, in the sixth night of *The Four Zoas,* in a way strikingly similar to the questions of *The Tyger.* And that similarity is all the more real since each question makes the inevitable comparison, implicitly and explicitly, between the universe that was (innocence) and the present condition of the world. With Lear-like despair Urizen laments:

"O what a world is here, unlike those climes of bliss
Where my sons gather'd round my knees! O, thou poor ruin'd world!
Thou horrible ruin! once like me thou wast all glorious,
And now like me partaking desolate thy master's lot.
Art thou, O ruin, the once glorious heaven? are these thy rocks
Where joy sang on the trees & pleasure sported in the rivers.

And laughter sat beneath the Oaks, & innocence sported round
Upon the green plains, & sweet friendship met in palaces.
And books & instruments of song & pictures of delight?
Where are they, whelmed beneath these ruins in horrible destruction?
And if, Eternal falling, I repose on the dark bosom
Of winds & waters, or thence fall into a Void where air
Is not, down falling thro' immensity ever & ever,
I lose my powers, weaken'd every revolution, till a death
Shuts up my powers; then a seed in the vast womb of darkness
I dwell in dim oblivion; brooding over me, the Enormous worlds
Reorganize me, shooting forth in bones & flesh & blood,
I am regenerated, to fall or rise at will, or to remain
A labourer of ages, a dire discontent, a living woe
Wandering in vain. . . ." (317)

Thus Urizen poses the alternatives for man in experience: remain "a
living woe" or rise out of the watery prison and enter into immortal
day; face the tiger and either fall down before his wrath or see in him
the lamb of redemption. "Generation, image of Regeneration," is the
way Blake put it. From the forests of the night, the fettered minds of
humanity and the fearful symmetry of *The Tyger* will rise to the
higher realm toward which all of *The Four Zoas* tends and which
Blake presents in all its splendour at the end of the ninth night:

The Sun has left his blackness & has found a fresher morning,
And the mild moon rejoices in the clear & cloudless night,
And Man walks forth from midst of the fires: the evil is all consum'd.
His eyes behold the Angelic spheres arising night & day;
The stars consum'd like a lamp blown out, & in their stead, behold
The Expanding Eyes of Man behold the depths of wondrous worlds!
One Earth, one sea beneath; nor Erring Globes wander, but Stars
Of fire rise up nightly from the Ocean; & one Sun
Each morning, like a New born Man, issues with songs & joy
Calling the Plowman to his Labour & the Shepherd to his rest.
He walks upon the Eternal Mountains, raising his heavenly voice,
Conversing with the Animal forms of wisdom night & day,
That, risen from the Sea of fire, renew'd walk o'er the Earth;
For Tharmas brought his flocks upon the hills, & in the Vales

Around the Eternal Man's bright tent, the little Children play
Among the wooly flocks. . . . (379)

And among those same wooly flocks lie the lion and the tiger, for it is immortal day.

The parallels are inexhaustible. To see them will perhaps not identify the multitude of prophetic characters, but it will place each of them in relationship to innocence and experience. To recognize the recurrence of a symbolic act from *Songs of Innocence* or *Songs of Experience* will not explain all the ramifications of that act, but it will establish its basic motivation and result. To find in the prophecies a symbol used in the *Songs* will not reveal completely its significance but it will provide a basis and a direction for discovering and examining that significance. In a sense Blake created his own tradition in the *Songs* and other early works, so that he could allude to it in the prophetic books. In that way he made his symbolic world, as Yeats said of Shelley's, "solid underfoot and consistent enough for the soul's habitation."[7] The cosmic higher innocence must be understood in terms of the humanity of the *Songs of Innocence and of Experience.*

NOTES

APPENDIXES

INDEX

APPENDIX A

A NOTE ON THE ORDER OF BLAKE'S SONGS

Blake did establish a definite order for the songs in 1815, after which all but one issue of the *Songs of Innocence and of Experience* appeared with the poems in the same order.[1] Yet even in this final configuration a reason for the songs' being in that particular order is not apparent. It is true that the *Songs of Innocence,* for example, progress generally from the more happy songs (*The Shepherd, The Ecchoing Green, The Lamb*) to the songs containing a mixture of joy and sorrow (*Night, A Dream, On Anothers Sorrow*); but interspersed throughout the former group the 1815 pattern has the far from insouciant *The Little Black Boy, The Chimney Sweeper,* and *The Little Boy Lost,* and throughout the latter group *Spring, Nurses Song,* and *Infant Joy.* Speculation as to whether Blake actually did have a purpose in mind has rested largely on the assumption that about 1818 he listed the songs in an index as they "ought to be paged & placed" in the engraved copy (see note 1). This index is now believed to be in someone else's handwriting.

Thus, Blake's constant changing of the order of the songs, combined with the apparent futility of searching for reasons behind those changes, seems to lead to but one conclusion: Blake simply wanted variety. Each copy he engraved was to be different. Even here, however, there is evidence to the contrary. If Blake wanted each copy of the *Songs* to be unique, it would have been simple to avoid repetition of the same order entirely, either the order of the whole book or even of a few songs. There are nineteen songs of innocence—at one time there were as many as twenty-three[2]—and Blake's output was far less than the maximum number of different combinations of nineteen possible. There is no duplication; no copy is quite unique, even before the 1815 arrangement became standard.

[1] Geoffrey Keynes, *A Bibliography of William Blake* (New York, 1921); Keynes and Edwin Wolf, *William Blake's Illuminated Books* (New York, 1953). Keynes and Wolf have been able to locate and examine eight issues of the *Songs of Innocence and of Experience,* which can be dated with certainty after 1815. All of them have been foliated by Blake. The one issue which is at variance with the 1815 pattern is the one which corresponds to an index originally thought to be Blake's but now suspect.

[2] *The Little Girl Lost, The Little Girl Found, The School Boy,* and *The Voice of the Ancient Bard* often appeared in *Innocence* before 1815. The first two of these were transferred permanently to *Experience* in 1794 in the first issue of the combined *Songs of Innocence and of Experience; The School Boy* was transferred sometime between 1799 and 1801; and *The Bard* appeared in *Innocence* as late as 1802-1808.

APPENDIX A

I see no ready solution to the dilemma. On the one hand I cannot agree with those who believe that the arrangement of the songs has no significance at all, simply because I am impressed by the obvious pains which Blake seemed to take to establish a definite order. On the other hand I cannot agree with Wicksteed's creation of an order merely to substantiate a thesis, though I certainly must sympathize with his apparent frustration in the face of Blake's fickleness. Finally I can offer reasons neither for the 1815 standard arrangement nor for Blake's changes before and after that date. In view of this paradoxical situation I have proceeded in my explications with little regard for the poem's position in the book except insofar as a knowledge of that position definitely contributes to a greater understanding of any one poem or symbol. For, in the final analysis, innocence as a state precludes the necessity for a rigid internal progression; each poem, regardless of its position in the *Songs of Innocence,* is a contribution to the formation of the state and its major symbols, not a step in the mystic way or a day in the private life of William Blake.

APPENDIX B

A NOTE ON THE FORM OF TIRIEL

The first few lines quoted are symptomatic of the many technical failings of *Tiriel*. The lines range from nine to seven feet, from the regular iambic of the second line to the half iambic, half trochaic first line, which trails off to nothing at the end; from the ineffective tragedy of the third line to the awkwardness of the last. To be sure there is some semblance of Blake's poetic architecture in the symmetry of first and last lines and in the subtle distinction between "beautiful palace" and "delightful palace," but it is obvious that he was not able to cope with the laxness of the basic line, especially when engaged at the same time in polishing the gems of the *Songs of Innocence*.

There are many stylistic and dictional details in *Tiriel,* indeed, which show a marked similarity to those of the dramatic and quasi-dramatic pieces in the *Poetical Sketches*. The over-all form of *Tiriel* resembles a closet drama, in which Blake was never at ease whether it was written in rhythmic prose, blank verse, or the strange hybrid prosody of *Tiriel* itself. The dialog form, made up for the most part of short speeches, and the general stiffness, lack of feeling, and immature, melodramatic effects, all confess to the author's embarrassment outside the lyric form. For example, a passage early in the poem demonstrates Blake's inability to convey intense feeling in the new verse form; the poetry rapidly disintegrates with each successive, desperate exclamation:

> Hark listen ye serpents listen
> What Myratana. What my wife. O Soul O Spirit O fire
> What Myratana. art thou dead. Look here ye serpents look

This difficulty is largely a holdover from the Gothic tale of terror and the terrified damsel in distress, which Blake had already tried to harness in poetic form in *Fair Elenor*:

> "Ah, woman's-fear!" she cry'd; "Ah, cursed duke!
> Ah, my dear Lord! ah, wretched Elenor!
>
> "My lord was like a flower upon the brows
> Of lusty May! Ah, life as frail as flower!
> O ghastly death!" (5)

In another passage from *Tiriel,* in which Blake intends to convey Tiriel's fierce hatred and the concomitant terror inspired by his curse, the language so overflows with fogs, clouds, and poison that the effect desired is lost amid a jumbled confusion of unassimilated sounds (106). There is no thematic tie to control the extravagance of near-madness as there is in Lear's anguished cries to the elements in Act III. To be sure, this kind of blood and thunder held a certain fascination for Blake. To this the prophetic books amply attest. But there he learned, at least in the better passages, to subvert mere violence and noise to a distinct pattern or aim. And—a smaller point—he learned to eliminate almost entirely the eighteenth-century personifications which play so prominent a part in the *Prologue to King John, The Couch of Death, Contemplation,* "Then she bore Pale desire," "Woe, cried the muse," and the passage from *Tiriel* just referred to.

That Blake was learning, however, is not to be denied. Mixed in with the triteness of much of *Tiriel* we can find such basically fine passages as Tiriel's concluding speech, including the searing condemnation of Har in the unaccountably deleted twelve lines:

> Dost thou not see that men cannot be formed all alike
> Some nostrild wide breathing out blood. Some close shut up
> In silent deceit. poisons inhaling from the morning rose
> With daggers hid beneath their lips & poison in their tongue
> Or eyed with little sparks of Hell or with infernal brands
> Flinging flames of discontent & plagues of dark despair
> Or those whose mouths are graves whose teeth the gates of eternal death
> Can wisdom be put in a silver rod or love in a golden bowl
> Is the son of a king warmed without wool or does he cry with a voice
> Of thunder does he look upon the sun & laugh or stretch
> His little hands into the depths of the sea, to bring forth
> The deadly cunning of the scaly tribe & spread it to the morning

Blake's later efforts at dialogue tend toward long formal speeches, much like the one just quoted, with very little gesture or implied stage business. More and more his characters become mere mouthpieces for cosmic argument and "prophetizing" rather than living, breathing characters in personal strife. Yet these elemental forces retain a certain precision of characterization that prevents them from falling into the stereotyped mold of personification. The distinction is between personalized—perhaps even human—character and essential, even quintessential, character. In *Tiriel* there are elements of both, but the general sharpness of Tiriel, Har, and Heva contrasts with the voices heard in *Thel* or the vague shapes of *Visions of the Daughters of Albion.*

CHAPTER I

1. *William Blake: A Critical Essay* (London, 1906), p. 140.

2. Letter to Trusler in Geoffrey Keynes, *The Complete Writings of William Blake* (London, 1957), p. 794. All subsequent page references in the text to Blake's works will be to this edition, though for the major works under discussion I shall retain consistently Blake's punctuation rather than Keynes's.

3. *William Blake: A Critical Study*, p. 140.

4. *Ibid.*, p. 161.

5. There has been considerable discussion about how much of his system Blake derived from others, particularly Boehme, Swedenborg, and various neo-Platonists. The ideas of a primal unity, a fall into division, and a return to unity are of course not new, and no one can deny that there are many isolated instances of congeniality between Blake and various philosophers, theologians, pseudo-scientists, Gnostics, Cabbalists, and so forth. In none of them, however, is there an adumbration of Blake's system as I shall define it, except insofar as many of their symbols turn up in Blake's poetry. Even here Blake's mind did with them what it would, and my occasional references to a "source" are more as an aid to clarification than a suggestion of indebtedness. That Blake's system only gradually developed, with many fits and starts, is adequate proof of its essential originality. For the controversy over the influence of other writers see especially Mark Schorer, *William Blake: The Politics of Vision* (New York, 1946), pp. 104-148; J. G. Davies, *The Theology of William Blake* (Oxford, 1948), pp. 35-49; Paul Berger, *William Blake: Poet and Mystic,* trans. Daniel H. Connor (New York, 1915), pp. 13, 55, 57, 198-208, 211-220; Helen C. White, *The Mysticism of William Blake* (Madison, 1927), pp. 128-164; David V. Erdman, *William Blake: Prophet against Empire* (Princeton, 1956), *passim;* and a group of scattered articles and essays by George Mills Harper and Kathleen Raine.

6. Blake never uses the former term in this sense, but for his use of the latter see *The First Book of Urizen,* 227 (hereafter referred to as *Urizen*).

7. *The Four Zoas,* 277, hereafter referred to as *Zoas*.

8. "To the Jews," *Jerusalem,* 649.

9. *Milton,* 483. Cf. *Zoas,* 264:

Four Mighty Ones are in every Man; a Perfect Unity

Cannot Exist but from the Universal Brotherhood of Eden, The Universal Man. . . .

10. Letter to Butts, 805. Cf. *A Vision of the Last Judgment*, 605-606, and especially the Annotations to Lavater's *Aphorisms*, 87.

11. See, e.g., *Zoas*, 374; *Jerusalem*, 664-665.

12. Annotations to Swedenborg, 89.

13. *Literature and the Occult Tradition*, trans. Dorothy Bolton (London, 1930), pp. 17-18.

14. Annotations to Lavater, 83; Annotations to Swedenborg, 90.

15. *The Marriage of Heaven and Hell*, 151, hereafter cited as *Marriage*.

16. See Blake's Annotations to Lavater, 77 (no. 409) and 88 (no. 640). See also *Last Judgment*, 615, par. 2.

17. Annotations to Reynolds, 471; Letter to Trusler, 794; Annotations to Reynolds, 473.

18. *Last Judgment*, 604. In this work is a good example of what Blake probably meant by "spiritual sensation." Speaking of his painting of the Last Judgment he says: "If the Spectator could Enter into these Images in his Imagination, approaching them on the Fiery Chariot of his Contemplative Thought, if he could Enter into Noah's Rainbow or into his bosom, or could make a Friend & Companion of one of these Images of wonder, which always intreats him to leave mortal things (as he must know), then would he arise from his Grave [i.e., this world], then would he meet the Lord in the Air & then he would be happy" (611). See also Chapter III of this study for an examination of Blake's technique as an application of his theory of the symbolic imagination.

19. Annotations to Wordsworth's *Poems*, 783; Annotations to Berkeley's *Siris*, 775; *Last Judgment*, 617.

20. This is what Blake scrupulously avoided in all of his work. In one place he wrote: " 'What,' it will be Question'd, 'When the Sun rises, do you not see a round disk of fire somewhat like a Guinea?' O no, no, I see an Innumerable company of the Heavenly host crying, 'Holy, Holy, Holy is the Lord God Almighty.' I question not my Corporeal or Vegetative Eye any more than I would Question a Window concerning a Sight. I look thro' it & not with it" (*Last Judgment*, 617). Cf. *Auguries of Innocence*, 433-434, lines 125-128.

21. *The Delights of Wisdom Pertaining to Conjugial Love after which Follow The Pleasures of Insanity Pertaining to Scortatory Love* (New York, 1910), p. 157, par. 143.

22. *The Everlasting Gospel*, 748-759. See also *Marriage*, 158.

23. I use the word "reorganize" here advisedly since Blake insisted, "Un-

organiz'd Innocence: An Impossibility. Innocence dwells with Wisdom, but never with Ignorance" (Notes written on a page of *Zoas,* 380). Cf. *Zoas,* 366, lines 363-374.

24. *William Blake's Circle of Destiny* (New York, 1938), pp. 123-124. See Blake's *Everlasting Gospel,* 753-757.

25. *William Blake: The Politics of Vision,* p. 268.

26. *A Man without a Mask* (London, 1947), p. 135.

27. *William Blake's Circle of Destiny,* pp. 11-12.

28. *Heaven and Its Wonders, the World of Spirits, and Hell: From Things Heard and Seen,* trans. Rev. Samuel Noble (New York, 1864), p. 134, par. 278.

29. *Poetry and Myth* (New York, 1927), p. 173.

30. Ellis and Yeats define this idea with admirable precision: Urizen falls "into chaos, which is memory, because memory is the record of the merely egoistic experience, thus differing from inspiration, which is direct experience."—*The Works of William Blake* (3 vols., London, 1893), I, 252.

31. *The Everlasting Gospel,* 750; statement by Lavater, underlined by Blake and called "true worship" (82).

32. *An Introduction to the Study of Blake* (London, 1927), p. 133.

33. *Heaven and Its Wonders . . . and Hell,* p. 9, par. 15; p. 13, par. 23; *Concerning the Earths in Our Solar System which Are Called Planets,* trans. anon. (London, 1787), pp. 116-117.

34. *Marriage,* 158. Swedenborg could never hold such a view as this, since he never identified the evil man with the all-good God. Indeed he probably would have reacted to this statement in the *Marriage* much as the angel did when he heard Blake's devil speak the words: "The Angel hearing this became almost blue but mastering himself he grew yellow, & at last white pink & smiling. and then replied, Thou Idolater, is not God One? & is not he visible in Jesus Christ? and has not Jesus Christ given his sanction to the law of ten commandments and are not all other men fools. sinners & nothings."

35. See, e.g., *Urizen,* 235-236; *The Book of Ahania,* 255; *Zoas,* 374; *Milton,* 517-518; *Jerusalem,* 679-680, 724-725.

CHAPTER II

1. See, e.g., *The Laocoön,* 776-777 *passim.*

2. *Fearful Symmetry* (Princeton, 1947), p. 21.

3. *William Blake* (London, 1909), pp. 76-77.

4. *Ibid.,* p. 96.

5. Annotations to Reynolds, 474. In view of Blake's obvious identification of intuition and imagination, it is interesting to note here what Helen White writes of these two faculties in the over-all context of mysticism: ". . . contrary to much current misunderstanding, intuition is not an act of the imagination, a faculty of which mysticism has been traditionally suspicious. Intuition is a super-rational apprehension of super-rational truth, an interior enlightenment, what a contemporary philosopher has called 'total working.' "—*The Mysticism of William Blake*, p. 66. One could scarcely find a better, more concise definition of Blake's idea of the perceptive imagination.

6. *William Blake*, pp. 92-93.

7. See Chapter III for the application of this principle.

8. *Fearful Symmetry*, p. 87.

9. See his comments on *Songs of Innocence and of Experience* in "The Symbolism of Poetry," *Ideas of Good and Evil* (London, 1903), pp. 255-256.

10. Jacob Bryant, *A New System: or, an Analysis of Antient Mythology* (6 vols., 3rd ed., London, 1807); Edward Davies, *Celtic Researches, on the Origin, Traditions & Language, of the Ancient Britons* (London, 1804).

11. *The Romantic Comedy* (Oxford, 1948), pp. 32-33.

CHAPTER III

1. A recent and excellent book on Blake, Stanley Gardner's *Infinity on the Anvil* (Oxford, 1954), employs a method similar to mine and, though I arrived at my conclusions independently, my confidence in their validity has been greatly strengthened by Gardner's analyses. See also Mark Schorer's *William Blake: The Politics of Vision* and David V. Erdman's *William Blake: Prophet Against Empire, passim*.

2. *Mysticism of William Blake*, pp. 166-167.

3. In this interval Blake also produced *America* and *The French Revolution*, which I have largely ignored except for occasional reference to a symbol or character.

4. *Ideas of Good and Evil*, p. 25.

5. See also *America*, 198, plate 6.

6. *Infinity on the Anvil*, p. 5.

7. *William Blake: The Politics of Vision*, p. 424.

CHAPTER IV

1. See Appendix A, "A Note on the Order of Blake's Songs."

2. The essence and symbol of the infant joy, intensified to the point of

syntactical obscurity, is established in the poem of that title. Without reference to its enigmatic punctuation and confusing dialog-monolog form I hazard here a very tentative partial paraphrase to point up the essential "thoughtlessness" of the Blakean innocent. "I am, I exist," says the infant joy; "and since I am happy in that existence happiness or joy must be my name." The adjective merely becomes a noun; the quality assumes concrete, symbolic form; the essence achieves identity. The Piper, aware of impending experience but unable to do anything directly for the infant innocent, speaks in the final lines the supreme prayer of the state of innocence: "Sweet joy" (Christ, higher innocence, imagination, wisdom) "befall thee." Cf. "Take thy bliss O Man! And sweet shall be thy taste & sweet thy infant joys renew!" (*Visions of the Daughters of Albion*)

3. "There is not an Error but it has a Man for its Agent, that is, it is a Man" (*Last Judgment*, 615).

4. See, e.g., *Jerusalem:*

There is a limit of Opakeness and a limit of Contraction
In every Individual Man, and the limit of Opakeness
Is named Satan, and the limit of Contraction is named Adam.

. . . .

But there is no Limit of Expansion; there is no Limit of Translucence
In the bosom of Man for ever from eternity to eternity. (670)

5. Here and elsewhere (in the *Songs, Tiriel, The Marriage, Thel,* and *Visions*) I have used Blake's punctuation, chaotic and confusing as it is, because many times editorial emendation has obscured or even changed Blake's meaning or intention. Though I hold no brief for Blake as a grammarian, it is nevertheless essential that we study the poems as he wrote them.

6. See my analysis of *Night,* pp. 120 ff., for a fuller explanation of the devouring of lambs.

7. See Blake's statement on beauty, ugliness, and strength, which he called the only "Britons" who escaped the last battle of King Arthur: "The Strong Man represents the human sublime. The Beautiful Man represents the human pathetic, which was in the wars of Eden divided into male and female. The Ugly Man represents the human reason. They were originally one man, who was fourfold; he was self-divided, and his real humanity slain on the stems of generation, and the form of the fourth was like the Son of God" (*A Descriptive Catalogue,* 578). See also 580, where Blake writes of "what is truly Ugly, the incapability of intellect."

8. J. H. Wicksteed, *Blake's Innocence and Experience* (London, 1928), p. 80.

9. *Ibid.,* p. 83.

10. See, e.g., Letter to Trusler, August 16, 1799: "I find more & more that my Style of Designing is a Species by itself, & in this which I send you I have been compell'd by my Genius or Angel to follow where he led. . . ." And, in the same letter, "And tho' I call them Mine, I know that they are not Mine . . ." (791-792). And, finally, in a letter to Butts, April 25, 1803: "I have written this Poem from immediate Dictation, twelve or sometimes twenty or thirty lines at a time, without Premeditation & even against my Will . . ." (823).

11. Blake too seemed to think the *Green* a suitable introduction to the song series for in five issues before the 1815 order was established it immediately follows the *Introduction. The Shepherd,* which follows the *Introduction* after 1815, also uses these elements of innocence but it is concerned mainly with the protection provided in innocence for the children (or lambs). This protection will be discussed more fully in the second and third groups of poems below.

12. The first attempt, that is, except insofar as the concept is inherent in *To the Muses* (10-11), the same muses to whom Blake later referred as the daughters of memory as opposed to imagination or inspiration. See, e.g., the Annotations to Reynolds, 452; *A Descriptive Catalogue,* 565-566; *Last Judgment,* 604; and Annotations to Wordsworth, 783. Most of these, of course, refer to Blake's theory of art, but as we have seen, that theory is inextricably bound up with his ideas on perception, poetry, indeed all life.

13. This kind of impotence and fear Blake infused more artistically and more satisfactorily in the figures of Har and Heva in *Tiriel.* See below, Chapter VII. In *Nurses Song* in *Songs of Experience* Blake portrays the ultimate result of such impotence, active evil. E.g., lines 3-4 of that poem read:

> The days of my youth rise fresh in my mind,
> My face turns green and pale.

14. See especially my analysis of *The Little Black Boy,* pp. 104-108.

15. Keynes supplies a comma after "rest" (116) even though it is clearly a colon or semi-colon.

16. In only one issue before 1815 does *Spring* appear adjacent to the *Green,* and after 1815 the two are separated by eleven poems. Before 1815, however, *Spring* does appear in conjunction with *Laughing Song* (four issues), the *Introduction* (one issue), *Infant Joy* (two issues), *Nurse's Song* (three issues); and after 1815 it is followed by *Nurse's Song* and *Infant Joy* in that order.

17. Perhaps it is also the poetic awakening from the night of dog-trot iambs and jingling, "Monotonous Sing Song, Sing Song from beginning to end" that Blake complained about in his *Public Address* (600). The whole idea of the first two lines is almost a rewriting of the first and last stanzas of *To the Muses*:

> Whether on Ida's shady brow,
>   Or in the chambers of the East,
> The Chambers of the sun, that now
>   From antient melody have ceas'd;
>
> How have you left the antient love
>   That bards of old enjoy'd in you!
> The languid strings do scarcely move!
> The sound is forc'd, the notes are few!

18. In *The Blossom* Blake complicates matters by using only half of the relationship between bird and child: the child is never mentioned in the poem, strong evidence in justification of cumulative reading.

19. For a full discussion of this important idea see my analysis of *Night*, pp. 120-124.

CHAPTER V

1. See, e.g., J. Bronowski, *A Man without a Mask*, p. 114. Wicksteed, in *Blake's Innocence and Experience*, p. 105, claims that the lower case letters in the titular "lost" and "found" prove that the two songs are one, despite the fact that in his own facsimiles the initial letter of "Found" is clearly capitalized. Indeed Blake himself kept the songs far apart in copy "A" of *Songs of Innocence and of Experience*.—Keynes and Wolf, *William Blake's Illuminated Books*, p. 56.

2. There is an interesting parallel to this idea of seizing corporeally that which must be approached imaginatively in a later poem by Blake, *The Crystal Cabinet* (429-430), and the result of the attempt, though in a greatly different context, is strikingly similar to that in *The Little Boy Lost*:

> I strove to sieze the inmost Form
> With ardor fierce & hands of flame,
> But burst the Crystal Cabinet,
> And like a Weeping Babe became.

3. I have commented elsewhere on the key problems in this poem and consequently I shall not offer a full analysis of it here. See p. 302, n. 4, and

also my two notes: "Irony in Blake's 'Holy Thursday,'" *MLN*, LXXI (1956), 412-415; "Blake and Wesley," *N & Q*, n. s., III (1956), 522-524.

4. A rare opportunity is afforded to study an earlier version of a key line in *Holy Thursday,* and Blake's change admirably dramatizes his distinction between being lost and found. In the second stanza all of the details contrast sharply with the cramped regimentation of stanza 1: "The hum of multitudes was there" and "Thousands of little boys & girls" raise "their innocent hands." The fourth line, however, as it originally appeared in *An Island in the Moon* (59) read: "And all in order sit waiting the chief chanter's commands." Not only is this a reference to an extraneous person (the chief chanter), but a reiteration of the very authority stanza 2 flouts. Moreover, the over-all effect is static: the second line emphasizes the fact that the children are seated and the fourth line awkwardly repeats it. What Blake wanted, and what he finally achieved, was a spontaneous vocal and gesticulative demonstration. In the revised stanza then, the hum that breaks the solemn silence is followed by the mass gesture toward heaven, not toward the beadles or a chanter. The children are the lambs of innocence, radiant in that innocence, raising their hands to the only law which for them has any authority, the law of freedom, infinity, vision. Thus their song bursts forth "like a mighty wind . . . to heaven," the human voice divine transcending the human voice human (the law, the beadle, the chanter); "like harmonious thunderings the seats of heaven among" it sounds. The solemnity of the first stanza has been transformed into a divine solemnity which Blake surely thought of as joy. The movement is up, out of Paul's and this world, as the flowers of the earth become cherubim around the throne of God. "Beneath them sit the aged men wise guardians of the poor." The sharp contrast is almost melodramatic. There is no movement here, no joyousness, no music. To the aged men in all their "wisdom" (a wisdom which sadly lacks understanding) the triumphant song is ritual, the children's duty, something which is right and proper when one is in St. Paul's. They remain earthbound while the children, who are not wise, ascend. True wisdom is that of the poet who can see the drama unfold. One reaches God not in processions, not by command, but by spontaneously going out to Him, as in song, creation.

5. *Milton,* 488. Cf. *Zoas,* 336:

. . . the arts of Urizen were Pity & Meek affection
And that by these arts the serpent form exuded from his limbs
Silent as despairing love & strong as jealousy.

6. *Zoas,* 347. Cf. *On Anothers Sorrow* and *Jerusalem* (648):

For not one sparrow can suffer & the whole Universe not suffer also
In all its Regions, & its Father & Saviour not pity and weep.

7. Significantly, before 1815 Blake placed *The Little Black Boy* next to *Laughing Song* (four issues), *Infant Joy* (three), *The Lamb,* whose symbolic value in *The Black Boy* is considerable (three), and *The Ecchoing Green, The Shepherd,* and *Spring* (one each). The idea of the selfless act as the key to being found in experience is also clearly reflected in Blake's arrangements of the songs before 1815, *The Blossom* appearing beside *The Black Boy* in three issues, *On Anothers Sorrow* in three, and *A Cradle Song* and *Night* in one each.

8. Cf. *Milton,* 511:

>Crave not for the mortal & perishing delights, but leave them
>To the weak, and pity the weak as your infant care.

9. See, e.g., S. F. Damon, *William Blake: His Philosophy and Symbols* (New York, 1924), pp. 269-270, and Wicksteed, *Blake's Innocence and Experience,* pp. 109-110.

10. This close alliance is reflected in Blake's arrangements of the songs before 1815. *A Dream* appears next to *Night* in four issues, to *On Anothers Sorrow* in four, and to *A Cradle Song* in four. After 1815 it almost always precedes *On Anothers Sorrow.*

11. Copy "B" in Keynes and Wolf's census, dated about 1794. The issue does not have Blake's foliation or pagination, but it is interesting to note that *A Dream* precedes *The Little Girl Lost,* in which the mother again effects a breach in the system of innocence.

12. Besides his persistent use of animal analogy, there is perhaps another reason for Blake's using an emmet here rather than simply a mother and her child. He believed not only that "every thing that lives is holy" (*Visions,* 195), but also that "God is in the lowest effects as well as in the highest causes; for he is become a worm that he may nourish the weak" (Annotations to Lavater, 87). In *The Four Zoas,* for example, he wrote:

>So Man looks out in tree & herb & fish & bird & beast
>Collecting up the scatter'd portions of his immortal body
>Into the Elemental forms of every thing that grows. (355)

In the *Songs of Innocence* he wrote of many links in this chain of being (another name for the human form divine): angels, children, lambs, lions, birds, blossoms. We have seen the winged joys which expand in realms of airy freedom and the unwinged joys of the ground-locked animal like the lamb; now we see the joys of the underground animal, the smallest of all, the emmet, guarded not by angels like the child nor by shepherds like the lamb, but by beetles. Thus Blake effectively brings to this poem implications and associations of other poems, making his song, like Whitman's, cosmic.

CHAPTER VI

1. Before 1815 *A Cradle Song* was adjoined to *The Divine Image* in three issues of the *Songs,* and, further reflecting its basic theme, to *Night* in three issues, *The Blossom* in two, *A Dream* in four, *Nurse's Song* in two, and *On Anothers Sorrow* in one.

2. Cf. Blake's use of the crown in *Thel, Tiriel,* and other poems concerned with father-priest-king. Usually it is associated, with the same connotations, with the sceptre of authority. See, e.g., *The French Revolution* (140, lines 144ff), *Europe* (241, lines 14-23), *Zoas* (278, lines 504-511; 310, line 220), and *A Vision of the Last Judgment* (608).

3. For the grammatical difficulty involved in this reading I have no ready solution. In both stanzas 3 and 4 the subject of "beguiles" is plural; both times the verb is singular. Blake was either so interested in the music of his words and rhymes that he deliberately violated grammatical rules to gain the song effect, or he was occasionally deficient in those rules as he often was in the rules of punctuation. I see no alternative reading in any case.

4. Cf. Blake's annotations to Berkeley's *Siris* (774): "Jesus . . . says I will not leave you Orphans and I will manifest myself to you; he says also, the Spiritual Body or Angel as little Children always behold the Face of the Heavenly Father."

5. As before Blake's use of the singular "beguiles" with a plural subject, "smiles," presents some difficulty. In this case, however, it is conceivable that Blake considered the implicit "he" or "divine image" as the subject.

6. The close relationship between *A Cradle Song* and *On Anothers Sorrow* is obvious, but in the latter poem there are one or two points worth mention here. Mainly the poem establishes the fact that no earthly sorrow can ever be ignored, either by humans or by Christ. Christ assumes both innocence and experience, joy and sorrow, infancy and maturity, just as each child must pass through these states to attain realms of eternal joy. Blake closes the poem with a powerful statement of the efficacy and power of the sigh and tear, which call Christ forth to accept his "sorrows share":

> Think not, thou canst sigh a sigh,
> And thy maker is not by.
> Think not, thou canst weep a tear,
> And thy maker is not near.

The sigh and tear of the infant not only move the mother and father to sympathetic "grief & care" but also inspire the human form divine to appear to the child "like his father in white" (*The Little Boy Found*). The speaker of the poem, then, whether he is interpreted as mother, father, Piper, or everyman, does as Christ does eternally, because Christ became "an infant small" and "a man of woe." That is, Christ became everyman. On the other hand, Christ does as we here on earth do, but he achieves the one higher step separating joy from eternal joy, Beulah from Eden, innocence from the higher innocence—that is, he assumes human woe in the night of experience so that that woe may be destroyed, "fled & gone." We have joy because Christ gives it to us; he gives it by taking on our sorrow: "He doth sit by us and moan" until our grief is gone. He has joy because we have joy; and his crowning greatness lies in the fact that, finally, he has joy because he has our sorrow. This is eternal love, the combination of mercy, pity, and peace, the condition in which joy and sorrow cease to exist separately but have become part of the body of love, the human form divine.

7. Blake was more than usually consistent in his placing of *Night* in the sequence of the *Songs of Innocence,* since only once did he precede it or follow it with a song not concerned with night or the mother or being lost and found. Outside of this issue, in which *Night* is followed by *Laughing Song,* before 1815 *Night* appeared next to *A Dream* in four issues, *A Cradle Song* in three, *The Little Boy Found* in three, *The Divine Image* in three, *The Blossom* in three, *The Little Boy Lost* in two, *The School Boy* in two, *Holy Thursday* in two, and *On Anothers Sorrow* in one. Three times *Night* ends the *Songs of Innocence* also.

8. See Blake's Annotations to Lavater: "Every man's leading propensity ought to be call'd his leading Virtue & his good Angel. . . . the omission of act in self & the hindering of act in another . . . is Vice, but all Act is Virtue" (88).

9. Cf. Gardner, *Infinity on the Anvil,* pp. 29-30.

10. See, e.g., Geoffrey Keynes, ed., *The Writings of William Blake* (3 vols.; London, 1925), Plate VII in vol. I, facing p. 182. See also Bromion and Theotormon in Plate VIII (I, 254), Urizen in Plates XVIII, XXIII, and XXIV (I, 312, 320, 322), "The Sun of Reason" in Plate XXVI (I, 338), "Hand" in Plate LIV (III, 200), "Vala, Hyle, and Skofield" in Plate LV (III, 240).

CHAPTER VII

1. Blake annotated Swedenborg's *Wisdom of Angels Concerning Divine Love and Divine Wisdom* in 1788 or 1789 and the *Wisdom of Angels Concerning Divine Providence* about 1790. A translation of Lavater's *Aphorisms*

was published in 1788 and Blake's annotations were probably made in that year.

2. The text of *Tiriel* was first printed by W. M. Rossetti in 1874. It was never engraved by Blake although there are twelve sepia drawings for it in existence. The text preceding this chapter represents the first accurate transcript, as far as I know, of the unique British Museum manuscript.

3. See Appendix B, "A Note on the Form of *Tiriel*."

4. In *The Little Girl Lost* and *The Little Girl Found* the lost child is not returned to the mother, and in *A Little Girl Lost* she is brought face to face with the father, the mother being conspicuous by her absence.

5. Cf. Blake's later version of this idea in *Jerusalem*: "He who makes his law a curse, / By his own law shall surely die" (652).

6. See Kathleen Raine's fascinating essay, "Some Sources of *Tiriel*," *HLQ*, XXI (1957), 1-36, for Blake's imaginative and corroborative use of Swedenborg, Agrippa, MacPherson, Mallet, *King Lear*, and the Theban tragedies of Sophocles and Aeschylus in developing his great father-priest-king figure.

7. For other examples of this Urizenic domination see *The First Book of Urizen*, Chapter VIII (234-235); also Chapter II, 6-8; Chapter IV, 3-4; Chapter IX complete.

8. Cf. Urizen's similar reaction in *The Four Zoas* (312-313).

9. *The Works of William Blake*, I, 401.

10. For a somewhat different reading of the Ijim section see Raine, "Some Sources of *Tiriel*," pp. 29-34; Frye, *Fearful Symmetry*, pp. 242-243.

11. Miss Raine quite rightly, I think, rejects Ellis and Yeats's interpretation of Hela as the sense of sight. She is rather "the goddess of death . . . specifically, the goddess of death through old age."—"Some Sources of *Tiriel*," p. 21. See also pp. 22-25 of her article for Hela's mythological antecedents in MacPherson's *Introduction to the History of Great Britain and Ireland* and *Ossian*, and in *King Lear*.

12. The west is the realm of darkness and experience, as opposed to the east and the rising sun. See *The Little Black Boy*, for example, in which the mother points to the east before instructing her child to bear the beams of love.

13. Cf. *A Vision of the Last Judgment*: "All Life consists of these Two, Throwing off Error & Knaves from our company continually & Recieving Truth or Wise Men into our Company continually. . . . to be an Error & to be Cast out is a part of God's design. . . . Whenever any Individual Rejects Error & Embraces Truth, a Last Judgment passes upon that Individual"

(612-613); "There is not an Error but it has a Man for its Agent, that is, it is a Man" (615). See also *Jerusalem,* 676, lines 10-15.

CHAPTER VIII

1. See, e.g., Annotations to Reynolds' *Discourses*: "Genius has no Error; it is Ignorance that is Error" (465). "Genius cannot be Bound" (472); "Inspiration & Vision was then, & now is, & I hope will always Remain, my Element, my Eternal Dwelling place" (477).

2. A complementary interpretation of the bowl and rod symbols is offered by Quentin Anderson in his provocative *The American Henry James* (New Brunswick, 1957), p. 224: "The golden bowl is usually held to be the head, the vessel of consciousness, and was so employed by Blake. . . . The rod, associated with the phallus, is here the form of human self-assertion, opposed to God's wisdom. . . ."

3. The only exception to this that I know of is Stanley Gardner in his excellent *Infinity on the Anvil,* pp. 35ff.

4. The "Mne" has been variously described as a misprint for "the," as the first syllable of "Mnetha" which Blake neglected to erase when he changed the parents to Seraphim, and as a corruption of "Bne Seraphim," a mystical term found in Agrippa's *Occult Philosophy* and elsewhere. Although I prefer to read the "Mne" as an abbreviated form of "mnemonic" and Seraphim, then, as angels of memory, the point is not worth the quibble over Blake's knowledge or ignorance of a Greek root.

5. Quoted by J. G. Davies, *The Theology of William Blake* (Oxford, 1948), p. 44. Cf. Swedenborg's *Divine Love and Divine Wisdom,* trans. R. Norman Foster (Philadelphia, 1923), pars. 65 (p. 45), 216 (p. 117), 271 (p. 154), 297 (p. 171), 307-308 (pp. 176-177). Davies believes *Thel* to be "a lyrical expatiation" of Swedenborg's doctrine (p. 44).

6. Cf. *The Four Zoas*:

> Man is a Worm; wearied with joy, he seeks the caves of sleep
> Among the Flowers of Beulah, in his selfish cold repose
> Forsaking Brotherhood & Universal love, in selfish clay
> Folding the pure wings of his mind. . . . (374)

7. It is at this point that I diverge from Gardner's otherwise excellent explication in *Infinity on the Anvil,* pp. 35-40.

8. Tiriel, we should recall, became

> . . . subtil as a serpent in a paradise
> Consuming all both flowers & fruits insects & warbling birds.

9. The universalization of the theme of brotherhood here suggests a

reason for the cloud's being male and the lily female. Both sexes give as well as take to create the ideal union symbolized in that of clay and God. Cf. *The Four Zoas:* "Rent from Eternal Brotherhood we die & are no more" (293); "Life lives upon death, & by devouring appetite / All things subsist on one another" (330). See also *Zoas,* 374, lines 627-642.

10. Cf. *Europe,* 237, lines 1-6.

11. For a detailed application of this idea, see my reading of *Visions of the Daughters of Albion* in Chapter X.

12. *The Four Zoas,* 310-311. Cf. the lament of Ahania in *The Book of Ahania,* 254-255.

CHAPTER IX

1 *Flaxman, Blake, Coleridge, and Other Men of Genius Influenced by Swedenborg* (London, 1915), p. 79.

2. Though Blake's copy has never turned up, it is certain that he had more than an acquaintance with this volume.

3. Blake's comments in *Divine Love and Divine Wisdom* (89-96) are generally favorable whereas the annotations to *The Wisdom of Angels Concerning Divine Providence* are all in the tone of the following: "Predestination after this Life is more Abominable than Calvin's, & Swedenborg is Such a Spiritual Predestinarian. . . . Cursed Folly!" (133)

4. But see Martin K. Nurmi, "Blake's *Marriage of Heaven and Hell,*" *Kent State University Bulletin* (April, 1957), p. 29: "*The Marriage* seems to resemble the A-B-A' of the ternary form in music, in which a first theme and its development are followed by a second theme and its development, followed in turn by a return to the first section or a modification of it. If a little intermingling of themes be allowed, *The Marriage* could be thought of as a rich philosophical rondo."

5. This is probably a reference to Blake's method of "printing" his poems. See the letter to George Cumberland, Dec. 6, 1795 (790); memoranda in the Rossetti MS. (440); *An Island in the Moon* (62). All further Blake quotations in this chapter are from *The Marriage,* unless otherwise noted.

6. The meaning of this "Fancy" is obscure. Blake may have intended something like the following. In the first chamber both the internal and external faculties of perception are cleansed and expanded. In the second chamber, however, the original faculties are restricted and then artificially adorned with a material point of view. That restriction and artificiality is abrogated, though, when the eagle of imagination takes over the perceptive process; and in the fourth chamber the lions of intellect melt the erstwhile

bounded perception of the infinite into living fluids to be cast into forms of knowledge suitable for human consumption. For a more elaborate and confident explication, see Nurmi, pp. 45-48.

7. *The Way to Christ,* trans. J. J. Stoudt (New York, 1947), p. 108. See Nurmi, pp. 31-37, for Boehme's influence on *The Marriage.*

8. See, e.g., *Heaven and Hell* (New York, 1864), par. 586 (p. 339): "In some hells . . . there are . . . dark forests, in which infernal spirits prowl about like wild beasts. . . . There are also deserts, where all is sterile and sandy; with, in some places, rugged rocks with caverns in them. . . ." Cf. Blake's *The Garden of Love.*

9. *Heaven and Hell,* par. 589 (p. 342). Swedenborg's "equilibrium," however, to Blake was only another basis for "what the religious call Good & Evil." For example Swedenborg asserts: "The reason that man would not be capable of being reformed, unless he were in the enjoyment of liberty, is, because he is born into evils of all kinds. These must be removed, in order that he may be saved: and they cannot be removed, unless he sees them in himself, and acknowledges them; and afterwards ceases to will them, and at length holds them in aversion. It is then that they are first removed. This could not be accomplished, unless man possessed in himself good as well as evil; for he is capable from good, of seeing evils, but not, from evil, of seeing goods."—*Heaven and Hell,* par. 598, pp. 348-349.

10. *Heaven and Hell,* par. 291, p. 143; par. 547, p. 314.

11. Swedenborg, on the other hand, thought of marriages occurring even in heaven, where, with both female and male spirits in existence, a marriage is little more than a reconciliation. See *The Delights of Wisdom Pertaining to Conjugial Love.* Cf. Blake's *Jerusalem:* "In Eternity they neither marry nor are given in marriage" (660).

12. In Swedenborg the emphasis is exactly reversed. For example, "Conjugal love has its physical aspect, for 'a married pair who mutually and reciprocally love each other inwardly, in mind, also mutually and reciprocally love each other as to their bodies.' "—Quoted by J. G. Davies, *The Theology of William Blake,* p. 49.

13. *Times Literary Supplement,* Oct. 22, 1925, p. 698.

14. Compare this with the Swedenborgian Satan listening to a lecture on God's "law of order": "When the satan had heard this his countenance, from being bright at first, turned ghastly, and then black, and thus speaking from his own mouth he said, 'You have uttered paradoxes on paradoxes.' " —*The True Christian Religion* (Philadelphia, 1923), par. 71, p. 98.

15. Cf. *Jerusalem:* "the Reasoning Spectre / Stands between the Vegetative Man & his Immortal Imagination" (663).

16. It is interesting to note that in one place Swedenborg came to almost the same conclusion, though his premises of angelic marriages or reconciliations and the separation of body and soul give to his terminology a meaning quite different from Blake's. The passage occurs in *The Delights of Wisdom Pertaining to Conjugial Love* (New York, 1910), par. 143, p. 157: "*Love truly conjugial is chastity itself.* The reasons are these: (1) Because it is from the Lord, and corresponds to the marriage of the Lord and the church. (2) Because it descends from the marriage of good and truth. (3) Because it is spiritual, just in the degree that the church is with man. (4) Because it is the fundamental love, and the head of all loves, celestial and spiritual. (5) Because it is the true seminary of the human race, and thence of the angelic heaven. (6) Because it therefore exists also among the angels of heaven, and with them spiritual offspring are born of it. . . . (7) And because its use is thus preeminent above all the other uses of creation. From this it follows that love truly conjugial, viewed from its origin and in its essence, is pure and holy . . . and therefore chastity itself."

17. D. V. Erdman has shown that, even though Blake appended it almost always to *The Marriage,* the "Song" is really a preliminary sketch for *America.—William Blake: Prophet Against Empire,* p. 177.

CHAPTER X

1. See my discussion of *A Little Girl Lost,* pp. 259 ff. See also *The Book of Ahania,* 255, lines 4-47.

2. Cf. D. V. Erdman's excellent explication in terms of "the parliamentary and editorial debates of 1789-1793 on a bill for abolition of the British slave trade."—*William Blake: Prophet Against Empire,* pp. 211-223. All in all Erdman's is the only accurate summary of the plot and meaning of the *Visions* that I know of. George Mills Harper's analysis is often blurred by his preoccupation with Blake's "sources" in Thomas Taylor's works; but see his valuable comments on *Thel* as well as *Visions* in "Thomas Taylor and Blake's Drama of Persephone," *PQ,* XXXIV (1955), 378-394.

3. Cf. *Jerusalem:*
    And this is the manner of the Sons of Albion in their strength:
    They take the Two Contraries which are call'd Qualities, with which
    Every Substance is clothed; they name them Good & Evil;
    From them they make an Abstract, which is a Negation
    Not only of the Substance from which it is derived,
    A murderer of its own Body, but also a murderer
    Of every Divine Member: it is the Reasoning Power,

An Abstract objecting power that Negatives every thing.
This is the Spectre of Man, the Holy Reasoning Power,
And in its Holiness is closed the Abomination of Desolation. (629)

4. In *Jerusalem*, e.g., the fallen cosmos is characterized by, among other things,

. . . ignorance with a rav'ning beak,
Every Emanative joy forbidden as a Crime
And the Emanations buried alive in the earth with pomp of religion,
Inspiration deny'd, Genius forbidden by laws of punishment. . . . (628)

5. Cf. the "Proverbs of Hell": "As the catterpiller chooses the fairest leaves to lay her eggs on, so the priest lays his curse on the fairest joys." In connection with the last two lines of the passage quoted from *Visions,* see *Night,* lines 45-48, and my analysis, p. 124.

CHAPTER XI

1. The most ambitious attempt heretofore to unravel the complexity of the two poems is Kathleen Raine's essay, "The Little Girl Lost and Found," in *The Divine Vision*, ed. V. de S. Pinto (London, 1957), pp. 19-49. My own essay was written some years before this appeared, but I have left it intact in the face of Miss Raine's persuasive reading to, I hope, stimulate further discussion of these important but very difficult poems.

2. Among other things seven is the number of a completed sequence—combining three (the soul) with four (the body)—and it is the number of virginity; the seventh year is the year of release, and seven in general is the number of redemption, whether the number of redeeming forces or the number of evil influences which make redemption necessary. That Blake was unacquainted with all these representations is impossible; they are to be found in the Bible if one misses them in the Cabbala, in Agrippa, Erigena, Boehme, St. Augustine, the Gnostics, and the Hermetics. All of the meanings of seven, of course, are not applicable to Blake's poem. See Milton O. Percival, *William Blake's Circle of Destiny* (New York, 1938), pp. 242-243.

3. Cf. my discussion of *A Little Boy Lost*, pp. 252-255.

4. In this connection it is important to remember that the mother in *A Cradle Song* stays awake while her child sleeps.

5. *A Man without a Mask*, p. 115.

6. In only two issues of the *Songs of Innocence* are *The Little Girl Lost* and *The Little Girl Found* preceded by any poem other than *A Dream,*

and both of these issues (Copy F in Keynes's *Bibliography* and Copy U in Keynes and Wolf's census of illuminated books) are without Blake's foliation or pagination. Copy F is paginated in pencil and may be Blake's arrangement, dated about 1789-94. Copy U, however, may be as late as 1818, after Blake moved *The Little Girl Lost* and *The Little Girl Found* to *Songs of Experience*. Its arrangement, then, is suspect.

CHAPTER XII

1. "And they heard the voice of the LORD God walking in the garden in the cool of the day: and Adam and his wife hid themselves from the presence of the LORD God amongst the trees of the garden."

2. Verses 16-24 read: "Unto the woman he said, I will greatly multiply thy sorrow and thy conception; in sorrow thou shalt bring forth children; and thy desire shall be to thy husband, and he shall rule over thee.

"And unto Adam he said, . . . cursed is the ground for thy sake; in sorrow shalt thou eat of it all the days of thy life;

"Thorns also and thistles shall it bring forth to thee; and thou shalt eat the herb of the field:

. . . .

"And the LORD God said, Behold, the man is become as one of us, to know good and evil: and now, lest he put forth his hand, and take also of the tree of life, and eat, and live for ever:

"Therefore the LORD God sent him forth from the garden of Eden, to till the ground from whence he was taken.

"So he drove out the man: and he placed at the east of the garden of Eden cherubim, and a flaming sword which turned every way, to keep the way of the tree of life."

3. I am clearly outnumbered in my reading of Blake's ambiguity, for Maud Bodkin, Stanley Gardner, and Northrop Frye all believe the Holy Word to be Christ and the Bard as the poet-prophet who receives his inspiration from Christ. The two voices, therefore, deliver the same message, without irony. See, respectively, *Archetypal Patterns in Poetry* (Oxford, 1934), p. 319; *Infinity on the Anvil*, pp. 118-119; "Blake's Introduction to Experience," *HLQ*, XXI (1957), 57-67. The latter two are especially valuable analyses.

4. *The Four Zoas* (311). Cf. *The Tyger*, stanza 5, and *America* (200-201, plates 12-14).

5. That this is Blake's intention is supported by earlier versions of the line. Blake first wrote, successively, "eyes fled" or "eyes dead" and then

"orbs fled" or "orbs dead."—Wicksteed, *Blake's Innocence and Experience,* pp. 237-248 and plates between pp. 236 and 237.

6. Cf. the imagery used to describe Oothoon's imprisonment in Bromion's den, *Visions* (190).

7. Cf. *The Human Abstract,* in which Cruelty "sits down with holy fears, / And waters the ground with tears."

8. Cf. my analyses of this concept in *The Little Black Boy* and *Thel,* pp. 105-108, 162-174.

9. The italics are mine. Cf. *The Book of Los:*

> The Immortal revolving, indignant,
> First in wrath threw his limbs like the babe
> New born into our world: wrath subsided,
> And contemplative thoughts first arose;
> Then aloft his head rear'd in the Abyss
> And his downward-borne fall chang'd oblique. (258)

10. Cf. Blake's use of the idea of "abstracting" in his tracing the origin of "Priesthood" in *The Marriage* (153, plate 11).

CHAPTER XIII

1. See *A Poison Tree* and *The Human Abstract* for Blake's effective use of this figure.

2. Cf. *Earth's Answer:*

> Break this heavy chain
> That does freeze my bones around.

3. Blake gave the children of innocence no cause to know of death, and it is not until *The Book of Thel* that the word appears, significantly in a speech by a non-innocent, Thel herself:

> Ah! gentle may I lay me down and gentle rest my head.
> And gentle sleep the sleep of death. . . .

4. Thel wanted to pass experience by—the very state from which she had already fled—and go on to the innocence of a higher, gentler Eden; she was concerned with physical immortality, not with the salvation of her soul.

5. Actually neither act would be correct in experience according to Blake: to cry now is self-pity; to curse the chain that binds, a misinterpretation of enslavement. As Blake wrote in *The Marriage,* "Those who restrain desire, do so because theirs is weak enough to be restrained; and the

restrainer or reason usurps its place & governs the unwilling. And being restraind it by degrees becomes passive till it is only the shadow of desire."

6. In the letter to Butts quoted in the text Blake concludes with: "Naked we came here, naked of Natural things, & naked we shall return; but while cloth'd with the Divine Mercy, we are richly cloth'd in Spiritual & suffer all the rest gladly" (813).

7. It is worthwhile noting here that Blake strategically has begun with the basic action, so to speak, upon which the all-important clash of viewpoints and attitudes depends, and by so doing forces the reader to choose immediately whether he will listen as priest or as Blake to the child. A bystander's role is impossible. The question must be asked: Is this selfishness or spiritual wisdom? If the former the poem falls apart, for Blake obviously believed the latter. To convince his reader he becomes almost propagandistic in his use of persuasive devices: the child as victim, the brutal and pompous priest, the violence of the punishment, and the final rhetorical question.

8. From this point of view the wisdom of Blake's change of title is suspect. Yet if one considers that the butt of his attack was not Christianity per se but the institution called Christianity on earth, his decision to allow the poem to speak for itself was most wise.

9. Cf. *Milton:*

> If you account it Wisdom when you are angry to be silent and
> Not to shew it, I do not account that Wisdom, but Folly. (483)

CHAPTER XIV

1. Cf. Har's and Heva's visible fear at the sight of Tiriel, even though they apparently live in peace (100-101, lines 10-26).

2. See also *My Pretty Rose Tree* and my analysis of it in the *Bulletin of the New York Public Library,* LXI (1957), 531-532.

3. *Eternity* (179). The third word of the first line Keynes records as "bends." I prefer Wicksteed's reading, which he gives in a footnote: "This word looks like 'bonds' and has generally been read as 'bends.' But Mr. [Max] Plowman points out to me that in the transcript the dot of the 'i' can be seen, and the word 'bind' is much more characteristic of Blake."— *Blake's Innocence and Experience,* p. 271. See also the untitled MS. poem:

> If you trap the moment before its ripe
> The tears of repentance youll certainly wipe
> But if once you let the ripe moment go
> You can never wipe off the tears of woe. (179)

NOTES

4. See, e.g., *To Nobodaddy:*

> Why art thou silent & invisible
> Father of Jealousy
> Why dost thou hide thy self in clouds
> From every searching Eye (171)

5. Cf. the following untitled MS. poem:

> Let age & sickness silent rob
> The vineyards in the night
> But those who burn with vigrous youth
> Pluck fruits before the light. (172)

6. Cf. the untitled MS. poem:

> An old maid early eer I knew
> Ought but the love that on me grew
> And now Im coverd oer & oer
> And wish that I had been a Whore
>
> O I cannot cannot find
> The undaunted courage of a Virgin Mind
> For Early I in love was crost
> Before my flower of love was lost (184)

7. *The Golden Net* (424). For Blake's worship of the "lineaments of gratified desire" see the two untitled poems numbered by Keynes 40 and 41 (178), *The Question Answer'd* (180), and *Several Questions Answered* (184).

8. The temptation to overcome the difficulty, in this and other songs, by falling back upon the illustrations should be studiously avoided. Comment on the pictorial aspect of *Nurses Song* admirably illustrates the pitfalls involved in such a procedure. For example, after deciding what the theme of *Nurses Song* is, Wicksteed examines the illustration on that basis. It pictures a young woman combing a young boy's or girl's hair—the sex is not clear. Behind them sits another figure, presumably a girl, while the whole picture is bordered with clusters of grapes and miscellaneous foliage. The expression on the woman's face is at best enigmatic, and the recipient of her attentions has an expression that rivals hers in its blankness. Wicksteed, however, sees in the illustration "a boy at the beginning, and a girl at the end, of their teens, in bitter spiritual conflict. The boy is burning with secret resolutions in defiance of her authority, and the girl is filled with distrust. The grapes symbolise the pleasures, and a younger girl sits demurely behind the boy."—*Blake's Innocence and Experience,* p. 155. S.

315

Foster Damon, on the other hand, concludes that "the nurse combs the hair of a boy with folded hands. In the majority of copies, the boy looks very unhappy and indignant. In the grape-wreathed cottage door behind sits a little girl."—*William Blake: His Philosophy and Symbols,* p. 285. Naturally the differences in these two views of the illustrations reflect to a certain extent the basic individuality of each man's approach to both poetry and art. Neither the approach to the poetry nor the approach to the art is inherently wrong by itself; together, however, the approach to one merely compounds the difficulties involved in a basic and healthy individualistic view of the other. However one looks at the page, it seems to me not only right but necessary to examine the poem as poem. Only in this way will it reveal itself as a carefully worked prosodic and artistic triumph, instead of an obscure commentary on an illustration or a simple song which requires elucidation (or complication) in another medium.

9. She has been mentioned of course in *Infant Sorrow, A Little Boy Lost, The Little Vagabond,* and *The Chimney Sweeper,* but in none of these, except perhaps *The Vagabond,* is her role delineated in such psychological detail.

10. I take "green" to indicate simply "envy," nothing more. In *The Human Abstract,* we recall, jealousy has a human face.

11. Damon, *William Blake: His Philosophy and Symbols,* p. 281.

12. On the name, Tirzah, see Frye, *Fearful Symmetry,* p. 127: of the five daughters of Zelopehad, one "is named Tirzah, also the name of an Israelite capital of the Ten Tribes, and therefore a symbol of opposition to Jerusalem, the City of God. This Tirzah is associated with a beautiful woman in the Song of Songs. The five daughters represent the five senses and imply the passive dependence on sense experience which is symbolized in our being born from a mother."

13. Cf. *The Everlasting Gospel* (751, lines 1-10; 757, lines 31-35) and especially the words of Blake's Milton:

"Obey thou the Words of the Inspired Man.
All that can be annihilated must be annihilated
That the Children of Jerusalem may be saved from slavery.
There is a Negation, & there is a Contrary:
The Negation must be destroy'd to redeem the Contraries.
The Negation is the Spectre, the Reasoning Power in Man:
This is a false Body, an Incrustation over my Immortal
Spirit, a Selfhood which must be put off & annihilated alway.
To cleanse the Face of my Spirit by Self-examination,

To bathe in the Waters of Life, to wash off the Not Human,
I come in Self-annihilation & the grandeur of Inspiration,
To cast off Rational Demonstration by Faith in the Saviour,

. . . .

These ["natural" images] are the Sexual Garments, the
   Abomination of Desolation,
Hiding the Human Lineaments as with an Ark & Curtains
Which Jesus rent & now shall wholly purge away with Fire
Till Generation is swallow'd up in Regeneration."

(Milton, 532-533)

14. The words Blake engraved on one of the figures in his illustration to *To Tirzah.*

15. That is, except for a few poems in the Rossetti MS. and the entire Pickering MS. These latter, however, are more lyric-prophecies than lyrics like those in the *Songs.*

CHAPTER XV

1. *An Introduction to the Study of Blake,* pp. 74-75.

2. Compare, e.g., the following passages from *A Vision of the Last Judgment:* "Whenever any Individual Rejects Error & Embraces Truth, a Last Judgment passes upon that Individual" (613); "The Last Judgment [will be] when all those are Cast away who trouble Religion with Questions concerning Good & Evil or Eating of the Tree of those Knowledges or Reasonings which hinder the Vision of God, burning all into a Consuming Fire" (604).

3. *Fearful Symmetry,* pp. 181-182.

4. See Martin K. Nurmi's excellent essay on Blake's synthesis of these (and other) opposites, "Blake's Revisions of 'The Tyger,'" *PMLA,* LXXI (1956), 669-685.

5. Of course one must know other poems as well. See, e.g., the use Erdman makes of *The French Revolution, America, The Book of Urizen The Book of Ahania,* etc. in his illuminating interpretation of *The Four Zoas* in *William Blake: Prophet Against Empire,* pp. 258-361 *passim.*

6. *William Blake: The Politics of Vision,* p. 251; *William Blake: Prophet Against Empire,* pp. 178-180; "Blake's Revisions of 'The Tyger,'" 672-674.

7. For a contrary view of Blake's prophecies see Gardner, *Infinity on the Anvil,* especially Chapter VI, "Disintegration." He feels that disinte-

gration is all but complete; "control is . . . rare in the later books. The mythology is so overpowering that Blake loses sight of the abstract connotations in actions of absurd fatuity, and is then obliged to explain the significance of the action."—p. 137. This is undoubtedly true in many cases, but I am convinced the essential control is there in greater measure than Gardner will allow.

INDEX

ॐ

Edited by George P. Solomos
Designed by Selma Tenenbaum
Set in Granjon Typefaces
Printed on Warren's Old Style Antique
Bound in Joanna Mills Pardiment Cloth
Manufactured in The United States of America